UNSCATHED

UNSCATHED

ESCAPE FROM SIERRA LEONE

MAJOR PHIL ASHBY QGM
ROYAL MARINES

MACMILLAN

First published 2002 by Pan Macmillan Publishers Ltd
20 New Wharf Road, London N1 9RR
Basingstoke and Oxford
Associated companies throughout the world
www.panmacmillan.com

ISBN 03339 8920 1 (HB)
ISBN 14050 0021 X (TPB)

1 3 5 7 9 8 6 4 2

A CIP catalogue record for this book
is available from the British Library.

Typeset by seagulls
Printed by Mackays of Chatham plc

For Anna

CONTENTS

AUTHOR'S NOTE

Many people in Sierra Leone helped us and without them we might not be here today. To try and protect them in turn, I have changed the names of certain individuals and villages.

ACKNOWLEDGEMENTS

I would like to thank:

My parents, James and Sue, for their love and forbearance, and my big sister Penny for rescuing me on numerous occasions when we were kids.

Alistair Hopkins, 'Iain' the Good Samaritan and the Dundonell Mountain Rescue Team for helping to save Anna's life.

Peter Babbington and fellow members of the BSA, especially Joe P-W and Mike E-G.

Andy, Dave and Paul for their bravery, mettle and for hanging in there.

Joss McCabe and the team at DNM for their support when I wasn't firing on all cylinders.

All at Macmillan, especially Charlie Carman, publisher, guru and provider of pizza; Annie Schafheitle, editorial assistant; Matt Richell, marketing manager; and Katie James, head of publicity, for their advice and encouragement.

The Royal Marines for supporting this book and for the best training there is.

Dan Bailey; Bob Baxendale; Lou Brown; Tony and Sophie Chattin; Amy Crook; Huan Davies; Robin Eggar; Mel Gibson; Richard Hamilton; Mark Higginbottom; Christine King; Richard, Kate and Isla Love; Andy Olliver; Richard Rochester; Marine Andy Tayler; Kevin de Val; Pete Webb; Edward, Musa and Usman in Freetown; Captain Moses Korir and Lieutenant Colonel Ngondi from the Kenyan Army; and the staff of Chelsea and Westminster Hospital, for all their help along the way.

And all those friends and colleagues who have had the (mis-) fortune to share a rope, tent, or bivvy ledge with me.

PICTURE ACKNOWLEDGEMENTS

I would like to thank all those individuals who have kindly let me reproduce copies of their photographs. Many of these photos were taken under difficult and dangerous conditions and I fully appreciate the extra effort needed in such circumstances.

All photos taken by the author, except those listed below:

Plate section 1:
Page 1, © Susan Ashby
Page 2, middle and bottom, © Pete Webb
Page 3, middle, © Robin Eggar
Page 3, bottom, © Matthew Ford
Page 4, bottom, © Kate Love
Page 5, top © Andy Olliver
Page 5, bottom, page 6 top left and bottom, © Royal Marines
Page 7 top left, © Huan Davies
Page 8, top, © Studio 16 Photography, Edinburgh

Plate section 2:
Pages 1-4, © Richard Rochester
Pages 5-7 © Paul Rowland
Page 8, bottom right © Huan Davies

LIST OF ILLUSTRATIONS

MAKENI DISARMAMENT CAMP, SIERRA LEONE, 29 APRIL 2000

The afternoon of my thirtieth birthday. Ten rebels approach me and ask to disarm. I hope they will set a precedent for others to follow, but still think it unwise to proceed until the local rebel commanders approve.

At UN headquarters in Freetown, however, they see things differently. They think it a risk worth taking to start disarming in Makeni. I suspect we understand better how the local rebel commanders will react, and our formal report is blunt: 'If we proceed as instructed, we risk provoking a violent reaction from the Revolutionary United Front without the military capacity to contain it.'

Our protestations are overridden and in the afternoon I dutifully disarm the ten rebels and issue them with their new ID papers. They are apprehensive and understandably so. Most of them have had to smuggle their weapons past RUF checkpoints and would have been executed if caught.

As I man my desk in the reception centre, I write in a letter to my wife 'if this leads to large-scale rebel disarmament, it'll be a fine birthday present'. I never get a chance to post the letter; it is soon stolen by rampaging rebels along with all my other belongings.

We have tried to keep the disarmament as low key as possible – there is no point in publicly humiliating the local commanders. But they know well enough what is happening and a hardliner - the barbarous Colonel Bao - turns up at the camp with several hundred rebel soldiers. They quickly surround the camp and the Kenyan platoon guarding it. The fragile cease-fire is about to come to a bloody end.

Kenyan 'A' Company position, 1 May

As night falls, the rebels start to attack. They first encircle our position, then begin rhythmic drumming and chanting. Then they start shooting. I am unarmed but take cover in the front Kenyan trench. I hope that if one of my trench-mates is shot I will be able to pick up his rifle and keep firing. After eight hours, the firefight begins to subside. I crawl up to the mud wall and everywhere I look I see a solid mass of rebel soldiers. I have no idea how many are attacking us – in the darkness it seems like thousands. If the rebels are trying to terrorize us they are certainly succeeding. I hear something land in the bushes nearby. A hand grenade? Ten seconds and no explosion. I crawl over to investigate. At first I can't see what it is so I pick it up. It's a freshly severed human hand. I do my best to stay calm outwardly, but inwardly I am terrified. I cannot describe the impotence I feel without a weapon in my hands. This goes on for three days.

Under siege, 4 May

I have a confab with two other Brits and a New Zealander who are seeking refuge in the same compound. We all reach the same conclusion: as white men, our presence is attracting the rebels' attention and endangering the lives of the Kenyan soldiers guarding the compound. The Kenyans are under intense pressure to hand us over to the rebels. We know the RUF intend to 'do a Somalia', referring to the debacle in October 1993 when dead US soldiers were dragged naked through the streets of Mogadishu, following a bungled US military intervention against a Somalian warlord. I feel particularly vulnerable – as a British Commando, my slaying would be good for rebel street cred. And just to cap it all, it's my signature on the disarmament forms of those rebels who have surrendered their weapons. In Conduct after Capture training you are taught to remain the 'grey man'. In rebel eyes, I could hardly be more colourful.

For the Kenyans' sake and ours, we need to get out. There is no more food and water. And it seems far better to do something positive than just sit around waiting for the end.

Under siege, 5 May

I have a long, soul-searching conversation on the satellite phone with Colonel Babbington in Freetown. I don't rate our chances of getting out alive if we try to break through the cordon, and tell him so. He still reckons we should try.

'Sir, if I told you I thought we had a 20 per cent chance of making it through the cordon, what would your advice be?'

'Go for it!'

The implied message is sobering. "Shit. He thinks we're all going to be butchered." We are deep inside the rebels' heartland, many miles from safety. No one is coming to rescue us. Our fate is in our own hands.

2:30am 6 May

With half an hour to go, we recheck our kit and talk through our escape plan one final time. I make everyone jump up and down to make sure that nothing rattles. We use charcoal from a fire to blacken our faces. Dave has recently been paid and has $1,000 in cash. We split this between us in case we are separated. The most secure means of carrying it is to swallow it. I wrap my share of the money in a condom I have in my survival kit. Swallowing the packet with a dry throat and no water is a real challenge. I eventually manage. Finally, we rip the UN badges off our uniforms.

These bright blue badges are a symbol of UN neutrality and are supposed to guarantee the safety of the person who wears them, but all they will do is make us show up more easily in the dark. As we remove the badges, we abandon our last symbol of neutrality. We are no longer Observers. From now on, despite being unarmed, we are combatants.

Dave and I share a last cigarette to calm our nerves, and then another one. He observes wryly that we've both become chain smokers. But with possible life expectancy down to thirty minutes, I'm not too worried about the long-term health implications.

Andy, Dave and Paul have only known me a few days. I ask them to trust me. I've had various brushes with death in my life when my nerve – and thankfully my luck – have held out. I also know my training has been the best possible preparation for whatever lies ahead. I hope I can live up to the reputation I've gained in the Marines for always landing on my feet. I pray that this time we can all get out unscathed.

2.45am: We have no more preparations to make and there seems little point in waiting any longer. I suggest we go now and the others agree. I whisper 'Good luck, guys. Stay close behind me.' Then I climb over the wall and drop into no man's land.

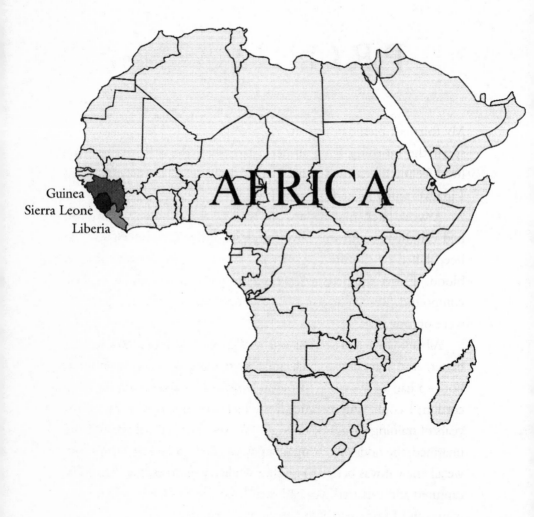

Guinea
Sierra Leone
Liberia

AFRICA

PROLOGUE

My thirtieth birthday was memorable for all the wrong reasons. I spent the morning lying under a tree, feverish with malaria, my head feeling like someone had parked a bus on it. In the afternoon, I inadvertently kicked off a civil war.

A week later, malaria was the least of my problems – the war had caught up with me. Five hundred of my UN colleagues had been killed or captured by rebels, who were now baying for my blood. I was trapped, with three other colleagues, in a small compound. Rescue attempts had failed. Diplomacy had failed. We were on our own.

All my life I had sought out challenges, the more extreme the better. And somehow – luck, military training or a combination of both – I had always come through. Now, as I looked out on the rebel cordon, I could only wonder if my luck would stay with me, if my years of training would be enough. We were hungry, dehydrated and unarmed: the odds of getting out alive seemed stacked against us. But we all knew it was better to be shot while trying to escape than to be captured and tortured. We had seen what these rebels would do to a man – and I was their Number One hate figure.

We would have to go over the wall. The longer we delayed, the weaker we would become. The decision had to be made. So I made it.

CHAPTER ONE

LANDING ON MY FEET

'But risk we must, because the greatest hazard in life is to risk nothing.'
ANON

If you're going to face the harshest conditions the world can throw at you, then you'd do well to grow up on the west coast of Scotland. If you can navigate in a snow-storm in the Cairngorm mountains, when you can't even see your hand in front of your face, you can navigate anywhere. And after Scottish midges, it's easy to cope with tropical mosquitoes or biting soldier ants in the jungle.

What's more, if you're going to be a Commando and ultimately a Mountain Leader – able to get through the most demanding physical and mental training – it helps to love the outdoor life and have a good head for heights. I started young in both respects, with a fun childhood that took me camping, sailing, swimming in the freezing River Clyde every New Year's Day and – particularly exciting – water-skiing on my father's shoulders on

Loch Lomond. When I wasn't immersed in the cold and wet, I'd be climbing trees: an early indication of a love affair with heights.

It must have been in the genes. My father, a nuclear engineer on Royal Navy submarines, was always a tough, outdoor type. Born in New Zealand and brought up in Canada, he was a firm believer in 'character-building' activities for all the family. It was only in later life that I realized not all fathers took their kids on long-distance, overnight hill walks. I remember asking on one occasion why everyone else at the Glencoe ski-centre was allowed to take the chairlift but we had to walk up carrying our skis. My dad said he didn't like queuing and we'd only get cold if we stood around waiting, which seemed reasonable enough.

My mother, on the other hand, was a bit of a worrier, but like most boys I refused to be mollycoddled, and her attempts to stem my adventurous impulses were in vain. She eventually resigned herself to letting me learn by my own mistakes. Not that I seemed to sustain lasting damage from any of my exploits. I remember a tree-climbing competition when I was only six. I was almost at the top of what seemed to be the tallest tree in the world when the branch I was on snapped. I fell through lots of greenery, bouncing off the branches – painful, but at least they broke my fall. Then, just before I hit the ground, my feet caught on a branch, and I was flipped over. I hit the ground face first and blacked out. I have no recollection of the rest of the day. Apparently, I did manage to complete a sponsored walk that afternoon, though with a splitting headache.

It wouldn't be the last time I walked away from a setback – though sometimes my companions weren't so lucky. I used to see myself as a talented amateur scientist and inventor, but tended to be inspired more by curiosity than common sense. One science project was almost the end for my friend Angus. I had heard from somewhere that bullets stopped within a few metres if fired into water and asked my father why this was. As he was an engineer, I was convinced he knew everything.

'Viscosity, son,' he informed me. In trying to explain what viscosity was, my dad added that Vaseline was even more viscous than water. This gave me an idea for an experiment. I reasoned that if a real bullet could be stopped by a few metres of water, then an airgun pellet could be stopped by a few centimetres of Vaseline. So, confident the pellet would be stopped, I asked Angus to put a tub of Vaseline on top of his head. (Science is always more fun when it involves a bit of drama.) Angus knelt down and I stood over him, took aim with my air rifle, and pulled the trigger. The gun went off, the tub of Vaseline shattered and Angus yelped; the experiment had failed. The Vaseline hadn't stopped the pellet, but Angus's skull had. Luckily the end of the pellet was still sticking out, so I was able to remove it with a pair of tweezers.

Before my boisterous antics developed into something more serious, my parents sent me to boarding school. I won a scholarship to Glenalmond College in rural Perthshire. This was one of those Scottish schools in the middle of nowhere, where boys' energies were directed into outdoor activities and sport – if only because there was scant opportunity for anything less wholesome. Glenalmond was not the social centre of the world but the teaching was excellent and, more importantly to me, the climbing was great. I don't know of many schools that offer ice-climbing as an alternative to football on winter Wednesday afternoons.

I began to develop a reputation for getting through scrapes in one piece, while others around me came a cropper. Bored at the back of a geography class one day, I was staring out of the window, watching a truck dump a load of coal against the school wall. I reckoned it would be possible to leap from the classroom window on the second floor and land on the pile of coal without injury. When I told my friends this, they thought I was mad. So I determined to prove my theory. I crept back to the classroom after dark, opened the window, climbed on to the windowsill, aimed for the coal and jumped. As I'd hoped, my fall was successfully broken by the coal. It felt like landing in a sand dune and I emerged jubilant and covered in coal dust. Word got around of this 'feat' and another would-be daredevil tried the same stunt the following night. Egged on by his mates, he jumped, plummeted and hit the ground where he lay screaming in pain and indignation. He had failed to notice that the workmen had come along that afternoon and shifted the pile of coal elsewhere.

I may have a bit of a reckless tendency – but I do know to look before I leap.

Moving on

I left school with good enough exam results to get a place at Cambridge University. I had won a couple of academic prizes but was much prouder of holding the unofficial school record in the pole-vault and being able to swim four lengths of the pool underwater. I had also been concussed a few times on the rugby pitch and almost expelled for (accidentally) setting my next-door neighbour's bed on fire.

I was seventeen when I left school and I wanted to do some growing up before going to university. I thought about joining the Army, but you had to be eighteen. And anyway, I was put off by the crusty old Army colonel who gave me a formal interview, then sent me a regimental Christmas card featuring pictures of castles and bagpipes. I was much more impressed by the Royal Marines careers officer who came to visit our school. A charismatic Falklands veteran called Lieutenant Malcolm Duck, he led a group of us on a long run, made us swim across a river and then took us to the pub. This was much more my kind of thing. Plus you only had to be seventeen and a half to join the Marines. So, at seventeen and a half and three days, I joined the Royal Marines as a Second Lieutenant on a 'gap year' commission. This made me the youngest officer in HM Armed Forces.

Within a few days of joining up, my lack of prowess on the drill square had earned me the nickname 'Shaggy'. I think the drill sergeant's exact words were: 'YOU CAN'T MARCH TO SAVE YOUR FUCKING LIFE, SIR. WHO ARE YOU – SHAGGY OR FUCKING SCOOBY-DOO?' From then on, I was known to all my Marines friends as Shaggy.

The highlight of that year was Arctic warfare training in northern Norway during the winter with 42 Commando. Our instructors were Royal Marines Mountain Leaders from the elite Mountain and Arctic Warfare Cadre, and I aspired to join their branch. Back in Britain, I passed an arduous Commando course, earned my Green Beret a few days after my eighteenth birthday and made some friends for life. I knew that if I were to join the Marines full time, I would have to go through this course all over again – and more.

When the Marines offered to sponsor me through Pembroke College, Cambridge, I signed up for a longer commission and spent three very enjoyable years as an engineering student. The academic side was challenging enough, without the numerous distractions on offer... and I was very easily distracted. For me, the highlights were the extra-curricular activities. For a start, there were more pretty girls than I'd ever seen in one place and a whole load of interesting, friendly people, to make up for a few spectacularly dull ones. And there were even opportunities for climbing.

Cambridge is famous for being the flattest place in Britain, with only one 'hill' to speak of. What I didn't realize until I got there was how good the climbing would be. Ironically for such a flat place, Cambridge has the second oldest climbing club in the world. What it lacks in mountains it makes up for with long holidays (trips to Scotland and the Alps), and architecture that is inspiring, not only to look at, but especially to climb on.

Climbing buildings is something of a cult activity in Cambridge and whole guide books have been published on it. The pastime has long been outlawed by the university authorities, for the good reason that student climbers periodically fall off and kill themselves. It always seemed bizarre to me that you could fail your exams or get caught taking drugs and only be told off. Get caught climbing once on King's College Chapel, however, and you were straight out.

This meant that die-hard climbers like me could practise our sport only at night. The climbing was unique: generally unroped and in the dark. Certainly, the fear of being rusticated (a quaint Cambridge term for being expelled) if caught, as well as the more traditional fear of falling off, made for some memorable nights. We ticked off all the 'classic' routes and added a few 'first ascents' of our own.

Continuing my love of all things watery, we also made a first descent that nearly went badly wrong. After weeks of rain, the River Cam was flooded and my friend Pete and I decided it was deep enough to jump six storeys from the roof of St John's College into the river. After a quick recce to check for submerged shopping trolleys, we climbed the conveniently ornate Bridge of Sighs, then up on to the roof to our take-off point. Once up there, we rapidly realized this was a stupid idea and agreed that if we both chickened out there'd be no face lost.

Unfortunately at this point, we were spotted by a concerned resident.

'Don't jump! It can't be that bad. The porters are coming, they'll help you down...'

We didn't think the college porters would be quite as sympathetic. Reversing our previous decision not to jump, we landed together into three feet of water and some soft mud. We had intended to keep a low profile during this outing, but had inadvertently become a public spectacle. Someone had called the police, who were now forcing their way through the crowd that had formed on the river bank. In all the commotion, we let the current sweep us downstream for about half a mile, before climbing out and walking across town back to my flat.

Looking back on such student escapades, I can see they were a little... unnecessary. But sometimes the gratuitous bits are the most fun. One thing I have always taken seriously, though, is safety in the mountains. The grounding I had had at home and at school had made me a competent and experienced mountaineer for my age. Furthermore, six months of holiday every university year, and financial independence thanks to my Marines sponsorship, gave me ample opportunity to broaden my experience further afield. Mountaineering highlights included trips to Greece, Spain, Kurdistan and Iceland, and numerous expeditions in the Alps. I felt confident in my own abilities and was convinced that accidents were easy to avoid if you knew what you were doing.

Another Cambridge night, memorable for more romantic reasons, was Valentine's Day 1991, when I met Anna for the first time. A pretty Scottish girl studying French and Arabic, she immediately shared my sense of fun and adventure. We quickly became inseparable and have been in love ever since.

As the end of my university days loomed, I felt I had to pack in as much as possible before joining the Marines again. Unfortunately, this was not the ideal revision strategy. Two weeks before my final exams in May 1991, the lure of a good weather forecast and a great piss-up was more than enough to overcome my guilty conscience for not revising. With three mates, I drove up to the Peak District late on a Friday night and dossed down in a pub car-park. We needed to get up early for the weekend's first activity, a bridge-jump from a disused railway viaduct at Monsal Head.

Bridge-jumping is the poor man's equivalent of bungee jumping and involves tying a climbing rope to one side of a bridge and jumping off the other side while tied on. You plummet downwards but, as long as you've got your calculations right, the rope becomes tight before you hit the deck. Then you swing like a pendulum until you can be lowered to the ground.

The last climbers to try this viaduct had somehow got it wrong and one of them had been killed. A memorial plaque at the bottom of the bridge was a thought-provoking reminder of the consequences of failure. Since then, the local police had tended to arrest any would-be bridge jumpers as they set up their gear. To avoid being apprehended, it would have been best to do the jump in darkness, but we needed a bit of daylight to take some photos. In the end, we went for it at four o'clock in the morning.

We drew straws for who would get to go first. Jim, a New Zealand climber with no apparent sense of fear, won the privilege. From 90 feet up, he launched himself into space, clearing the ground by at least 10 feet. No problem, I thought, until it occurred to me as I dropped off the bridge that I was three stone heavier than him and the rope was about to stretch that bit more. I kept my legs tucked beneath me and missed the ground by two or three feet.

We climbed all that day on gritstone outcrops and I was feeling confident enough to solo an E5 rock-climb. In climbing terminology, E stands for Extremely Severe. The 'Extreme' category is subdivided from 1 to 9, so there were only a few harder climbs around. From the ground, it looked desperate – 60 feet of smooth, sheer rock with tiny holds for your fingertips and relying only on friction for your feet. This was as hard a route as I'd done and, standing at the bottom of it, I felt extremely nervous. As soon as I left the ground, though, I felt calm and focused.

A steady nerve is useful in most walks of life, but in climbing it is essential. I have seen climbers lose their nerve, start to tremble uncontrollably and literally shake themselves off the rock face. For me, though, fear has often been a positive force – there is no better way of concentrating the mind. In fact, one of the reasons I love climbing is because it relieves stress. Overcoming physical danger puts the less immediate stresses of everyday life into perspective. Deadlines and workloads have no relevance when you're 300 feet off the ground and a small mistake could mean falling to your death.

Of course, there is an adrenalin buzz to be had from rock-climbing. After a while, being off the ground becomes more exhilarating than frightening, and intensive physical exertion just adds to the experience. But climbing is more than that. Most people can appreciate the rugged beauty of mountains. As a climber, this sensation is heightened by being intimately involved with often awe-inspiring surroundings.

For me, rock-climbing combines the mental challenge of problem-solving with the physical challenge of a good work-out in the gym. The best climbers have brains and brawn, as well as flexibility, balance and a cool head. Climbing also gives you a good reason to spend time in beautiful places with like-minded people... and something to talk about in the pub afterwards.

Climbing has taught me to stay in control. I find it enormously satisfying to know that I can stay in complete control in a potentially dangerous situation where a moment of panic could be disastrous. This has obvious military applications, as I was later to discover. Meanwhile, though, I was simply enjoying my climbing – convinced, as many young men are, that accidents only happened to other people. And if they did happen to me, I seemed to bounce. This rather cavalier attitude had been only slightly dented by an experience in July 1990, which brought me very close to death.

I had been climbing with a friend called Mark in the French Alps. Mark, a skinhead with bulging neck muscles and scars all over his face (the result of too many Rugby League matches), looked more like a bouncer than the Latin teacher he actually was. I trusted Mark with my life and we made a strong, if inelegant, climbing team.

One of the most impressive mountains near Chamonix is the Aiguille des Drus, or 'Druids' Needle', a 13,000-foot-high spire of granite that soars above a glacier called the Mer de Glace, or 'Sea of Ice'. Mark and I had climbed its south-west face the previous summer, a route called the Bonatti Pillar. We had climbed with the bare minimum of kit and had spent a very cold night, 13,000 feet up the mountain in a storm. We only had lightweight rock-climbing gear, no waterproofs or even socks. Happy – but cold – memories.

We now wanted to attempt its North Face. The North Face of the Drus is one of the six classics in the Alps and is a long, steep, exposed route on rock that is usually sound, at least according to the guide book...

The climb takes two days, and there are some excellent bivvy ledges half-way up the route. (A bivvy ledge is a ledge on a steep cliff where there is just enough room to sit or lie down to spend the night.) After 2,000 feet of climbing on the first day, Mark and I reached the bivvy ledges suggested in the guide book as the best place to spend the night. However, we still had a couple of hours until last light so, on the spur of the moment, we decided to continue climbing a few more pitches, even though we knew it would mean spending an uncomfortable night on a smaller ledge higher up. We had chosen not to carry sleeping bags, to save weight on a difficult climb, but had a small gas cooker and enough warm clothing not to freeze. The night was long and cold, but very atmospheric as we sat on our ledge, several thousand feet above the lights of Chamonix. We spent the time chatting and drinking tea, before eventually dozing off, still firmly anchored to the rock face in case we rolled off the ledge during the night. Every few minutes, I'd wake up shivering, move around for a bit to warm up and go back to sleep. Mark, on the other hand, is one of those people who seem able to sleep, uninterrupted, anywhere – as his loud snoring constantly reminded me.

An hour before first light, we were too cold to enjoy a lie-in. We got up and made breakfast by chipping chunks of ice from a niche in the rock and melting them on our cooker to make porridge. We had the kind of conversation that everyone has at breakfast: Mark was rude about my cooking and I grumbled about his snoring. We concluded that the food and bedding in our accommodation were not up to much, but the amazing view at sunrise more than made up for it. We both agreed that a night of discomfort had actually added to our experience of the mountain. (Though this didn't stop us looking forward to a warm bed and decent food back down in the valley.) We peered back down the face and could make out the head-torches of other groups of climbers on ledges further down.

The first pitch of the day's climb was a steep, overhanging crack, made even more awkward by the fact that there was still ice lurking in the back of it. With cold, stiff limbs after the long night on our ledge, this was not the most gentle of starts, but at least I was unlikely to stay cold for long. It was my turn to lead so I set off, wedging my numbed hands and feet into the crack to pull myself up. As the crack got wider, I ended up using my backside, shoulders and, at one point, my head to gain purchase on the rock. Mark congratulated me – sarcastically – on my style. He knew the banter would help me relax and get through this pitch, the hardest section of the climb. Struggling not to fall off, I shouted down to Mark to keep a close eye on me as I made the 'crux' move – the hardest part of the climb.

Just at that moment, we heard a rumble nearby. A massive rock-fall had started somewhere above us and was crashing down the steep rock face towards us. My stomach lurched as I realized there was absolutely nothing I could do to get out of the way. If the flying rocks were heading in my direction, then my time was up. If the rocks missed me, I still had to avoid falling off my climb. Resisting the urge to panic, I concentrated hard on the immediate necessity of hanging on, regardless of the rock-fall.

Huge boulders came crashing down just to our left and continued on down the face. The whole mountain shook with the impact of falling rocks, each one triggering yet more rock-fall. We could feel the rush of displaced air on our faces and smelt the sulphurous smoke produced as huge rocks crashed into each other at hundreds of miles an hour.

In fact, we were lucky and the rocks fell straight past us. But we watched in horror as, seemingly in slow motion, rocks swept over the ledge where we had previously intended to spend the night. Five climbers were killed: some buried under boulders, others ripped off the rock face, falling thousands of feet to the glacier below. Had we stuck to our original plan, that would have been us.

We wondered whether we should go back down but, realistically, with a rock-fall like that, the other climbers' chances of survival were minimal. In any case, rescue helicopters were on the scene within a few minutes and we didn't want to add to their problems by getting into difficulties ourselves.

We carried on to the top of the route, the safest way off the mountain. As we climbed we could see that the very shape of the mountain had changed. High-altitude Alouette rescue helicopters buzzed around beneath us looking for survivors. We arrived at the summit, relieved to be off the North Face and in the sunshine again. Sitting on the summit, Mark the 'hard, northern rugby player' and Shaggy the 'tough Marine' admitted we could both do with a hug.

For a few minutes, I thought I would be quite happy if I never did another dangerous climb in my life. This feeling later subsided but had left me with a more acute sense of my own mortality. I love adventure but I also love life and, unlike some mountaineers, I don't have a death wish – despite what some of my friends might say.

When we eventually reached Chamonix that evening after a long, difficult descent, we reported to the local Gendarmerie and told them what we had witnessed. They were surprised to see us as they hadn't believed anyone on the North Face could have survived. I couldn't help wondering: why had we survived? Not for the last time, I felt my guardian angel had been looking out for me.

Rowing round Spitsbergen

I knew I should make the most of the summer holidays immediately after graduation – such long breaks would not come round again very often once I was in the world of work. There were still countless mountains left to climb but, when a mate suggested an 'ocean-rowing expedition in the Arctic', I was intrigued. Pete, an intrepid geology student who had also spent time in the Marines, invited me to join him in an attempt to circumnavigate the island of Spitsbergen in a small, wooden rowing boat.

I had scarcely heard of Spitsbergen before and initially found it hard to share Pete's enthusiasm for what seemed a distinctly eccentric scheme. A bit of research and a few alcohol-fuelled nights with Pete poring over maps soon whetted my appetite. Spitsbergen lies 600 miles south of the North Pole, is about the same size as Scotland and almost totally covered in ice. It has more polar bears living on it than humans. The ocean around it is just about navigable because the Gulf Stream melts the pack-ice for a couple of months during the short polar summer, but no one had ever successfully rowed or kayaked round Spitsbergen before. I was beginning to see the attraction.

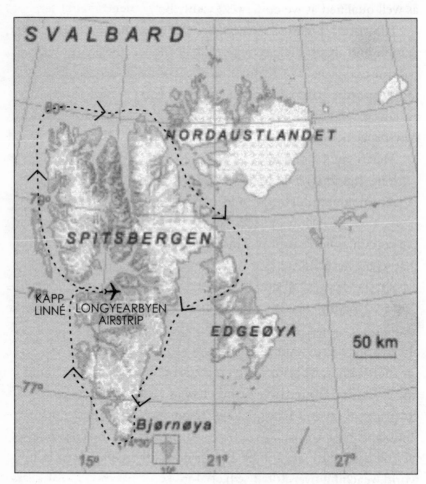

Map of Spitsbergen

I had never been on a major rowing expedition. Neither had Pete, for that matter. But he was an experienced off-shore sailor and I had also done a fair amount of in-shore sailing, as well as being used to very cold weather conditions. We reckoned we were as well qualified as we could reasonably be.

Ultimately, I trusted Pete's judgement that the expedition was feasible and that we had a reasonable chance of getting round and back in one piece. We both knew it would be a serious undertaking, but made light of it. For inspiration, Pete dug out a copy of an advertisement Sir Ernest Shackleton had placed in a London newspaper before his ill-fated Antarctic expedition of 1914:

Men wanted for Hazardous Journey. Small wages, bitter cold, long months of complete darkness, constant danger, safe return doubtful. Honour and recognition in case of success.

We certainly didn't expect honour and recognition, but we knew that whatever happened we would have a good laugh.

So, the day after graduation, Anna saw us off at the airport. We flew to Norway then on to Longyearbyen, Spitsbergen's capital. Our wooden rowing boat, 17 feet long and with an open top, was already out there, waiting for us. After a delay of ten days waiting for the weather, we set off from our start point, Kapp Linné, heading clockwise around the island. It was to take us six weeks to cover the thousand miles, half of them through pack-ice, round the island back to our start point. To the best of my knowledge, we still hold the record for the most northerly rowing boat in the world, reaching over 80° north.

Our little boat was named *Kotick* (after Kotick the White Seal in Rudyard Kipling's *Jungle Book*). She was a fine boat but very leaky and we had cold, wet feet solidly for all of the six weeks. She had a small sail, which meant we could sail downwind, but the wind was seldom in the right direction and it was normally quicker to row.

My experience in in-shore sailing, and Pete's in off-shore sailing, led to some amusing conflicts of interest. If I was frightened I tended to head for land. Pete's natural instinct, on the other hand, as an ocean-going yachtsman, was to keep as far away from land as possible. Land for him represented danger, so he would try to head out to sea. I'm sure we covered many extra miles by zigzagging to and fro along the coast, as we took turns steering.

The boat itself weighed only about 80 kilograms but, fully laden with all our food and equipment, it weighed in at nearly half a tonne. The difficulty of beaching and launching the heavily laden boat meant that we came ashore as little as possible. If the weather and sea were calm, we preferred to sleep, cook and eat in the boat. This far north, we at least had the advantage of twenty-four-hour daylight and soon found that our bodies adjusted to a thirty-six-hour cycle. Throughout the trip, thirty-six hours became our standard 'day', though our final day was a marathon forty hours of rowing.

The rowing itself was physically very hard work but, after the first few days, our bodies adjusted to the prolonged physical effort. When we were rowing together, I sat in the bow of the boat, so spent a lot of time staring at the back of Pete's head. We may have had wrecked feet and blistered hands, but at least we built up good upper body strength. A combination of long days and not enough food meant we quickly shed any excess body fat. By the time we got home, we were lean, mean... and sunburnt. This close to the North Pole, the ozone layer has been partially destroyed so the ultraviolet radiation from the sun is intense. The ice and snow both reflect the fierce polar sunlight, so any exposed flesh soon becomes burnt to a crisp. We did have sunblock with us but it was stored at the bottom of a waterproof barrel lashed in the back of the boat. Unpacking while at sea was a risk we wanted to avoid, so we just let our faces burn. The irony did not escape me that my toes, at one end of my body, were going down with frostbite while, at the other end, my face was being badly burnt.

We had arranged for a Dutch survey ship, the MV *Waterproef*, to pre-position six food and fuel caches at strategic points around the island. Each cache was supposed to contain cooker fuel and ten days' food in an airtight, waterproof barrel (to keep out both the weather and marauding polar bears). I had prepared all six barrels in my room in Cambridge, stuffed with freeze-dried rations and huge quantities of chocolate. The barrels may have been polar bear-proof in the Arctic but unfortunately they weren't protected against students with the munchies passing No 4 Pembroke Street. Cold and hungry when we finally reached one of the food caches, Pete and I were a tad disappointed to find empty Mars Bar wrappers among the rations. Some of my friends had at least left amusing IOU notes: 'Hello Phil, it's 2 a.m., I'm trashed and you're not in. Hope you don't mind if I borrow a Mars Bar or two. I'll buy you one later. Love, Andy.'

We had to laugh…

What we didn't know was that unusually thick pack-ice had prevented the *Waterproef* from reaching three of our cache sites. So food was very short and we were forced to ration ourselves. An advantage of thirty-six-hour days was that we could row much further than in twenty-four hours, but for the same amount of rations. As half of our caches failed to materialize, this became crucial to our success.

While we were forced to ration ourselves, our day and night routines were as follows:

Daily routine for both of us
Start with a cup of black coffee and a hand-rolled cigarette.
Row for two hours.
Eat a biscuit each.

Row for another two hours.
Eat another biscuit.
Row for another two hours.
Have some soup.
Row for another two hours.
Attempt to cook in boat. Petrol cooker leaks and catches fire.
Have main meal (freeze-dried, everything tastes of petrol).
Take life in hands answering call of nature, Pete leans out one
side of the boat and I lean out the other.

My night routine
Sleep for four hours, while Pete rows.
Row for four hours, while Pete sleeps.
Four hours' sleep...
Four hours' row...
Begin whole cycle again.

As I rowed along, I thought incessantly about two things: food
and Anna. For me, every stroke of my oars took me closer to
Anna. I wrote her letters every day in my journal, even though I
had no way of sending them to Cairo, where she was studying at
the time.

Smeerenburgfjorden
20° 30' W, 79°50' N
21 July 1991

Darling Anna,
    In the tent after another bastard long day. 30 km closer
to seeing you again, but it's taken a hell of an effort. The
pack-ice was really dense today. I had a soporific 'afternoon'
in the boat. With 36-hour daylight, we have long days and

I keep falling asleep at my oars. We've put the tent up for once, mainly for psychological protection as the fabric's not bear-proof.

Sleeping with a loaded gun in your sleeping bag is not the best, especially when you roll over.

We've turned food rationing into a game – you earn points by discarding 'unwanted' food into a special bag for later. There is an unexpected bonus of being constantly hungry: it takes our minds off fear. If another bear attacks, I'll be more interested in eating it than running away...

The first time I saw a polar bear, it was six inches from my face when it woke me up. We were sleeping in a derelict trapper's hut, when I felt something nudging against me. I assumed it was Pete until I smelt its breath. Not even Pete's breath smelled that bad, so I peered out of my sleeping bag to investigate and saw a bear looking back at me. Luckily it seemed more curious than hungry, otherwise it would have gone straight for us. Polar bears are fierce predators with no natural foes and they are particularly hungry in the summer, when it's harder to catch seals. That's why polar explorers always carry powerful rifles – just in case.

I kicked Pete to wake him up, and we sat there with our rifle and our camera, arguing with our eyes over whether to shoot at the bear or take his picture. In the end, I pointed my camera at him and took a photo. The flash went off, which freaked him out but he still wouldn't leave us alone. This bear weighed nearly half a tonne and sitting just a few feet away from him was not a healthy plan. We didn't want to shoot him – he had done us a big favour by not eating us as we slept and he was not attacking us. Eventually, we fired a signal flare over his head and he ambled off.

Something terrifying happened nearly every day on that expedition. We capsized once and, on more than one occasion, found ourselves being swept downwind away from land faster than we could row towards it. The nearest land in this direction was Siberia, 3,000 miles away, and we were starting to feel very alone.

Kotick's gunwales were only six inches above the water so waves regularly broke into the boat. The sea temperature went down to minus 4°C (the freezing point of salt water), which made life in the boat fairly uncomfortable. Rowing kept the top half of our bodies warm, but our feet suffered constantly.

In among the pack-ice, the ice-floes acted as breakwaters and kept the water calm. Here, at least, the rowing was easier but sometimes the ice was so thick that the channels would completely close up. We discovered we could make progress by pushing giant lumps of ice apart using one of our oars. Sometimes it would take an hour of pushing to create enough momentum to create a channel wide enough for *Kotick* between floating lumps of ice, some of which weighed several thousand tonnes. In places, though, the ice just closed in completely. Then we were forced to winch the boat out of the water and pull it like a sledge across the frozen sea.

Despite the hardship – in fact partly because of the hardship – it was a privilege to be in places normally only visited by ice-breakers, nuclear submarines, polar bears and itinerant whales. We witnessed some of nature's most savage and beautiful terrain, weather and wildlife. It became easier to ignore blistered hands and aching muscles as we rowed passed stunning ice-sculptures, watched new icebergs calving off the ends of glaciers and saw whales, rare birds, walruses, Arctic foxes and reindeer. For me, though, the polar bears were hard to beat.

On the rare occasion that the sea was totally calm, we allowed ourselves the luxury of setting up our Walkman and a small pair of loudspeakers in the boat. To save weight, we had taken only a couple of tapes with us – *Sunshine on Leith* by the Proclaimers, and the sound-track from *Grease*. A pretty random choice by any standards. At one stage, Pete was asleep in the front of the boat and I was rowing on my own, chilling out, listening to *Grease* for the hundredth time. Every few strokes, I checked over my shoulder in case we were heading for a 'growler' (small icebergs that can damage a boat if you hit them).

As we were over ten miles from the nearest land or any ice floes, I did not expect to see a polar bear. Suddenly, though, I noticed that the lump of ice a few metres ahead was covered in fur and swimming towards us. I turned the boat around and started rowing for my life. Our rifle was lashed in a waterproof barrel at the bottom of the boat. If the bear caught up with us, it could easily tip us into the water before we could get the rifle out. I shouted at Pete to wake up, but he thought this was just a ruse to get him out of his sleeping bag.

The bear was gaining on us while, in the background, John Travolta and Olivia Newton-John were singing 'You're the One That I Want'. I got ready to use an oar as a weapon. Pete now realized this was no joke, scrambled out of his sleeping bag and hurriedly started rowing. With the two of us pulling together, we were able to shake off our pursuer. I still get butterflies in my stomach when I hear that song.

Although I'd been scared before, it had never been for such a prolonged period of time: six weeks of being continually frightened was emotionally draining, and I did a lot of growing up very quickly. I didn't stop taking risks after this, but it did make me think harder about things. And in terms of physical and mental effort, it was to make Commando training seem almost tame in comparison.

Officer training

I returned from Spitsbergen with just enough time to spend a few days with Anna before reporting to the Commando Training Centre Royal Marines in Lympstone, Devon.

Thirty-five individuals started officer training on 4 September 1991. All of us were high achievers in our own right and had been through a rigorous selection process just to be there. Fifteen months later, twenty-six older and wiser individuals passed out as Royal Marines officers, fully prepared to lead thirty experienced Commandos in any operational environment.

Unlike any other service in the British Armed Forces, Royal Marines officers are trained alongside the other ranks, and the award of a Green Beret is an absolute standard that all have to meet. This really does help build mutual respect and a bond between all Commando soldiers. You are a Commando first; the rank comes second.

The hardest part of officer training is the Commando Course, which you have to pass to earn your Green Beret. For me it was second time round. Four weeks long, it consists of a combination of demanding field exercises, which wear you down both physically and mentally, ending with the Commando Tests. These tests have hardly changed since the Second World War and comprise a series of load carries, forced marches and assault courses. Then there's the appropriately named Endurance Course, which involves running and crawling over a six-and-a-half mile course, while carrying an assault rifle and 22 pounds of ammunition over steep hills, through deep pools of water and a series of underground tunnels. You've got to be careful to keep your weapon clean and dry, as the final part of the Endurance Course is on the rifle range, where you have to hit seven out of ten targets. If your weapon fails, or you're too tired to shoot straight, then you fail the test. The final Commando Test is a 30-mile forced march across Dartmoor carrying weapons and equipment. Officers must complete this final test in seven hours, other ranks in eight.

Derived from the experience of battle-hardened men in the Second World War, the Commando Tests still have relevance today. As I was to find out, the brutality of war has not changed and only the toughest training can prepare you for it.

Training was hard work but a great laugh at the same time. By the end, we calculated we had run or 'yomped' 2,500 miles; done 40,000 press-ups and 60,000 sit-ups; climbed 7,500 feet of rope... and Greg Barr had slept with 120 different women.

Many of the men in the 'Batch' had girlfriends when they started. Many also had girlfriends when they finished – but different girls. Royal Marines officer training was not conducive to maintaining a steady relationship and it was hard to devote effort to anything except work. Weekends were valued for catching up on sleep and painstaking preparation of kit. I was desperate to keep things going with Anna and we both made the extra effort necessary to see each other whenever possible. Particularly hard were the long, sleepy car journeys back to Devon from Cambridge, where Anna was still a student. I remember driving 270 miles on a Sunday night with all the car windows down in the middle of winter, slapping my face to try to stay awake. I was all too aware that I would only have two hours in bed when I got back to Lympstone before getting up again to prepare my kit for the first parade on Monday.

My reputation for landing on my feet followed me into the Marines. On one occasion, we were woken in the middle of the night and told to be seated in the classroom ten minutes later with pencil and paper. We were given a current affairs test with some near-impossible questions. The more questions we got wrong, the further away from camp we would be dropped off before having to run back. So, as none of us managed to guess the name of the President of Ecuador or on what day of the week Saddam Hussein had invaded Kuwait, we psyched ourselves for a long run. A 4-tonne truck drove us out of camp to our drop-off point. As the truck stopped, I managed to clamber on top of its canvas canopy. The training team searched inside the truck, but failed to look on the roof. I stayed where I was and the truck drove me back to Lympstone. Back inside the camp gates, I jumped down, fetched my car and started ferrying my colleagues back to base.

Outside work, too, there was still time for the occasional adventure. The south coast of Devon has some impressive sea cliffs and I'd spotted a possible new climbing route on a sea-stack just offshore at a place called Ladram Bay. You could only get to it at low tide unless you were prepared to swim. After work on a balmy summer evening, I asked if anyone fancied giving it a go. One of my closest Batch-mates, Dan Bailey, was up for it, and we set off. When we arrived at Ladram Bay, the tide was on its way out but it would be dark well before low tide, so we decided to swim out with our climbing gear on our heads. In fact, the water was only chest deep and we were able to haul ourselves out on to a seaweed-covered ledge at the bottom of the climb. The sea-stack was only 50 or 60 feet high so I wasn't too bothered if I fell back into the water. The climb itself was hard, loose and frightening but I got to the top without falling off, trailing the rope behind me. I took the rope tight and Dan climbed up. We sat there for a few minutes admiring the view, then untied ourselves from the rope, ready to abseil back down.

I asked Dan to coil the rope, then to throw it down. In climbing parlance, this means you throw one end of the rope down, but hold on to the other one. Dan, a relatively novice rock-climber, took a more literal interpretation and threw the whole thing off. Without a rope, there was only one way down. With the tide still going out, the longer we delayed, the shallower the water would get. I had no intention of waiting overnight until the tide came in again. As the lead climber, it was my ultimately my cock-up so I jumped first. The water was just deep enough. We both hit the bottom but luckily the sand on the sea-bed was soft.

At the end of training, I was surprised and proud to be awarded the Commando Medal for 'Leadership, Unselfishness, Cheerfulness in Adversity, Determination and Courage'.

Jungle training

At the end of Officer Training, I was posted to 45 Commando, based in Arbroath, Scotland, which was due to go on a six-month operational tour to Belize in Central America. In that ex-British colony, the presence of a small British force helps maintain stability in a volatile part of the world. In preparation, I was sent on a Jungle Warfare Instructors' course, with fifteen other officers and NCOs from 45 Commando, in Brunei in South-east Asia. This was an intensive, ten-week training package, where we gained first-hand experience of the skills we would be teaching to the rest of the unit in Belize. The skills I picked up here were to prove invaluable to me in a real survival situation in the African jungle several years later.

In the jungle, hi-tech gadgetry doesn't work very well as the trees get in the way, so you have to rely on basic soldiering skills such as patrolling, ambushing and good camouflage and conceal-ment. These skills, together with iron discipline, are needed to stay one step ahead of your enemy. Although patrolling in the jungle is hard work, at least you get lots of sleep, as the total darkness beneath the jungle canopy makes it impossible to move at night. If you're well away from the enemy, you can afford to put your hammock and mosquito net up and get a good night's sleep.

Life becomes a lot less comfortable if you're on 'hard routine'. This means you're too close to the enemy to risk putting up a hammock, cooking food, or even taking your shirt off to wash. You sleep on the ground, with your weapon by your side, using your webbing as a pillow. The best way to stay hidden is to crawl under a bush and keep very quiet. This is easy enough in itself, though there are plenty of unpleasant distractions. During a long overnight ambush, I still remember the sensation of a leech crawling up my leg, inside my trousers, heading for my groin. (This is the tastiest part of the human body, if you're a leech.) Had I been able to stand up, remove my trousers and use a torch, it would have been simple to remove, but this would have compromised the ambush. So I lay there as the leech attached itself to my right testicle. When a leech bites you, it's not painful. It tickles slightly, but the thought of it sucking your blood, as this one was now doing, is a bit unnerving. Gorged on blood and swollen to the size of a human thumb, the creature eventually dropped off of its own accord.

Before the final, two-week jungle exercise, we were given a long weekend to explore the region. A number of us ended up in a hotel in the town of Kota Kinabalu in nearby Malaysia. After a night on the town, we decided to hold a shallow-diving competition in the hotel pool. I led the way, by jumping off the hotel roof into the children's pool, clearing five storeys and the pool bar. Inspired by this, someone suggested using the disinfectant foot bath as the next landing zone. The water here was just a few inches deep and anything less than a perfect belly flop was likely to result in injury. The 'diving platform' was only a couple of feet above the water, which didn't seem too bad. So, again, I went first. To my relief, my technique seemed to work. A couple of Marines officers followed suit with no problems.

Next up was Jim, an officer from 5 Airborne Brigade's Pathfinder Platoon. He launched himself from the platform, in a perfect sky-diving position, belly-first towards the water. But at the last minute, he appeared to lose his nerve, bringing his arms round in front of him to break his fall. Instead he broke his elbows.

Soon afterwards, in April 1993, we deployed to Belize, and I spent the majority of my six months there helping run a Jungle Warfare Training Camp, where I was now an instructor. We hired some local Mayan Indian trackers who taught me some unusual survival skills. My favourite was hunting iguanas using 'traditional methods' (that is, not shooting them). Iguanas are large lizards that grow up to 5 feet long and live in the branches of tall trees above rivers. Catching them involves one member of the hunting party climbing a tree with an iguana sitting in it and everyone else treading water in the river below. The tree-climber chases the iguana higher and higher up the tree until it jumps into the water to escape. Iguanas are excellent swimmers but when they hit the water from 70 feet up, they are momentarily stunned and the swimmers have an opportunity to grab them. Perhaps not the most efficient hunting method, but a lot of fun. We would always eat the iguana we caught – the meat on its own was a bit bland, but delicious grilled with hot pepper sauce.

While I was away in the jungles of Brunei and Belize, Anna was on the other side of the world, having adventures of her own studying Arabic in Yemen and Syria. Communications weren't easy. One Valentine's card I sent took over four months to reach her via assorted offices and mailrooms. Being apart was hard enough, but the next time we were together was to prove even harder, though for very different reasons.

Avalanche

Anna and I were both in the UK for Christmas 1993. We had invited a group of friends to Edinburgh for New Year, including Alistair, my oldest climbing partner from school and university. We all spent Hogmanay among the drunken masses on the streets of Edinburgh and had a great night. We crashed out late so I was not popular when I bullied the others into getting up early on New Year's Day. The fine weather forecast for the next two days was too good to ignore and I was unable to resist the lure of the fresh snow in the Highlands.

Alistair, Anna and I set off by car heading north, intent on climbing some isolated mountains in a remote area north of Inverness. We were aiming for a group of six Munros (Scottish mountains over 3,000 feet) in the Fisherfield and Letterewe Wilderness. These hills are too far from a road to climb in a single day. So, having parked the car and with the winter sun setting behind the hills of Skye to our west, we walked the 12 miles or so through fresh snow to a bothy (mountain refuge) called Sheneval. There we cooked by candlelight and caught up on the sleep we should have had the night before.

The next day, 2 January, turned out more overcast but, with just a gentle breeze blowing from the west, it was still a fine day for a ridge walk. We started out soon after first light – this far north, about nine o'clock in the morning – hoping to make the most of the available daylight. Even in the best weather, Scottish hillwalking involves getting wet feet and we had to wade across a small river before heading up the east ridge of our first Munro of the day. This was Beinn a' Chlaidheimh, a beautiful, craggy peak, whose name is Gaelic for Mountain of the Sword.

As we gained height, the snow deepened, but conditions seemed excellent. We had stopped to dig a snow pit, examining the layers of snow to check for avalanche danger. Everything seemed fine but, as we were soon to discover, the safe snow conditions low down the mountain were not replicated higher up. Luck is always a factor in these things. After two hours of straightforward walking and scrambling, we had climbed the steepest part of the hill and were making our way up the now easy-angled slope towards the summit. The scenery around and beneath us was stunning. Knowing that it would be uncomfortable and windy on the very top, Anna and I stopped a few metres beneath the summit, to admire the view. Alistair, fed up with playing gooseberry, continued on and disappeared from sight over the other side of the ridge. After a quick kiss, Anna and I followed on.

Suddenly, I was aware of a dull thud and felt the slope beneath my feet give way. We had triggered an avalanche. A huge chunk of snow had detached itself from the mountainside and started sliding back down the hill – with us on top of it. I was slightly higher up than Anna and contemplated jumping to the side and jabbing my ice axe into something solid to stop myself. Then I heard Anna scream and decided to stick with her. I dived down the slope, grabbed her and we fell, clinging on to each other for dear life.

For the first few seconds, we rode on top of the large slab of snow and the slope was not too steep. But then we went over a cliff. I felt us fall through the air and muttered a silent prayer. Anna displayed a less spiritual approach and was swearing like a trooper.

I tensed up, anticipating a violent impact...

WHOOMP! We hit the ground with a thud and for a brief moment I thought it was over. The snow slab carrying us had cushioned the blow and we seemed alright. But the giant slab, about 50 metres square, had now broken into smaller chunks and was travelling on downwards, sweeping us along with it. We were tumbling wildly and I did my best to protect Anna by cocooning her in my arms, while frantically trying to dig my feet into something solid. We were being thrown around like rag dolls and buffeted by falling chunks of snow and ice. Everything around us was white. Disorientated, I struggled to dig my feet into firm ground.

Eventually, more through luck than judgement, my feet caught behind a large, stable boulder and we lurched to a sudden halt. I was lying on my back with my feet facing downhill and Anna was more or less sitting on my lap. For a split second, I thought we had made it intact. But now the remnants of the avalanche swept over us and we were being crushed. It seemed as if thousands of tonnes of snow were landing on our heads and I dreaded being buried. By a quirk of fate, though, we had stopped so suddenly that nearly all the snow swept past us, and we ended up near the surface of the avalanche debris.

'Anna, are you OK?'

She could only moan a weak reply: 'My back.'

There had been no time to feel frightened as we fell. But now I could feel fear rising in my throat and had to concentrate on staying calm. I looked around to see what had happened. I was pinned underneath Anna, who was clearly in a lot of pain. Looking down the hill, I saw we had come to a halt on a steep slope, just above another large cliff. Without the cushioning effect of a large slab of snow, we would not have survived this next drop. Looking back up, I was shocked to see how far we'd fallen – well over 300 feet. I checked my body for broken bits, in case I was injured and the adrenalin had numbed the pain. Everything seemed normal. In fact, the only thing broken was my watch strap. Perhaps I had been partly protected by my rigid-framed rucksack. Anna, however, had not been so lucky and was badly crushed.

'Sweetheart, I need you to try to move off me.' We were wedged, precariously, on a steep slope above a large drop, and I had to stop us falling further. She tried to lift herself up but screamed in agony and couldn't move. 'Can you wiggle your toes?' She could – a good sign. 'OK, take a deep breath and try standing again.' Another yelp. I could only imagine how much pain she was in. I found it distressing listening to her suffering, when I could do nothing more than dig my feet in, hold on to her and hope that Alistair had not been caught in the avalanche.

After what seemed an eternity, he emerged above us on the ridge. Considerate as ever, he had assumed we were still canoodling and had not wanted to invade our privacy. Eventually, though, he retraced his steps to see what was happening.

'What are you doing down there?' he shouted down to us.

'We enjoyed the walk so much, we wanted to do this bit again! What the hell do you think we're doing?'

'Oh right. Hang on. I'm on my way.'

He made his way back down towards us, gingerly in case he dislodged more snow. By chance, he saw something lying in the snow – our ice axes that had been ripped from our hands as we fell. By the time Alistair reached us, we had been wedged behind our boulder for twenty minutes. Anna had stopped moaning: a bad sign. Shock and cold were making her start to lose consciousness.

I kept talking to her. 'Hang in there – we'll look after you.' Alistair and I had come through a few scrapes together before. We both knew what we were doing and this gave me confidence. We had a quick 'team talk'. If Anna stayed where she was, she could soon die of cold. Her clothes were full of snow, which was now starting to melt. We needed to move her somewhere flatter and safer, where we could put extra clothes on her and get her inside the sleeping bag and bivvy bag I had in my rucksack. I was very glad of these 'safety stores' I had taken the trouble to carry, on what should only have been a six-hour walk to and from the bothy.

I suspected Anna had broken her back. I knew moving her would cause her terrible pain and possibly further injury, even paralysis. But if we did nothing, she could well die, either by falling further from this precarious position, or from cold. Raising the alarm would take hours (mobile phone technology had not yet reached this part of the Highlands) and rescue, especially if the weather deteriorated, could even take days. It was a hard decision to make.

'Sweetheart, we're going to have to move you. I'm sorry. It's going to hurt.'

Ignoring her groans, we lifted her up. We did our best to keep her in the same hunched position she had landed in, to minimize further damage to her spine, and carried her across the slope towards a decent-sized ledge. On the steep slope, covered with snow and boulders, this was not an easy task. Anna is light, though, and incredibly tough, and we reached the ledge without losing our careful grip on her.

As gently as possible, we tried to brush the snow from her clothes, then manoeuvred her into my sleeping bag and bivvy bag. Once again, we had to ignore her screams. Although I had some painkillers with me, I couldn't risk giving them to her, as they would have reduced her level of consciousness and made her even more susceptible to exposure. Far better to endure pain than die of cold. The ledge was not completely flat and Anna couldn't use her legs to stop herself sliding downhill, so she was constantly slipping down inside the sleeping bag. This contorted position was causing painful cramp in her legs, but even minor movements were causing the broken bones in her spine to rasp. So she lay still and suffered stoically in silence.

Another team talk. I would stay with Anna to look after her and Alistair would go for help. I was struck by the irony of the situation. We had deliberately chosen to get away from it all, but now this was playing against us. We were stuck at the top of about the most remote mountain in Britain, on one of the shortest days of the year. It was now just after midday, and we had about four hours till nightfall. Alistair set off back down the hill to raise the alarm. We hoped there might be someone in the bothy who could walk out to the road and find a phone, leaving Alistair to come back up the hill with more survival gear. Although risky for him, Alistair decided to travel light, leaving us with most of his clothes.

For Anna and me, it was a long, cold wait. I made her as comfortable as I could, then set about doing everything possible to improve our chances of survival. The snow was too loose to make an igloo, but I managed to make a windbreak, using rocks chipped from the frozen turf with my ice-axe. I also used rocks to make a large cross on the hillside, which would improve our chances of being seen from the air. As I worked, we chatted to keep our spirits up. This more or less worked, even though the only stories I could remember unfortunately seemed to involve mountaineering accidents. When the stories dried up I started singing (badly) to keep her entertained. Poor Anna. The cold and pain were bad enough, but my contrived cheerfulness must have been a harder test of her endurance.

Although I felt quite calm at the time, with hindsight I was perhaps acting a little oddly. Apparently this can happen after a traumatic incident. At one point I asked Anna if she would mind if I went back up the hill to bag the peak. A string of colourful expletives suggested this was not such a good idea. I still haven't made it to the summit of Beinn a' Chlaidheimh. But it would be nice to go back there some time with Anna, perhaps in summer...

It was well below freezing, the wind was strengthening and I was staying warm by keeping active. Anna, on the other hand, was lying motionless in a damp sleeping bag (still full of melted snow, despite our efforts). I knew her injuries were unlikely to kill her now, but the cold might. To avoid worrying her, I kept my thoughts to myself, but things were not looking good. As daylight began to fade, the wind strengthened and it started to snow. Anna had been shivering violently all afternoon, but now she stopped – and not because she was warming up. As a hypothermia victim's body starts to close down, the shivering stops. The next stages are coma and death. This was now happening to the love of my life.

I was beginning to get seriously worried. I lay on the snow next to Anna and tried to hug her to let her share my body heat. The sleeping bag was not big enough for both of us (we had tried this out under happier circumstances) and the damp fabric was preventing much heat passing between us. I cajoled her into talking and stroked her face, the only part of her not buried in the sleeping bag. Anything to keep her conscious.

As the light faded so did my morale. I now felt helpless, realizing that, with hypothermia, Anna could die there in my arms and there would be nothing I could do about it. Without further assistance and another sleeping bag, I didn't think she would make it through the night. Survival now depended on others. If there were climbers down at the bothy, I knew Alistair would be back before too long with the kit we needed. If the bothy was empty, Alistair would have to make the long hike out to the road, and we would be on our own for the night. I decided to myself that if Anna lost consciousness, I would have to drag her off the mountain, whatever the damage. I started psyching myself for the descent, and wandered a few metres from the ledge, looking for the easiest way down. Below, in the gloom, I saw a lone figure coming towards us. My best friend Alistair was back.

Alistair had run and slid back down the mountain. Having left us with his warm clothes, he needed to move fast to keep warm. To his relief, another group of walkers had just reached the bothy. They must have thought it odd seeing a scantily clad, manic stranger come running through the river, then bounding across the snow towards them. Nevertheless, one of this group volunteered to go for help. To this day I have no idea who the good Samaritan was. Alistair didn't catch his name but told me he looked like an 'Iain'.

Alistair packed a rucksack with more survival gear, then started the long slog back up the hill. To prevent a mix-up, he had given 'Iain' a written note, stating who we were, our exact location, what our injuries were and the equipment we had with us. I suspect Iain was a fell-runner as he covered the 12 miles back to the road in three hours, a remarkable feat given the deep snow. We heard later that when he reached the road, he attempted to flag down passing motorists, but the first few drove past him, blowing their horns rudely. He was about to break into and hot-wire a vehicle (mine, I hope), when a passing car finally stopped. The nearest telephone was several miles down the road, in a village called Dundonnell. There, he dialled 999. By a stroke of luck, an RAF mountain rescue Sea King helicopter was on a training exercise on Ben Nevis. This was just forty minutes' flying time away and the chopper was re-tasked to come to our assistance. After touching down briefly in Dundonnell to refuel and pick up the local mountain rescue team, the helicopter was on its way to search for us.

Back up on the mountain, Alistair's arrival was timely. With the extra gear he had carried back up, we were able to start re-warming Anna. Almost as importantly, our morale picked up. We fed Anna some hot chicken soup (vegetarian for ten years, she temporarily waived her principles) and began settling down for the night. Alistair and I would keep warm by jumping up and down. Anna was still in pain but now seemed quite cheerful. We knew helicopter searches were rarely carried out at night, and didn't expect to be picked up before morning. Luckily for us, however, our rescuers had made an exception, since we had given them an accurate grid reference for our location.

A couple of hours later, we heard the distinctive throb of rotor blades, then saw the flashing tail lights of a Sea King helicopter flying up out of the glen. We flashed our head-torches to show exactly where we were (though not directly at the helicopter – the pilot would be flying on night-vision goggles and we did not want to dazzle him). A hovering helicopter produces a powerful down-draught, so we made sure Anna was firmly tethered. I would not have enjoyed the irony if the rescue helicopter had blown her off the slope. We zipped Anna's bivvy bag firmly shut to stop too much spindrift blowing in. Endearingly, though, she kept unzipping the bag to peer out at what was going on.

The rescue team placed Anna on a spinal stretcher and she was winched carefully up into the helicopter and flown to Raigmore Hospital in Inverness. In Accident and Emergency, showing traditional Scottish priorities, Anna wouldn't let the doctors use scissors to cut her out of my expensive sleeping bag. 'Fair enough,' they shrugged. Advising her to take a deep breath, they simply whipped the sleeping bag off her, like a trick with a tablecloth.

X-rays showed that one of her vertebrae had shattered, with shards of bone now lingering 'literally a hair's breadth away' from her spinal cord. We were later told that, had we been less careful manhandling her around the mountainside, her spinal cord could have been severed. She had only just escaped permanent paralysis and was going to have to spend 'some months' in hospital.

I had to steel myself to call Anna's parents. Her father, himself an experienced mountain man, received the news with characteristic calm and generosity, but I felt horrible. I might have saved his daughter's life in one sense, but she wouldn't have been on the mountain in the first place, were it not for me. Nearly losing Anna was a defining moment in my life and made our relationship even stronger. We had never taken each other for granted before and we never will.

Anna spent a month immobile in hospital on a special spinal bed and many months in a plaster 'jacket', then a back brace. After a few months convalescing at her parents' home, she was suffering 'cabin fever' and wanted to get out of the house. She couldn't walk very far and couldn't sit up for more than a few minutes, so she travelled in the boot of my car lying on an old mattress. On a couple of occasions, she even braved train journeys to see me. She would lie across two seats or in the guard's van – apparently, British Rail gin and tonics were the best form of pain relief available. After an extra year out of university, Anna gradually got herself back to full fitness and now finds regular exercise is the best way to stop her back hurting.

As a bonus, Anna has since got into rock-climbing, which has turned out to be great therapy for keeping her back strong and supple – and great for me! She is an excellent rock-climber and together we have conquered some adventurous and memorable routes all over the world. I am really lucky to have a soulmate in life who is also such a close partner on the rock face. We both know – from real experience – that we can catch each other's fall.

CHAPTER TWO

MOUNTAIN LEADER:
Training for Survival

'Remember, men, you're all volunteers.'
'SNOWY' SNOWDEN, MOUNTAIN LEADER COURSE SERGEANT MAJOR

Talk about rubbing salt into your wounds. When you're freezing cold, wet and knackered, being reminded that you're going through all this of your own volition and you can quit at any time is not what you want to hear. Dead on my feet, I tried to remember why I had chosen to try to become a Royal Marines Mountain Leader.

One of the tasks of the Royal Marines is to provide a specialist Extreme Cold Weather Warfare capability, spearheaded by instructors known as Mountain Leaders. To become a Mountain Leader (ML) involves passing the longest, and arguably the hardest, specialist infantry training course in the world. This qualifies you for membership of the Mountain and Arctic Warfare Cadre, also known as the Brigade Patrol Troop, or BPT. Within the

Royal Marines, Mountain Leaders have a reputation second to none and I was keen to join their number. For me, one of the highlights of Commando training had been a day we had spent on Dartmoor, learning cliff assault techniques with the Mountain Leaders – a physically hard day but immensely satisfying. The MLs were the embodiment of what I thought all Commandos would strive to be: highly trained, well-motivated, professional soldiers, working in small teams behind enemy lines in the harshest climatic conditions.

The origins of the Mountain and Arctic Warfare Cadre go back to the Second World War. Following the Nazi conquest of Western Europe, and the ignominy of Dunkirk, Britain needed soldiers who could strike back at the Germans in occupied mainland Europe. To achieve this, Winston Churchill ordered the creation of Commando forces (so named as a mark of respect to the hard-fighting Boer 'Kommandos' of South Africa). Marine Commandos, acting as the Navy's infantry, infiltrated from the sea. Small raiding parties, relying on stealth to reach their targets, could substantially improve their chances of success by landing where there were no enemy forces. To avoid the slaughter of landing on easily defendable beaches, so graphically demonstrated by the US Army landings on Omaha Beach on D-Day, the Commandos developed a method of entering hostile territory known as cliff assault. This involved them climbing from small boats directly on to steep sea cliffs. Highly trained lead climbers scaled the cliffs (usually at night), before securing ropes for follow-on troops to ascend with heavier weapons and equipment. The specialist unit responsible for this dangerous and demanding task was the Commando Cliff Assault Wing, and it was originally based in Cornwall.

The imposing sea cliffs of Cornwall, continuously pounded by the Atlantic waves, provided a formidable training area, and those who made it through cliff assault training played a crucial role in raids both on occupied France and, further north, on the coast of occupied Norway.

As the Second World War turned into the Cold War, the Cliff Leaders of the Cliff Assault Wing needed to broaden their skills. The Royal Marines' Cold War task was now to defend NATO's northern flank. The only place where NATO and the Soviet Union shared a border was deep in the Arctic between Norway and Russia, so the Marines had to learn to survive and fight in this harsh environment. The experience of such episodes as the Battle of Stalingrad during the winter of 1942–3 and the Korean War in the early 1950s showed that the cold can cause as many casualties as enemy action. At Stalingrad, nearly a million German and Soviet soldiers lost their lives, half of these to the cold. During the Korean War, 10,000 American soldiers were evacuated with cold injuries such as frostbite and hypothermia. The Commando Cliff Assault Wing became the Mountain and Arctic Warfare Cadre (known throughout the Marines simply as The Cadre) and the Cliff Leaders became Mountain Leaders.

The Cadre's main role throughout the Cold War was instructional, teaching mountain and Arctic warfare to the rest of the Royal Marines. Though the Mountain Leaders did sometimes work together on operations, this tended to be on an ad-hoc basis. For example, in 1982, the Mountain Leaders deployed to the Falkland Islands. There, as well as long-range patrolling, they carried out a highly successful raid on an Argentinian Special Forces' position at Top Malo House, an incident that has entered Royal Marine folklore. During this raid, on 31 May 1982, nineteen members of The Cadre, commanded by Captain Boswell RM, deployed behind enemy lines by Sea King helicopter. They crawled through the snow to within 150 metres of the Argentinian Special Forces' HQ before assaulting. They achieved total surprise and killed or captured all the Argentinians, sustaining only three injured casualties themselves. And at the end of the Gulf War in

1991, as part of the Coalition effort to prevent Saddam Hussein's oppression of the Kurds, the Mountain and Arctic Warfare Cadre deployed to the mountains of Northern Iraq. Patrolling in small teams in the steep mountains of Kurdistan, their job was to monitor the movement of Iraqi forces operating against the Kurdish population.

In 1992 The Cadre was finally given a formal operational role and became Brigade Patrol Troop, based in Stonehouse Barracks in Plymouth, Devon. It is co-located with the Headquarters of 3 Commando Brigade, and provides the 'eyes and ears' of the Brigade in the form of a number of highly skilled, six-man reconnaissance teams. Each of the three Commando units (the Marines' version of a battalion) also has its own specialist recce troop commanded by an ML officer, with ML corporals and sergeants commanding its individual recce teams. In addition to their recce role, MLs organize and run the annual winter training that 3 Commando Brigade undergoes in Norway. The Mountain and Arctic Warfare Cadre may not have achieved the cult status of other specialist units such as the SBS or SAS but, in our field of expertise, our reputation is unrivalled.

The Acquaint

As Snowy Snowden, our course sergeant major, had kindly reminded us, all those who attend the Mountain Leader course are volunteers. You must be an officer or an NCO with a specific written recommendation from your commanding officer. In other words, you've got to be good even to apply. Only two or three officers and about twelve corporals are accepted each year, so the competition is stiff. Occasionally members of the Army are allowed to apply, but normally only Royal Marines are accepted.

First, though, you must pass the innocuously named 'Acquaint'. On paper, the Acquaint sounds reasonable, especially as it is only a week long: 'Candidates must be able to perform at least sixty press-ups... maintain the highest standards of personal fitness... have a head for heights... enjoy working in small teams... candidates must bring at least five sets of physical training kit...'

What the brochure doesn't say is that squeezed into the one-week Acquaint is about a year's worth of physical activity. And that those sixty press-ups have to be performed over and over again. And that 'working in small teams' is a euphemism for yomping all night, 'in a small team', across Dartmoor. About the only bit I didn't find too bad was the 'head for heights' part. On some Acquaints, not a single candidate passes (six out of twenty passed on mine). ML training is extremely demanding, both physically and mentally, and the Acquaint filters out those who lack the requisite strength and determination. It consists of a series of physical and mental tests, including difficult night navigation and a climbing aptitude test.

A typical day starts at two a.m., when we are rudely awoken by one of our instructors: 'Get up! Get your running kit on. You've got two minutes to be outside in two ranks, ready to go. Make sure you've had something to drink. Don't be late.'

Bleary-eyed and half-asleep, we turn to in the car-park. After two minutes of stretching, the instructor says: 'Follow me. Make sure you keep up.' We know that if we drop too far behind we will fail the Acquaint.

For the next two hours, we run uncomfortably fast around the streets and parks of Plymouth. People are still spilling out of nightclubs, as if we need reminding how ridiculously early our own day has started. If anybody starts lagging behind, the rest of us are made to do squat thrusts or press-ups until they catch up again. This ensures we are all constantly 'hanging out' – Marines' slang for 'knackered'.

There are seven parks in Plymouth. We run to each, stopping for ten minutes of circuit training: sit-ups, press-ups, tuck-jumps and pull-ups from tree branches or goal-posts. If we come to a grassy hill, we are made to sprint up and down until our lungs feel like exploding. Or worse, carry each other up and down the hill until our legs feel like jelly. Not surprisingly, this makes for blood, sweat... and vomit. I'm paired off with a big Brummie corporal called Matt and, as I hoist him on to my shoulders for a fireman's carry, he retches from physical exertion and throws up down my back – but we're both too knackered to care.

Today's instructor's speciality is an exercise called 'Orgasm', but there is little pleasure involved. We are made to run backwards up a long hill for nearly a mile. It doesn't seem too bad at the time, but when we reach the top of the hill we are suddenly ordered to turn around and sprint forwards. Our legs burn as if they're on fire and we all moan as if we were having an orgasm...

After this session, we collapse back into bed for a couple of hours, getting up in time for the first official period of the day: a timed 10-mile run over Dartmoor, to be completed in under seventy minutes. If we were fresh this would be hard enough, but our legs are knackered before we even start. I, for one, find it desperate but make it just in time. Several don't. When I stop running, I nearly faint and have to be helped on to the transport.

The rest of the day involves tests of our professional and military knowledge, practical map-reading tests and a climbing acquaint on the aptly named Devil's Rock on the edge of Dartmoor. After climbing up the steep rock face on the end of a rope, we are suspended upside down 150 feet above the ground. We know the rope will not break, so this is just a test of nerve. We are allowed to have a healthy respect for heights, but anyone with a fear of heights is in the wrong line of work. The final test of the day is a written exam in the classroom, as much to assess our ability to keep alert when tired as to test what we actually know.

The official working day ends at five o'clock in the afternoon. The unofficial day is far from over.

'Right, men, you've worked hard today, so this evening's PT session will be a gentle leg stretch.' I begin to see why we've been told to bring five sets of PT kit with us... Two hours later, we finish our 'gentle leg stretch' and another four would-be MLs have dropped out. The day now over, we all eat as much as possible and drink as many isotonic drinks as our stomachs will take before preparing our kit for the next day's activities. Finally, we crash out on our beds and fall into a dreamless sleep, waiting for the next midnight shake from one of our instructors.

The final pass/fail test is a 20-mile forced march across the steep hills of Dartmoor carrying a 50-pound bergen, and must be completed in under four hours. This is the equivalent of running from Liverpool to Manchester carrying a bag of cement – except that the route cuts across steep hills and deep valleys, and includes a total of about 3,000 feet of ascent and descent. Apart from on the steep uphill sections, you have to run all the way.

Mountain Leader training

Each year, fifteen to twenty men who have passed the Acquaint start the ML course. Eleven months long, the course is the longest and arguably the hardest specialist military training course in Britain. (I must be a glutton for punishment – whenever I see a course described as 'longest' and 'hardest', I seem to sign up straight away.) I felt privileged even to be starting the course. All my instructors and fellow students, even the ones who failed mostly after injuring themselves, were professional soldiers of the highest calibre and the training facilities were second to none.

My course assembled for the first time at Stonehouse Barracks, Plymouth in August 1995. I knew some of my fellow course members from the Acquaint but most were strangers. There was one other Royal Marines officer and fifteen corporals. Ranks don't matter on a course like this, and we were all to become close friends over the next year, bonding through shared experiences and hardship.

We were issued with a mound of specialist kit including top-of-the-range technical climbing equipment. (In comparison, my own stuff looked suspiciously old and frayed.) The first week was spent learning about the theory of climbing, including rope-work and how to tie twenty-five different types of knot. We had six periods of teaching or practicals every day and two periods of physical fitness training, intended to build up further the physical and mental stamina we would need throughout the course. This is known in Royal Marines slang as 'being beasted'.

The course then moved to Cornwall. For the next month we learnt the basics of military climbing on the sea cliffs around Land's End. Initially, this was just civilian climbing with a uniform on, but then we had to do the same in the dark. You don't have to be Chris Bonington to pass this part of the course, but climbing above the sea on a dark, wet night with your fingertips feeling desperately for holds hidden in the darkness needs strong arms and a cool head. We learnt skills such as 'steep earth climbing', which involves using ice-climbing equipment to climb up rock or earth too loose for normal rock-climbing techniques. We erected aerial cable ways to hoist heavy equipment up a cliff or casualties down it, and used grappling hooks to scale completely smooth cliff faces (throw it and, if it catches, keep your fingers crossed and send the lightest man up first!).

We learnt how to set up abseil ropes and how to dispatch a group of Marines from the cliff top. After a successful cliff assault and night raid, an amphibious raiding force return to their boats by abseiling down a number of fixed ropes, using friction devices to brake themselves before they reach the ground. Unlike civilian abseiling, the military version has to be done as quickly as possible and each man should be on the rope for no more than a few seconds. Later on the course, we would all qualify as helicopter abseil instructors. From a helicopter hovering 200 feet off the deck, we were expected to be on the ground within five seconds. To stop the rope burning your hand as you slide down it, you wear a thick pair of Kevlar and leather welding gloves. Without the gloves, at this rate of descent, you would lose all the skin on the palms of your hands.

One particular afternoon's climbing training involved a circuit up and down the cliff face at a place called Sennen Cove. We had to ascend wire caving ladders or climb hand-over-hand up a thick, hemp rope on one part of the cliff before sprinting round to a different part of the cliff and abseiling back down again. We were doing this to perfect our technique, until we could do it without thinking, even when dog-tired.

As each of us waited at the bottom of the cliff for the man in front to reach the top, an instructor would quiz us to check we had been taking in the lectures. Each wrong answer was worth fifty press-ups. 'What is the breaking strain of 11mm nylon rope?' *Easy enough.* 'Name three climbing areas in Snowdonia.' *Still easy.* But if you knew the answers to all the straightforward questions, the questions just got harder. One of the instructors had just returned from six months on the Antarctic island of South Georgia and had an obscure line of questioning that even the climbing know-it-alls couldn't answer. 'How deep can the leopard seal dive?' *Ummm...* 'Name seven types of penguin.' *Emperor, King, Chinstrap. Shit, that's only three...* At least the press-ups were making us stronger.

As a relatively experienced climber, I thoroughly enjoyed this phase but not everybody could hack it, and our numbers soon dwindled. As well as the practical climbing training, we received lectures every evening on such diverse topics as geology and navigation using the stars.

Every day started with a long run along the cliff tops ('to warm up') and ended with an even longer one along the cliff tops ('to warm down'). To keep us on our toes during the day, any minor misdemeanour would be punished, in traditional military fashion, with press-ups. The consequences of cocking up for real while climbing can be fatal and, as future instructors, it would not be just our own lives at risk. So, until they knew we were proficient, our instructors kept us under constant, close supervision. This kept us alive, but did make for an awful lot of press-ups. In the end, it didn't really matter how few genuine mistakes you made – the press-ups never eased up. We realized they were there to test our will to hang in there and to build us up, physically and mentally, for the rigours of the course ahead. In a moment of madness I queried the training value of press-ups to the course sergeant major, Snowy Snowden. I thought pull-ups, for example, seemed a more relevant exercise for budding mountaineers.

'Well, sir, if I make you do pull-ups before you go climbing, you'll run out of energy and fall off.' (This seemed reasonable to me.) 'But since you've asked, give me ten pull-ups and fifty press-ups.'

I didn't query his logic again.

Despite stringent safety measures, two members of the course had to drop out after breaking their ankles. Others just gave up because of the incessant physical beastings. And as a test of nerve and confidence, we had to pass a series of 'bottle-tests'. One of these was the 'Land's End Long Jump', which involved jumping across a 12-foot gap between two rock pinnacles, 200 feet above the sea. Just when you were pleased with yourself for making it, though, they made you come back a few days later and do it again in the dark.

Each Friday afternoon, the training week ended with a special 'Friday PT session': a three- to four-hour beasting designed to test our will-power as much as our physical fitness. The hardest session was 'the Sandbag Run', when we each carried a 50-pound sandbag as we ran along the undulating cliff-top footpaths. Every time we passed a beach, we had to run down to the water's edge for a lung-busting circuit training session. Then we had to sprint up and down nearby sand-dunes. Dropping out meant failure. We ran in and out of the water then rolled in the deep sand till our clothes were waterlogged and our shoes were full of sand. Every time we went into the sea, our sandbags soaked up water, making them even heavier than before. Our lungs felt like they would explode, and there were people coughing up blood.

At least we had the weekend to recover. Although it wasn't quite as hard, the next Friday session had its moments as well – this time we were made to run carrying old tractor tyres. Not an easy task, especially once they were covered in sand. The chafing of the rubber and sand on our shoulders stripped the skin off them. You don't have to be superhuman to do this sort of stuff. Of course, you have to be fit and strong, but it's additional, mental stamina that keeps you going.

Our instructors always accompanied us on these sessions and led by example throughout. So the good news was that they didn't expect us to do anything that they couldn't do themselves. The bad news was that our instructors set such a high standard it was difficult to keep up. The guy who took us on our hardest Friday PT sessions, Sergeant Bill Wright, was a former Olympic biathlete – which didn't make trying to keep up with him easy for mere mortals like me. (The biathlon involves cross-country skiing and shooting and is reckoned by some to be the most gruelling Olympic event.)

Although the physical training was brutal, we had to learn to cope with prolonged hardship, and it certainly toughened us all up.

By the end of the Cornwall phase, we were down to twelve students. The course now moved to North Wales for four weeks of climbing in Snowdonia; longer, harder rock climbs and a progression of ever more demanding mountain marches: first by day and then by night, carrying heavier and heavier equipment. We honed our navigation skills using map and compass, counting paces to work out exactly how far we'd walked. As a Mountain Leader, you have to be able to navigate confidently even under the harshest conditions and it takes a lot of practice. If you're leading a group of 100 Marines in the mountains and you take them the wrong way, you will not be a popular man. A navigational error of as little as 10 metres can mean the difference between staying on safe ground and walking off the edge of a cliff. Personally, I got a buzz just from being in the mountains but the heavy packs and often miserable weather did not always make it much fun. Our numbers dwindled further for a while when Jim Milne, one of the corporals on the course, took a serious fall on an exposed rocky ridge on Snowdon, after his heavy pack caused him to lose his balance. He fell nearly 100 feet, sliding down steep wet rocks, before coming to a halt on a rocky ledge; he was lifted off by helicopter. Luckily, nothing was badly broken and he was able to rejoin the course several weeks later.

There were many other technical skills to master, first in the classroom and then in the field: advanced rope-work, aid-climbing and fixing lines for less experienced troops to follow over difficult terrain. We also practised mountain river crossings. They were the sort of rivers normally tackled by white-water canoeists – but we had to go across them, not down them. We'd learnt the theory in the classroom, but it had been raining solidly for two or three days before the practical, and the water was surging down out of the hills. We arrived at the river bank, distinctly unenthusiastic. Snowy Snowden could sense our gloom – none of us was keen to jump into the cold, dark waters.

'OK, men, when you teach Marines river crossing, they're so nervous about getting in the water that they don't listen to anything you've got to say. As I'm sure you'll agree, the reality of being cold and wet is never as bad as the anticipation of being cold and wet. So, get them used to it straight away.'

And with that, he ran into the water. We followed.

We all now shared a vested interest in getting the job done as quickly as possible, and nobody pussy-footed around about trying to stay dry. The basic drill was for the first man to swim across, dragging a rope behind him. Not an easy task in a fast-flowing river, but at least the rope meant your mates could drag you back to safety if you didn't make it to the far bank. The rope was then strung between two trees and tensioned, giving the rest of the team a rope bridge to climb across. Easy in theory, much more difficult in practice, when it's raining hard and the temperature's only just above freezing.

Snowy debriefed us at the end of the session: 'Well done. The next time you do this will be in six weeks' time in Scotland, tactically and at night. And if it's a warm winter in Norway and the rivers don't freeze over, you could be doing it with skis.'

Oh, great.

Every morning we dragged ourselves out of bed for an hour of PT in the dark before breakfast. We soon realized that if we wore black tracksuits, it was almost impossible for our instructors to see what we were doing.

'Fifty press-ups, GO!' (Everybody lies on the ground and grunts a bit but doesn't do any press-ups.)

'Fifty sit-ups, GO!' (Everybody rolls over on to their backs and keeps grunting.)

And so on…

Most PT sessions ended with a bracing swim in a nearby river. On one occasion, our run ended in the village of Betws-y-Coed. Our instructor, Sergeant Al Willis, led us on to an old bridge over the River Llugwy. It was still dark and we could hear the water flowing 40 feet below. I could guess what was coming next. Sergeant Willis stood on the parapet in front of us and told us to peer over the edge. I looked down towards the river. It was too dark to tell the difference between the rocks below us and the water. But I could see two luminous markers directly below where Sergeant Willis was standing.

'Right, men. As an ML, you must learn to trust your fellow Mountain Leaders without hesitation. Down there, you can see two lights. Each one is on a rock two metres apart. But between them, the water is deep enough for you to jump into. Follow me.'

And with that, he jumped. I clambered on to the parapet and made the leap of faith, my colleagues close behind. We all missed the rocks.

The Welsh phase of the course culminated in a twenty-four-hour forced march across North Wales's highest peaks. Our training was paying off and we all made it.

Operational training

So far so good: we had learnt a lot about mountaincraft. But now we had to learn the practicalities of mountain warfare. There's no military point in being there unless you can fight there. Mountain Leaders must be able to operate in small reconnaissance teams, acting as the eyes and ears of the commander of 3 Commando Brigade. Yet, until now, we'd not even been carrying weapons. So we now learnt how to operate in small teams of four to six men, behind enemy lines, going in by helicopter or on foot.

We were taught how to establish covert observation posts (OPs) inside bushes or dug underground on a hillside, from which to observe enemy positions using long-range optical telescopes and hi-tech thermal-imaging equipment. We also learnt how to conduct a close-target recce, or CTR, which involves using good fieldcraft skills to sneak right up to an enemy position, while remaining undetected. We were shown how to record important tactical information such as sentry routines, and how to recognize 'key signature equipments' – that is, something that gives the game away and tells you what the enemy is really up to in a position. For example, you may not be able to see what type of equipment is hidden in a tent or building, but if you see a certain type of generator or antennae nearby then you can make an educated guess that it's attached to powerful radios; then you know you're probably looking at an HQ.

We practised making detailed sketch maps in our heads, then later on paper. We also developed the specialist communication skills needed to send encrypted radio messages back to our own headquarters, sometimes hundreds of miles away, using long-range, burst transmission, high-frequency radios. We learnt to mark a drop zone on the ground using infra-red beacons (for logistical re-supply from low-flying aircraft).

We also learnt how to operate as snipers. Like all well-trained Commando soldiers, we already had the requisite basic marksmanship skills. Even the standard SA80 rifle issued to servicemen is highly accurate – you should be able to achieve a first-round kill at 300 metres. As MLs, we could easily end up behind enemy lines. If a high value opportunity target presented itself to us (such as an enemy general or visiting politician), then we needed to know how to take him out. A successful sniper has to try to crawl to within 200 metres of the target, kill the target with a single shot, and, if possible, escape.

We also learnt specialist technical skills, such as how to differentiate between different types of bridge and measure the dimensions of the most vulnerable parts of the bridge for later demolition. Then we were taught how to assess what weight of vehicle could pass over a bridge before it collapsed – but I'd be the first to admit that this was never much more accurate than an educated guess.

In a small reconnaissance team, your main weapons are your eyes, ears and radio. It's somebody else's job to come along later with more manpower and bigger weapons to do the fighting proper. So as recce teams, you try to avoid contact with the enemy but when things go wrong you have to be able to fight your way out. We learnt how to use special lightweight weapons such as the M16 assault rifle and its shortened version, the Colt Commando. It takes a long time to become a good shot; first in the classroom and then on the rifle range. Everyone has a slightly different way of holding and firing a weapon, so it's a matter of trial and error, overseen by an experienced coach, to work out exactly where you have to aim to hit a particular target. In fact, as I was to find out a couple of years later in Sierra Leone, troops with no previous formal training are often very bad shots, even if they are 'battle hardened'. Firing a burst of automatic rifle fire from the hip may look good in the movies or on TV, but you don't actually hit anything useful.

As an ML, you have to be able to climb with a weapon on your back, so short-barrelled rifles or sometimes just pistols are your preferred weapons. We were taught anti-ambush techniques: first put down such a high rate of fire that the enemy has to take cover and can't shoot accurately. Then run away. In a four-man team you need a set drill so that even in the dark every man knows where every other member of his team is. To 'break contact' (get out of a fire-fight) with a numerically superior enemy, you fire and manoeuvre in pairs out of the danger area. This means two men give covering fire while two of you move. If a member of the patrol is hit, things become much more difficult: the drills stop working and it's time to make some hard choices. As Special Forces patrols in the Gulf War showed, you sometimes have to leave men behind if they're injured – a soldier's worst nightmare. I hoped I would never be faced with this dilemma: abandon your mates and live, or stay with an injured colleague and maybe die in the process.

We learnt how to locate and recover pre-hidden caches of food and ammunition buried in the ground and how to establish contact with a friendly 'agent' in enemy-held territory. Finally we learnt E & E (Escape and Evasion) techniques – which were to come in very useful later on in Sierra Leone. If our E & E failed, we were briefed on what we could expect to endure if we were captured. The harsh experience of 'Conduct after Capture' and 'Resistance to Interrogation' practical training was to come later.

We practised all these skills for four weeks on the bleak hills of Dartmoor, in preparation for moving on to the colder, even less forgiving winter mountains of Scotland and Norway.

Scotland: a testing time

The course moved to Scotland in mid-November. We knew this would be the toughest part of the training and arrived in Kinlochleven, near Glencoe, with a feeling of trepidation. If we could make it through to Christmas, we thought, the rest of the course would seem easy. The first snows of winter had already fallen on the surrounding mountain tops. But I knew it was the combination of cold, wind and rain that would make this such a difficult place to operate in.

The first few days were easy enough – non-tactical mountain marches on hills that I knew and loved, including Ben Nevis. Then we travelled to a remote estate in the Western Highlands near Glen Shiel (the Moidart Estate, owned by an ex-Royal Marines officer) to learn the rudiments of survival. We slept in a teepee made out of an old parachute and huddled together at night to keep warm. Extra clothing, waterproofs and sleeping bags were all banned, but at least we were issued with that little-known publication *Beginners' Guide to Edible Fungi*. For three days we practised skills such as shelter-building, fire-lighting and trapping wild animals. Under the supervision of the estate's gamekeeper, we learnt how to butcher a variety of wildlife, including rabbits, birds and deer. We discovered there is nothing more cruel than being tentative or squeamish when you have to kill an animal, as the poor beast then dies slowly. Sometimes, though, we were a little too enthusiastic when it came to wringing the necks of rabbits or grouse, and more than one of us managed to rip their heads right off by mistake. Kinder to the animal, but very messy... We even received a lecture on how to find water in a desert – someone's idea of a bad joke as we sat there in the pouring rain.

In a nearby fishing village we were shown how to collect shell-fish and cook seaweed. Seaweed can be highly nutritious, but you have to boil it for four hours first to make it easier to digest (the stuff you buy in the supermarket has already been boiled before it is freeze-dried). In a survival situation, you can expend more energy collecting the firewood needed to boil water for this long than you gain from actually eating the seaweed. While this makes seaweed a good choice if you're on a diet, it's not ideal when you're weak through lack of food. The water in this part of Scotland is so clean that you can consume the shellfish raw. We ate mussels, limpets and even periwinkles straight from their shells. I've never liked seafood, and found it easier just to swallow the things whole.

We had been told to prepare waterproof sketch maps of the area on silk that could be sewn into our uniforms as 'escape maps'. As part of our survival kits we were allowed a miniature button compass each and we tested our 'escape maps' on a short night navigation exercise. The final checkpoint was a pub in the middle of nowhere. The barmaid was not allowed to sell us any food but we were able to boost our intake of calories with beer! We slept well that night, back in our teepee. But this three-day package had just been the 'teaching phase' of our survival training. The 'test phase' was still to come. At least we now knew the sorts of things to keep in our survival kits. Each of us carried a waterproof metal tin in the chest pockets of our shirts, containing stuff such as fire-lighting kit (waterproof matches, magnesium powder, potassium permanganate and some cotton wool as kindling), wire snares, fish hooks, scalpel blades, chlorine tablets to purify water for drinking or washing wounds, strong painkillers, a couple of sugar lumps and a cigarette, for when it got really bad.

We returned to Kinlochleven to prepare for our next tactical field exercise and spent two days studying maps, planning routes, resting, eating, drinking, packing and re-packing our bergens. As well as weapons, ammunition, spare clothing, a week's supply of food, radios (with a week's worth of batteries), thermal-imaging equipment, long-range telescopes and medical kit, we also had to carry mountaineering kit, including ropes, helmets, ice-axes and crampons. Each bergen was so heavy that it was near impossible to put it on single-handedly. Now I realized why we had done so many press-ups back down in Cornwall: to build up the muscle bulk on our backs and shoulders. My bergen weighed nearly 120 pounds – heavier than Anna. We made a group decision not to take any tents, as they were simply too heavy. Lightweight ponchos would have to suffice. In hindsight, this was the wrong decision and, in the end, it was to have devastating consequences.

At last light on a wet and windy mid-November night, we clambered into a Sea King helicopter and deployed on to Exercise Gaelic Venture. We would not be sleeping in a bed again for nearly a month. We split into two groups and each moved independently from different start points. Our orders were to go in by helicopter to a remote landing site behind notional enemy lines, then move across mountainous terrain to locate a probable enemy position three nights' march away.

After forty minutes' flying on NVGs (the pilot using night-vision goggles), we landed near Loch Arkaig on the remote

Knoydart Peninsula. I stepped off the helicopter straight into knee-deep mud. I struggled to put on my bergen and sank in even deeper. We set off on a compass bearing, heading slowly towards our target. Within minutes we were drenched. It was raining hard – the sort of driving horizontal rain that waterproofs can only slow down, not stop – and the going underfoot was truly horrendous. We struggled in complete darkness through peat bogs and across steep, waterlogged hillsides where every minor stream had become a raging torrent of white water. We repeatedly cursed the cripplingly heavy packs on our backs. If you fell over, you couldn't get up again without assistance. As long as we kept moving, though, we stayed warm enough.

We yomped all night through peat bogs and heather and lay up at first light under our ponchos. The ground was waterlogged and the damp soon seeped into our bivvy bags. After a few hours our sleeping bags were soaking wet. Tents wouldn't have kept us dry but they would have kept us warm.

We were in a part of Scotland that I knew well, and weather like this wouldn't have stopped me going for a brisk hill-walk in my own time with my father or friends. The difference was that when you're there as a civilian, however bad it is, you know that within a couple of hours you can be back in the pub. On this exercise, though, there was no respite from the elements. On top of that, you wouldn't normally choose to go hill-walking at night. Operating at night, the darkness can feel very oppressive. Your colleagues around you are just shapes in the dark and, because you're tactical, you can't chat to each other as you're walking along. It's hard to think of much else apart from the cold, the wet and your aching shoulders.

When day breaks and you have to stop, everything is completely soaked. When you go camping as a civilian, you take off your wet clothes at night before getting into your sleeping bag. We couldn't afford this luxury as we had to be fully dressed with our boots on even in our sleeping bags, ready to move at a moment's notice if we were spotted by the enemy. A side effect was that our sleeping bags also got wet and so were not particularly inviting. Even the sheep had come down off the hills because the weather was so miserable – we were the only living things up there. I knew we were not the first people to have such a low opinion of this place, since the hill had been named 'Gulvain' – 'Hill of Shite' in Gaelic.

The rain got harder and harder throughout the day and by the time we set off again we were walking into a storm. We dropped down off the high ground and followed a track through a forestry plantation for several miles. To communicate with our HQ, we had to stop every six hours on a prearranged schedule to set up our communications equipment. In mountainous terrain, normal military radios don't work very well because the mountains obstruct the radio waves. So we used long-range, high-frequency radios, which worked by bouncing radio waves off the ionosphere. This involved erecting a 20-foot-high mast and a long, fiddly antenna. This isn't an easy task at the best of times and on a dark, stormy hillside it was near impossible.

During the midnight radio schedule, we could hear that the other team was having difficulties. Their radio signal was weak, but we distinctly heard the word 'casualty' being repeated over and over. Our headquarters told us they would send a team out to investigate and we were ordered not to get involved. The other team were in a different glen, and it would be quicker to approach them from the road at the foot of the glen than for us to try to walk over the mountain tops to find them. We guessed that somebody had broken an ankle, which would have been painful but not too serious. As instructed, we continued on.

We dropped right down to sea level, and as we crossed the West Highland Railway Line near Loch Shiel we sheltered for a few minutes underneath a bridge. Taking advantage of the only dry ground for miles, we spread some of our kit out on the railway. We joked about a train coming but, on the West Highland Line, at this time of night in November, it seemed highly unlikely. In the distance, we could see headlights on the road that ran parallel to the railway line. We sat on our packs and got our cookers out to make a hot drink. Out of the corner of my eye, I saw another set of headlights. Again, someone asked if there was any chance of it being a train. 'Definitely not,' I predicted confidently.

A few seconds later, the shrill whistle of an Intercity sleeper cut through the wind and rain. *Shit!* In a frenzy as the train approached, we threw our kit off the railway... and straight into a large puddle. Cooking on a railway track is definitely not to be recommended.

As my team struggled on, we were unaware of the tragedy that was unfolding nearby. One of the other team had fallen into a ravine and broken his arm. Without a tent to shelter in, they were now trying to help the injured man down to the nearest road to be evacuated. This was why we had heard 'casualty' over the radio. To improve communications, Snowy Snowden had driven out from Kinlochleven in a Land Rover nearer to the exercise area with a signaller and a powerful, vehicle-mounted radio.

The signaller, Corporal Chris Brett-Iversen, had been sitting in the back of the Land Rover, tuning the radio while Snowy erected the radio mast. In the darkness, both were unaware that their vehicle was parked near power lines. While Snowy was erecting the antenna, a 20,000-volt electric shock arced through the wet night air and flowed down through the antenna that was connected to the radio. The fibreglass mast that Snowy was holding did not conduct electricity, and he was unharmed. Corporal Brett-Iversen, however, bore the full brunt of a massive electric shock and was killed instantly.

Two days later, we reached our first target. Morale was low following this tragic accident and the exercise was beginning to feel pointlessly difficult. As we lay in our observation posts high on the hillside above the 'enemy' position, the weather now turned really cold and our wet clothing and equipment began to freeze. Jim, the patrol commander, asked for volunteers to leave the OP that night and conduct a close-target recce. A Dutch Marine (the Dutch don't have their own mountains so train their MLs with the British Royal Marines) and I volunteered. I reasoned I couldn't get any colder and wetter than I already was, so I might as well do something to keep busy. We slid down the hillside, first through snow but lower down through slush and, lower down still, just through the mud towards the target. It was so dark and misty we were able to crawl right into the enemy position without being spotted. Recce complete, we scrambled back up the steep hillside to spend the rest of a long, cold night huddling under our ponchos in the OP.

In the morning, several members of the course were suffering from hypothermia so the patrol commander took the decision to retreat to a mountain bothy, where we could light a fire and dry our kit. The exercise was starting to grind to a halt and we were way behind schedule. The horrendous weather conditions just made the going too slow on this type of terrain with such large packs, and lying out without tents on top of exposed mountain tops in the freezing weather might have ended in further casualties.

We expected little sympathy from our training team but they too realized how difficult conditions were and respected the patrol commander's decision to retreat. In order to salvage the training benefit of the exercise, the training team called in a Sea King helicopter from Northern Ireland to fly us closer to our next target. Relieved, we climbed aboard.

We should have known not to relax too much. The training team was never going to let us off that lightly. This was dislocation of expectation. Only a few minutes into the flight, still deep in 'enemy' territory, the helicopter landed abruptly in a nearby glen. We were unceremoniously kicked off the helicopter to fend for ourselves again but at least we were now 20 miles closer to our next target. As the last man disembarked, he was handed an envelope containing a set of written instructions, informing us the helicopter had been shot down by an enemy missile. We were the only survivors (*what a surprise*) and had to escape and evade to an emergency rendezvous 50 miles away where we would be picked up by boat in a week's time. The instructions also gave the grid reference of a food cache buried nearby so at least we'd have something to eat. And it was good to be back together as a course – we compared notes on what we'd been through and enjoyed the banter: 'Well, if you think you had it hard, you should've seen the river we had to cross...'

Wearily, we slung our packs on our backs and trudged on over the hills. The weather slowly improved and we successfully evaded capture as we made our way to 'safety'.

This 'helicopter crash' gave me a philosophy that I have tried to stick to ever since: 'Hope for the best but plan for the worst'. Planning only for the best is living very dangerously.

A week later, we were picked up by boat from a remote, desolate beach near the end of the Ardgour Peninsula and were all looking forward to being warm and dry again. We had learnt our lesson from the 'helicopter crash', though, and were expecting the unexpected. Most of us, for example, had ceremoniously swallowed £20 notes wrapped in condoms just in case we were separated from our kit and had to get ourselves out of trouble. Sure enough, when we got on board, something was not quite right. We were expecting our instructors to pat us on the back, say well done and give us a nice cup of tea. Instead, there was a distinctly unfriendly atmosphere. It now dawned on us, once again, that the exercise was far from over.

Living off the land

Our kit was taken off us, along with our clothes, our watches, everything we had and we were left standing naked except for our underpants and boots. We were then strip-searched and told to put on new uniforms provided for us. Mine was far too small and all the buttons had been ripped off. Our survival kits (in small tobacco tins) were taken off us, searched for contraband such as money or credit cards and returned to us. We were not allowed to talk to each other and were forced to sit out on deck in the cold and wet and await further instructions. After a few hours of shivering, the chief instructor of the Mountain and Arctic Warfare Cadre, Colour Sergeant Brent Hushon, came up on deck to tell us what would happen next.

> 'Gentlemen, welcome to Exercise BLUE – the test phase of your survival training. We will shortly reach the Isle of Islay. You will be taken to an exercise area, where you will remain until further notice. If you are caught cheating, you will be thrown off the course. The rules are these:
>
> One: Do not build survival shelters less than 1 kilometre from any forests, roads, or houses.
> Two: Do not speak to any locals.
> Three: Do not leave your shelters during the hours of darkness.
> Four: Do not enter buildings.
> Five: Do not kill any farm animals or domestic pets.
> Good luck.'

When we reached Islay, the Hebridean island famous for its whisky and foul weather, we were all cold, wet and seasick. We still only had the clothes we stood in – all our other kit had been confiscated. We were split into groups of four and blindfolded with sandbags over our heads. This made it hard to breathe but at least they offered a bit of warmth. We were led ashore and manhandled onto the back of a truck. An hour later, we were dragged off again, and forced face first into the cold, wet mud. The truck drove off. I took the blindfold off my head, turned it into a hat and put it back on again. I looked around me, disorientated and shivering uncontrollably. The wind was whipping across the barren moorland, but at least it had stopped raining. With my three teammates, Zippy, Rob and Jim, I set to work. We had two hours before last light. Our first priority was shelter.

For the next ten days, we lived off the land as best we could. This was real survival as opposed to 'playing at survival', which you normally do on exercise. I doubted the training team would let us die of cold, but they'd let us get half-way there before rescuing us. Ending up in hospital would mean we had failed the exercise and would be chucked off the course.

We built a small but sturdy shelter (or 'hooch') out of logs, scraps of corrugated iron and turf. With a fire at the entrance to the hooch, we stayed warm but smoky. We caught brown trout from a nearby lochan. They were not much bigger than goldfish but they added variety to our diet of cattle feed and seaweed. Our traps were less successful but we enjoyed the road-kill we scraped off nearby roads. As long as we checked the same stretch of road every day, we knew it was fresh. The sheep began to look more and more tasty but the prospect of an irate local farmer – or worse, one of the training team – finding us out was deterrent enough.

To stay warm at night, we heated rocks in our fire then wrapped them in sacking and used them as hot water bottles. We also made a 'duvet' out of agricultural sacks stuffed with bracken. Our hooch was about the same size as a single bed, so it was a tight squeeze to get us all in at the same time. At least we had each other's body heat. Apart from Jim's snoring (which drove the rest of us to distraction), the only bad thing about our hooch was the lack of space. It was too cramped to lie down on our backs, so we lay on our sides and made like spoons. If anybody wanted to turn over, we all had to turn over. Unlikely as it sounds, once our hooch was up and we got a fire going, we managed to stay warm enough for the whole exercise, despite our lack of clothing or equipment. In fact, it was a relief not to be carrying our heavy packs any longer and, though hungry, we were kind of enjoying ourselves. Suddenly our only responsibility was survival.

We scavenged for food and collected firewood all day, dressed like scarecrows with 'waterproofs' made out of plastic bags, and chatted at night if we couldn't sleep. We even tried stalking deer, but of course never got close enough to rush them and club them to death. Legend had it that an ML on Islay once jumped off a cliff on to the back of a stag and broke its neck with his bare hands. Knowing the individual involved, I think it's probably true. The good news for this man's hooch mates was that they all dined on venison for the rest of the exercise. The bad news was that humans are not designed to eat a meat-only diet and they all made themselves ill by gorging on too much rich meat.

I kept myself going by dreaming about all the fun things I'd do during Christmas leave. Rob was a Dutchman, and he invited Anna and me to Amsterdam to stay with him and his girlfriend for Christmas. He and I discussed exactly what we'd eat and what drinks we'd have in which bars. (In the end, every bit of the fantasy came true. Except the bit involving Rob's 6-foot, blonde, international volleyball-playing girlfriend...)

We had been allowed to keep the contents of our survival tins: fish hooks, wire snares, four matches, a small amount of kindling, potassium permanganate (which can be used as a disinfectant and a firelighter as it burns very well), chlorine for purifying water, a couple of sugar cubes, a few decent scalpel blades and some painkillers. Those of us who had swallowed £20 notes in anticipation of a survival exercise did not see them again for several days, due to a combination of lack of food and constipation. In any case, spending money was also strictly against the rules and none of us wanted to get thrown off the course. We had been through enough discomfort not to want to have to repeat it.

On the tenth night, I woke in the middle of the night when I felt something land by my feet at the entrance to the hooch. Half-asleep, I wondered what it was.

BANG!

My head ringing, I realize it's a stun-grenade.

Someone is ripping the roof off our hooch and I can hear men shouting: 'GET THE FUCKERS!'

Dazed and confused, we are dragged out by a group of about thirty soldiers in balaclavas. I can smell the alcohol on their breath and they're really aggressive. We struggle but, outnumbered and weak through lack of food, we get a good kicking. We're blindfolded, thrown into a frozen pond, then led at gunpoint to a road. We're shoved on to the back of a truck and are well and truly suffering the 'shock of capture': fear, confusion and extreme discomfort.

Conduct after Capture

We more or less know what to expect: this is the 'Conduct after Capture' phase of the course. All UK service personnel who are deemed 'prone to capture', including Special Forces, MLs and front-line aircrew, have to undergo Conduct after Capture training. You cannot be taught how to resist torture but, by introducing you to the mind games that interrogators will use against you, you at least know what to expect. You must try to remain the 'grey man' to avoid unwanted attention, and hold out for long enough not to jeopardize the lives of any of your colleagues who might have evaded capture.

We spend the rest of the night in stress positions in an aircraft hangar at Islay's airport. Stress positions involve kneeling or standing in contorted positions for hours on end, such that your joints seize up and your muscles cramp. They are exceptionally painful and are an effective way of wearing down a prisoner without actually torturing him. Stress positions do not have to be complicated. One simple stress position involves standing with your arms stretched up above your head. If you don't believe me, try it for twenty hours in a row. If you let your hands drop, at any stage, get somebody to punch you in the kidneys. Another stress position they get us into is sitting cross-legged on the concrete floor with our hands behind our heads and our elbows pushed back. If we let our elbows come forward we are kicked in the small of the back. Given that it is impossible not to move at all after a while, we get kicked a lot. Not too painful to start with, but we are always kicked in exactly the same spot, and the pain of being struck on already bruised flesh is excruciating. Most of us take it stoically, but some can't help screaming and moaning.

By now it is the second week in December and very cold. As the thin cotton uniform I'm wearing is too small, my midriff, ankles and forearms are all exposed to the bitterly cold wind. By now, we have been out in the field for nearly a month, the last ten days of which we've effectively not eaten, so we are all run down already. As an added bonus, I've also had the shits quite badly for a couple of days but we aren't allowed to go to the toilet, so I just go where I'm sitting. I don't care about the smell, but it does mean that my trousers are damp and even less warm than before. At some stage I imagine the £20 note must have come out and jokingly wonder whether I could bribe one of the guards with it. One way or another, though, the opportunity doesn't arise.

If we collapse through cold or exhaustion, we are dragged into a warm room for a few minutes and sat in front of a heater until we stop shivering. Then, after a few precious minutes in the heat, we are dragged back out into the cold again. Going in and out of the cold is far worse than just staying in the cold. At one stage, I am given a pair of socks and told to put them on. This seems too good to be true. And it is. As I struggle, blindfolded, trying to undo my bootlaces with numb fingers, the socks are taken off me again – a cruel ploy.

In the morning, still blindfolded, we are led on to an aircraft, and fly for about an hour, still in stress positions. I later hear that we had been led past astonished passengers at the airport (who thought we were being kidnapped) and on to a Lear jet. This is the first and probably the last time I will have the opportunity to travel in such 'luxury'.

On landing, we are bundled into yet another truck and driven to what feels like an old stone fortress and thrown into a dungeon. For the next thirty hours we are kept in stress positions. The monotony and discomfort are alleviated every six hours when we are fed half a slice of bread each and a sip of water. Despite the blindfold I'm aware of day turning to night. As I stand there all night with my hands in the air, I begin to hallucinate from lack of sleep and sensory deprivation. We are being 'conditioned' for interrogation.

The next day we are moved again, this time to an interrogation centre. Our blindfolds are briefly removed and we are spoken to by a doctor. We are told that we will not be physically harmed and that, if we choose to give up, our request will be respected. Only when we see this same doctor will the exercise be over. Until then, anything else that happens is just a ploy by our interrogators and we must not be taken in. Dazed, confused and weak through lack of food and sleep, and weeks in the field, we are good candidates for a tactical interrogation. From then on, the blindfolds are removed only during our visits to the interrogators.

We are led to a 'holding centre'. The sensory deprivation is total. White noise blares out from loudspeakers around us and, blindfolded for days on end, we lose all sense of what is happening. We don't know where we are, who we are with or what the time is.

It's difficult to explain the effect this has on you. Time seems to creep by and, more than anything else, it starts to make you lose your grip on reality. The clichés of every second taking an hour become true. I try counting an hour's worth of seconds but it's too depressing as it seems to go on for ever and I never get beyond 100. We also have no idea of how many guards there are around us. They have a policy of never talking to each other in our presence. All we know is that if we move or make a noise, someone is there immediately to slap us in the face or push us around.

For the interrogations we are taken into a brightly lit room, and suddenly have our blindfolds removed, so we are completely disorientated. At first the interrogators shout at us in different languages: Russian, Arabic, Spanish – and I'm sure one of them is speaking Welsh. Although we know they aren't going to do us any serious physical damage, they make a good show of breaking up the furniture around us and we are slapped around a bit.

The physical stuff doesn't bother me so much: the real problems are in my head. I am pretty close to flipping out at times. I have a mental strategy of saying to myself, 'OK, whatever you want to do now, just wait for five minutes and see how you feel then.' I have to do my 'five-minute plan' over and over again until something changes, either mentally or physically, and it seems to do the trick. It's hard to describe just how grim it all is.

For the next twenty hours, we are subjected to a series of interrogations: some aggressive, some friendly and some downright
boring. We are not allowed to give away any more information
than our name, rank, number and date of birth. This may sound
easy but the interrogators are very good at their jobs and, given
our current state of mind, it is hard not to say the wrong thing.
During one session I am stripped naked and subjected to an
extended, internal 'body-cavity' search in front of a scathing group
of female interrogators. Though I'm not sure who finds this
more unpleasant, given the lack of personal hygiene facilities I've
enjoyed over the last month or so...

After the search, I am handed a set of overalls and told to
put them on. I think this is a trick, believing I will then be
photographed in what will appear to be an 'enemy uniform'. So I
refuse. My interrogators eventually lose their patience and I am
told: 'OK. Have it your way.' This turns out to be a big mistake on
my part. I have been too suspicious and later discover the overalls
were given to me just to keep me warm!

I am led outside and left spread-eagled, stark naked, against a
wall. It's a cold, frosty night and in my weakened state I grow
dangerously cold very quickly. For ninety minutes I stand there,
literally freezing. As I feel myself slipping into hypothermia, I think
maybe the exercise has gone wrong or that someone's cocked up.
In fact, I am being monitored via a hidden camera and, on the
point of collapse, I am brought back inside to a warm room, given
a blanket and a cup of tea and spoken to gently by a kind lady. She
tries to coax me into speaking freely, offering me more tea and
some biscuits if only I tell her where I am from. I refuse and am
led back to the 'holding area'.

In the holding area, as well as being blindfolded, we are made
to stand for hours on end with our hands pressed against a cold,
wet wall which numbs our sense of touch. White noise (like a badly

tuned TV) blares out deafeningly from loudspeakers, which is designed to test our sanity to breaking point... and in some cases does. One of my hooch mates from Islay finally cracks. He is taken into a cell and his blindfold removed. He is joined by another 'prisoner' he does not recognize and they are left alone. The 'prisoner' is really an interrogator, but my mate doesn't realize this and chats openly to his cell-mate. He tells the interrogator who we are, everything we've been doing and that there's an officer in his group called Phil. I'm dragged into the cell, my blindfold's removed and I see my friend and the other 'prisoner'. I twig what's going on and tell him to shut up, but the damage has been done. My friend's gone a bit mad. I have time to give him a reassuring squeeze on the arm, and tell him to hang in there, before I'm dragged out again.

There is one moment of light relief. For a few minutes, we are forced to lie down on a soft, padded floor, but no longer in a stress position. The idea is that we all fall asleep, but as soon as we nod off the guards rush in, grab us and lead us, half-asleep, into the next interrogation. Groggy and confused, we might say the wrong thing. The guards haven't taken Jim into consideration, though. He falls asleep at the drop of a hat and is the loudest snorer I've ever heard. He is asleep within seconds. The noise of his snoring keeps the rest of us awake but it's good to hear a familiar voice. I hear the titters of my colleagues and, for the first time in several days, we know we are not alone. It's a good feeling.

My next interrogation lasts for three and a half hours, during which I am asked the same question over and over again.

'What is your regimental number?'

'N034354T.'

'Number?'

'N034354T.'

And so it goes on, over and over again.

For the first half-hour this is easy and I wonder what the point of the interrogation is. But as I get sleepier, it becomes harder to concentrate. Soon, the interrogator is also struggling to stay awake. A colleague takes over. Again the same question. My mind starts to play tricks on me. I picture my regimental number in my mind's eye and try to read it out aloud each time I am asked. It's like I'm reading off an autocue. While the autocue gives me the right answers most of the time, every now and then an inappropriate word or number appears and it's difficult not to blurt it out. The nearest thing I can compare it to is playing a drinking game, where you get so wasted that even if you know the answer to a question, the words come out wrong. It's as if the co-ordination between your brain and your mouth has stopped working.

'Number?'

'N034354T.'

'Number?'

'N034354T.'

'Number?'

'I'll have the chocolate cake, please.'

I'm only glad it was something as inoffensive as food that had appeared on my 'autocue' and not something of more tactical significance.

After asking the same question over a thousand times, the interrogators start to slip in different ones.

'Number?'

'N034354T.'

'What unit are you from?'

In my mind-numbed state, it's hard not to answer. I can see how false confessions could easily be dragged out of prisoners.

After what seems an eternity, our blindfolds are removed for the final time and we see the doctor. We have successfully resisted

Four years old. Stuck up a tree, but still smiling.

Rock climbing as a teenager in France in 1987.

Ice climbing with my father. He's just been hit in the face by
a falling lump of ice, but seems to be enjoying himself.

Summitting on the Fitzwilliam Museum, during a night climb in Cambridge.

Spitsbergen, 1991. Stuck in pack ice at 81° North.

After rowing 1,500 miles in a 5.5 metre open-top boat, Pete and I were burnt, blistered and frozen-footed, but it was worth it to be in one of the most beautiful places in the world.

Spitsbergen: sometimes we had to force our way through the pack ice, and it could take more than an hour of constant pushing to move the chunks of ice apart.

Summer 1992. Exercise 'Crash Action' in the Brecon Beacons during my Commando Course. (I'm fifth from the right in the second row).

Officer training. On a 'collective punishment' mud run with fellow officers in the River Exe estuary.

1 January 1994. Approaching Beinn a' Chlaidheimh in the Scottish Highlands. The last photo before the avalanche.

3 January 1994. Anna lying on a spinal bed in hospital after the avalanche. She was to spend six months in plaster.

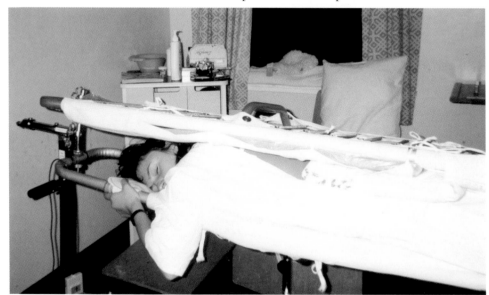

Mountaineering in the French Alps, near the top of the Dent du Géant (Giant's Tooth).

(From l to r) 'Zippy' Howard, Rob de Leeuw and me in our survival shelter on the Hebridean island of Islay, December 1995. All we had were the clothes we stood up in.

Ice-breaking drills in Norway. On one occasion I gave my five-minute lecture on self-rescue whilst treading water. I'm told that a man lasts eight minutes without losing consciousness in these conditions.

ML training in Norway. We were taught to soldier in temperatures down to −30°C.

Resistance to Interrogation training. We were given a small sip of water every six hours. Only troops designated prone to capture, such as aircrew, MLs, SAS and SBS, receive this training.

*Sacré Cœur (E2 5c) on the
North Devon coast.*

*New routing on a frozen waterfall in Norway.
(The icicles are known as chandeliers, and
like chandeliers they are very beautiful
but also very fragile...)*

*At the summit of Mount McKinley in Alaska – the coldest mountain in the world.
I don't know exactly how cold it was here as my thermometer stopped at –40°C.
(From l to r: Ian Marsh, Mark Dornan, me.)*

27 July 1997. Getting married at the foot of Arthur's Seat in Edinburgh was the happiest day of my life.

On our honeymoon in the Italian Alps, 1200 feet up a 2000 feet rock climb. We stayed in hotels, a mountain hut and a tent but we weren't forced to bivouac – this was our honeymoon, after all!

interrogation. All except my old hooch mate, who is thrown off the course. We sympathize, but this is no game.

A few years later, I ended up sharing an office with an experienced Joint Service interrogator who admitted that the trainee Mountain Leaders were his favourite subjects as, after everything we had been through, we most closely resembled captured PoWs.

Ice-cold in Norway

After an all-too-brief Christmas leave, we deployed to a village called Haugastol on the edge of the Hardangervidda National Park in the mountains of western Norway. For the next three months, we underwent the Extreme Cold Weather Warfare phase of the course. Haugastol is 3,000 feet above sea level, and the Hardangervidda is the wilderness area where the Norwegian resistance fighters of the Second World War, including the 'Heroes of Telemark', hid from the occupying German Army for years. A memorial in the nearby settlement of Finse is dedicated to Scott of the Antarctic as it was here he did his training before setting off for his infamous expedition to the South Pole. More recently, the snowy scenes from *The Empire Strikes Back* were also filmed here.

All of us were already trained in Arctic warfare from previous deployments to Norway with regular Royal Marines units. Now we were being trained to be instructors and would have to do more than just fend for ourselves. In the future, we would all need to have the 'spare capacity' to look after our subordinates and students in the most demanding of conditions.

After everything we had been through together, it was a shame to lose our hooch mate. But we were joined for the Norway phase by an old friend of mine, Huan Davies, who had just finished a year on exchange with the Chilean Army. He had completed the Chilean version of the ML course in the Andes, where he had acquired some unusual skills. He could claim to be the only trained 'mule-handler' in the UK Armed Forces and probably the only 'South American telemark ski instructor'. Sadly, these two claims to fame were only useful as chat-up lines! Chile had only recently stopped being a fascist dictatorship and the harsh military discipline had been something of a culture shock. On one occasion, Huan had been made to sleep outside in the snow for a week as punishment for farting during a senior officer's lecture. Huan had gastro-enteritis at the time but this was not seen as a good enough excuse.

For the first three weeks we ran our own 'Novice Ski and Survival Course', taking it in turns to be the instructors while the rest played the part of students. This gave us the chance to rehearse the lessons we would have to give to real novices once we were qualified as MLs. It also gave us ample opportunity to regain our 'ski-legs' before progressing on to more demanding tactical training. In the deep snow of the Norwegian mountains it is impossible to move around without skis or snowshoes. We covered vast distances on lightweight telemark skis until skiing, even by night with a heavy pack, became second nature. Despite the weight on our backs, we could move about much more quickly than in the mountains of Scotland. If we had to carry equipment too heavy or bulky for a rucksack, we dragged 'pulks' (small sledges with a harness attached) instead. To climb up steep slopes without taking our skis off, we fitted synthetic animal 'skins' to the bottoms of our skis (which let skis slide forward over snow, but not backwards).

Navigating on skis is not easy. When you navigate at night on foot you have to count your paces to work out how far you've been. Wearing skis, you obviously can't do that, so I mentally ticked off each time I had travelled 10 metres or so. With practice, I was able to do this subconsciously, even while holding a conversation. If you know exactly where you are to start with, stay on a compass bearing and keep track of exactly how far you've skied, then you can work out precisely where you are at all times. This a particularly good idea if you've got to find your way back to a small tent in a storm or find a food cache hidden in the snow. Skiing on a bearing on flat ground is hard enough, but down a steep hill it is near-impossible – just as when you're on the downhill ski slopes, you have to zig-zag backwards and forwards to slow yourself down. The other downside is that you might inadvertently go over the edge of the mountainside since you can't really see what's in front of you. Sometimes the only way to do it is to tie a 50-metre-long rope on to one of your colleagues, and send him forward until the rope has paid out. That way, you know he is exactly 50 metres away. If he holds his compass towards you, you can see the luminous dial that glows in the dark so you can move him left or right until he is on the correct compass bearing. When he is in the right place, you ski to him, then start the process all over again. It's slow going but better than skiing off a cliff.

We lived in tents, igloos or snow-shelters. The easiest type of shelter to make is a snow-cave. You find a bank of snow at least 3 metres deep, then hollow out enough space for four people to sleep in. Snow is a good insulator, so a good snow-hole is much warmer than a tent and it doesn't blow away in a storm. But it takes a couple of hours to dig one, so we mainly slept in small three-man tents.

Inevitably, people get pretty stressed on a course like this and occasionally come to blows. I shared a tent with Mick, a dour Glaswegian, and Matt, the big Brummie corporal I'd trained with earlier. They had been getting on each others' nerves for several weeks – Matt had accused Mick of having a 'stupid accent' and Mick had accused Matt of having a 'pointy arse'. Neither offence seemed serious to me, but living in a small tent together can do strange things to you. I was sleeping between them with my head at the far end of the tent. I awoke when I felt them rolling around on top of me, fists flying. They didn't seem to be doing each other much damage so I let them get on with it. It must have acted as a good form of tension relief, as there was far less arguing afterwards.

We were taught how to identify avalanche-prone slopes and what to do if caught in an avalanche. After my experience with Anna, this was something I had a particular interest in. By studying the interaction of temperature, wind and snowfall, we were able to predict when an avalanche was most likely to occur. The best way to avoid an avalanche was never to go on an avalanche-prone slope in the first place, but sometimes this was unavoidable. So we learnt how to search for victims buried in the snow and, for our own safety, wore radio beacons so we could be found much more easily if we ourselves were buried. If you survive the initial traumatic injury of being hit by an avalanche, you can expect to suffocate in less than ten minutes. So we buried 'victims' in the snow and repeatedly practised using our transceivers until we could rescue them in much less time than this, even in the dark.

We also practised finding safe routes for BV206 oversnow vehicles through difficult terrain. BV206s are Swedish-made, lightweight, fibre-glass vehicles with rubber tracks. They're like a cross between a skidoo and a tank and carry up to twelve people. Unlike a tank, though, they have a very low ground pressure so do not sink too deep into the snow. Their suspension is so good that you can lie down in the snow and let the BV206 run over your body without doing yourself any damage. Try this with a tank and you'll come out flat as a pancake.

We learnt how to test the thickness of ice on frozen lakes using an ice-augur (a device like a giant pneumatic corkscrew). If the ice is over a metre thick, for example, you can drive a 50-tonne tank over it or even land a Hercules C130 transport aircraft on it. Ten centimetres is fine for a man on skis, but if the ice is less than 5 centimetres thick, then you're living dangerously.

We also learnt how to teach 'ice-breaking' drills – what to do if you fall through the ice into a freezing lake or river. As long as you don't panic, it's relatively straightforward. You know the ice behind you is strong enough to take your weight, as you've just been standing on it. But the problem is climbing out with all your equipment before your body weakens with the cold. If you abandon your equipment, even if you don't drown, you will probably freeze to death. All your dry clothing, your sleeping bag, tent and cooker are in a waterproof bag inside your bergen, so you need to hang on to it.

The drill goes like this. If you have to cross a stretch of thin ice, you first loosen your ski-bindings and sling your weapon and bergen over one shoulder (to make them easier to take off if you fall through the ice). If the ice breaks and you fall into the water, the cold around your chest makes it hard to breathe but, if you don't panic, you soon get used to it. As an adult male, you can expect to stay conscious for about eight minutes in water at 0°C (longer if you're a woman or if you're wearing thick clothes), which is plenty of time to sort yourself out. To prove the point, in a lecture to a course I was running in Norway a couple of years ago, I gave the whole of the 'Ice-Breaking' lecture standing in freezing water.

Your skis and bergen (which has air trapped inside it) float, so you can worry about them later. First, you turn round to face the point at which you fell in. Then, as you tread water, you pass your weapon out on to the ice, then your skis, then your bergen. Next comes the tricky bit. Holding your ski-poles at the bottom, and using the sharpened tips as 'daggers' to grip on the ice, you haul yourself back out, keeping your body spread flat to minimize the pressure. You drag yourself back towards the thicker ice, then roll in the snow to absorb much of the water on your body and clothes before it has time to freeze. Snow has the unusual property of absorbing water like a sponge, and the colder the snow, the more effective it is. It's then a race against time to put up a tent, or get in a vehicle before you freeze to death. The coldest still air temperature in which I have ever done this drill was minus 27°C, so cold that any water on your body freezes almost instantly – including the water on your eyeballs. You must work quickly but not rush around like a madman. If you do and your heart rate goes up too much, the blood that has cooled down in your extremities will not have time to re-warm before entering your heart – and the shock can make your heart stop.

As a Mountain Leader, you have to demonstrate this technique to worried novices. It's crucial to do it confidently to show them it's no big deal (as well as being a matter of personal pride). So any of us showing distress while carrying out the drill had to practise it again and again until they could do it 'properly'. Luckily, most of us sussed it first time but a couple of the lads had to repeat it four or five times during the same afternoon. They were given only twenty minutes between each dunking to warm up. I was not jealous.

After the teaching phase, we progressed to more specialist skills and a series of tactical exercises. Once again working in four- to six-man teams, we deployed on long range ski-patrols, moving only at night to infiltrate deep behind enemy lines. We learnt how to create 'deception tracks' to prevent an enemy from following our own ski-tracks, how to dig covert observation posts into banks of snow, and how to fire our rifles while skiing up or down a hill. All Marines are expected to be able to live and fight in temperatures as low as minus 30°C. While this seems very cold by British standards it is, in reality, much easier to cope with than the cold and wet conditions of Scotland because it is dry. A comfortable working temperature in Norway is minus 10°C. Any warmer than this, and you start to sweat and dehydrate through the effort of skiing through deep snow with a large bergen on your back. To avoid overheating, we had to be disciplined to take our warm clothes off before setting out on a long ski-march. The best way to keep warm was to keep moving. While on patrol, we stopped for five minutes every hour to take our bergens off and relieve the strain on our shoulders. After five minutes, you are so cold that it is a relief to start moving again.

Many of the difficulties of operating in an Extreme Cold Weather Environment are the same as those encountered in a desert or jungle. Navigation is difficult, as there are very few landmarks. In the desert there aren't any; in the jungle they're hidden by trees; and in the Arctic they're buried under several metres of snow.

Water is a big problem too. You use a great deal of energy staying warm, and need to drink lots of fluid for your body to do this. But, although there's snow everywhere, there's no water. You have to carry fuel and a cooker and melt snow every day for drinking water, which you can then store in a vacuum flask. You can't cook at night because the glow of your cooker inside your tent can be seen from miles away, so you have to make do with just one litre of water in your flask – not a lot, if you're skiing overnight for twelve or thirteen hours. During the day, if you're not on sentry duty, you melt snow on a cooker inside your tent and make like a camel. But the limiting factor is the size of your bladder – if you drink too much, you have to get out of your nice warm sleeping bag to relieve yourself. Even with a 'pee bottle', this was a real pain. Ironically, dehydration causes more casualties in the Arctic than the cold.

For me, the highlight of the Norway phase was a week of ice-climbing in the Rondane mountains of central Norway – climbing steep, frozen waterfalls using ice-axes and crampons. The week nearly ended in disaster, though, after a large avalanche swept on to two of my colleagues, Huan and Jim, who were on an ice-climbing route on the far side of a valley from where the rest of us were climbing. We saw the avalanche start, far above their heads, and shouted to warn them. Both looked up, saw the avalanche approaching and managed to take cover in a small cave. As the spindrift from the avalanche subsided, we rushed towards the bottom of the cliff face thinking they must have been swept off or buried and fearing the worst, only to see Huan and Jim still standing in their cave, completely unharmed and grinning from ear to ear.

We didn't spend much time back in Haugastol itself. When we did, it was more lectures, including extensive combat medical training. But we had most Saturday afternoons and Sundays off, which gave us the chance to unwind a bit. Saturday afternoons were spent waxing skis, sharpening ice-axes and drinking heavily. We enjoyed some memorable piss-ups and cleared our hangovers on Sundays on the nearby downhill ski slopes at Geilo. MLs tend to be excellent skiers so there was plenty of scope for dodgy competitions. My party trick was known as the 'chairlift game'. All you had to do was climb out of your seat on the chairlift, climb hand-over-hand down the cable then drop on to the chair behind next to some confused-looking Norwegians. If you didn't climb quickly enough along the cable, you'd have the choice of dropping off and falling to the ground or losing your fingers between the wire and the rollers when you approached the pylon supporting the chairlift's cable. I seemed to be the only aficionado of this sport.

Of course, sometimes the last thing you wanted to do on your one day off a week was yet more skiing. On more than one Sunday we slobbed all day in front of the telly, watching all three *Star Wars* films back to back.

By the beginning of March, we could see light at the end of the tunnel. Although we had months of training still to go, we would be 'badged' at the end of the Norway phase. This would mean having the ML badge sewn on to our parade dress uniform and, just as importantly, receiving specialist ML pay for the first time.

First, though, we had one final major hurdle: a two-week exercise called Norge Finale. This was a 200-kilometre ski patrol that would test all the skills we had learnt: skiing, reconnaissance and attacking a target deep behind enemy lines before escaping and evading the inevitable enemy follow-up and search. After our experiences in Scotland, we were keen not to be captured again.

As small teams, we once again went in by helicopter to a remote drop-off point, infiltrating towards our targets on foot. Skiing only at night to avoid the enemy patrols we knew were looking for us, we crossed the Hardangervidda to reach our target a week later – an airfield near a village called Dagali. From a covert observation post in a nearby forest, we recorded the details of all vehicles and aircraft arriving or leaving the area, studied the routines of the enemy guards and formulated a plan to destroy the air traffic control tower. Our plan was approved over the radio and we linked up with the other team to carry out a night raid against the airfield. We knew that our target, the airfield's control tower, was only lightly defended at night, but that the main body of the enemy forces was camped just a few minutes' drive away. We would have to use speed and stealth to attack our target, and make our escape before enemy reinforcements arrived. We dumped our skis and bergens at the far end of the runway, and approached the control tower on foot from a direction out of sight from the sentries. With our white camouflage suits on, we were well hidden and crawled to within 50 metres of our target, unnoticed by the guards.

At H-hour, with the temperature a chilly minus 25°C, we attacked. First we took out the sentries, then stormed the control tower. Surprise had worked but, as anticipated, we soon heard the rumble of the enemy's reinforcements approaching in over-snow vehicles, and set up some booby traps to slow them down: logs across the road to stop the vehicles, and hand-grenades on a trip wire to take out the lead skiers of the enemy's follow-up. Our mission completed, we legged it back down the runway across the tarmac to avoid leaving footsteps in the snow that the enemy troops could easily follow. We picked up our heavy kit and detoured through a thick forest impassable for the enemy's oversnow vehicles, then just skied as fast as possible through the night to escape. There was no great subtlety to our escape plan – we just dug deep into our reserves of strength to out-ski our pursuers.

One of the best compliments Snowy Snowden ever paid us was when he said how impressed he was that we had managed to escape. He had joined the pursuing enemy forces and chased us for 6 kilometres on skis carrying no kit. We, on the other hand, were still carrying 120 pounds of operational equipment in our bergens.

At first light, we met a friendly 'agent' – a local farmer – at a prearranged rendezvous. He hid us on the back of a pig truck and drove us to within two nights' ski of a notional border with a neutral country. Once we had crossed this border, we would be safe and the exercise over. But the 'border' followed a mountain chain and we were told enemy patrols were guarding the mountain passes so they were too dangerous for us to use. We would have to find an ice-climbing route up and over a mountain called the Hallingskarvet, whose summit plateau was guarded by steep, icy cliffs. We had been carrying ice-axes, crampons and ropes throughout the exercise. Now we would have to use them.

As we slogged up the long, gentle slopes towards the Hallingskarvet, it was a beautiful, starlit night and we could see a snow-filled gully that might be climbable. As we approached the foot of the climb, though, the weather began to deteriorate. It clouded over and the wind was picking up. The slope soon became too steep to ski up. We strapped our skis on the outside of our packs and put on our crampons. Now the problems really started. The gully was about 1,000 feet high but, without our skis on and weighed down by our heavy packs, we were sinking in the deep snow up to our waists. The gully got steeper towards the top and we tied on to the rope for moral, if not physical, support. If one of us fell, we would all go. With 200 feet to the top, it was too steep to climb with a rucksack on. As the most experienced climber, I volunteered to lead this section. I took off my pack, strapped my rifle over my back and pushed on towards the top of the gully, trailing the rope behind me.

I climbed delicately, knowing that if I triggered an avalanche it would sweep my colleagues from the mountainside. I inched my way up. An overhanging cornice of snow barred my way out of the gully, so I buried my ice-axe deep in the gully wall, tied myself to it with a loop of rope, then started digging a groove into the cornice to crawl through. I pulled myself precariously on to flat ground. The gully itself was sheltered but, on the mountain plateau, the wind was ferocious, 80 or 90 miles an hour. It was too windy to stand up without risk of being blown back over the cliff edge, so I crawled around in the darkness searching for a strong point to attach the rope to. I found a patch of solid snow and hammered in my ice-axe up to the hilt and tied off the rope. I then abseiled back down to my companions. One by one, using the rope as an aid, they climbed to safety and I brought up the rear.

By lunchtime that day, we were back in Haugastol. By tea-time, we were officially Mountain Leaders. And by dinner-time, we were very drunk. We all thought our antics that night were hilarious, but you probably had to be steaming drunk yourself to appreciate them. Suffice to say, after hugging everyone and slurringly telling them they were the best, I phoned Anna to tell her how lovely she was, then flushed my best mate's head down the toilet after he fell asleep in the ladies' loos. We missed the last bus back to camp and decided to walk – 'It's only 18 miles and we're MLs so it'll be easy.' In our jeans and T-shirts, though, we weren't likely to get very far. To survive the rigours of Arctic training only to end up dying of exposure on a piss-up would have been ironic, to say the least. As we shivered by the road side, the duty Land Rover came back and scooped us up. When we eventually got back, we had the bright idea of warming up in the sauna. Needless to say we fell into a drunken slumber and woke up a couple of hours later having lost half our body weight in sweat. A great time had by all!

Back in the UK, we had a whole series of technical qualifications to acquire but we had now finally earned the respect of our instructors, which meant no more press-ups. The qualifications included helicopter abseil instructor training, parachute training and, for the officers, a Special Forces Operations Planning course.

The course ended in July, with a month's Alpine climbing in the Bernese Oberland in Switzerland. I was being paid extra money to do what I loved doing and I made the most of it. A highlight was a quick ascent of the Eiger with a fellow ML officer called Kev. We summited in a storm, but after some of the conditions we had endured during the course, this seemed almost tame.

From trainee to trainer

After all this training, I was looking forward to getting a job putting everything I'd learned into practice. My appointer told me there was a job going for an ML officer with the Parachute Regiment, whose 3rd Battalion had a cold weather warfare role as part of a NATO reaction force. This opportunity was too good to miss and I enjoyed two years working with some of the best of the British Army.

There is considerable rivalry – and mutual respect – between the Paras and the Marines. As the only Bootneck (slang for Royal Marine) among several hundred Paras, I received my fair share of stick, learnt a lot, taught a lot, and thoroughly enjoyed myself. Every time I went drinking, it turned into a challenge as to who could down more: Paras or Marines; every time I went running, it became a competition. Although I couldn't beat everyone at both of those, when we got to Norway I beat them all hands down on skis, so honour was preserved.

During this time, I spent nearly four months each winter back out in Norway, planning and running Arctic warfare training courses. As well as the formal, military training, there was ample opportunity for adventures in the mountains outside work.

One of my partners-in-crime was the unit chaplain, Frank Collins, a former SAS soldier who had been ordained as a Church of England vicar. He had recently rejoined the Army as a Para-trained chaplain and was game for anything. Frank and I went ice-climbing together in Norway and also partnered each other in a ski-jumping competition I organized.

The venue for the competition was a 40-metre hill, small by Olympic standards but massive when you're standing at the top of it. We were given some basic training by a local instructor and were all quite good at taking off but had failed to master landing. On the night of the competition, we were egged on by our colleagues and several hundred locals who had turned up, anticipating carnage. They weren't disappointed. Even when competitors managed to land the right way up, it was beyond our skill level to stop before the end of the piste. So we stopped either by steering into trees or on reaching the freshly gritted road.

Each competitor had to jump twice. My partner Frank had decided there was as much risk of injury in the training as in the competition itself, so had missed out the training part altogether. Therefore, when he stood at the top of the hill with his ungainly ski-jumping skis in front of the cheering crowd, it was as a complete novice. Frank had decided to compete in fancy dress and was wearing long robes, a bishop's mitre and carrying a crook. As he launched himself off the ramp, he jettisoned his mitre and crook and positioned himself for landing. He made no effort even to try landing on his feet, reckoning it would be safest to land instead on the fleshiest part of his body – his backside. That way, even if bruised, he would be fit enough to jump again.

I managed to stay more or less on my feet during my two jumps and when we totted up the results it appeared that Frank and I had accumulated the best overall score. Given that we had organized the competition, people were going to smell a rat if we awarded ourselves the crate of beer, so we disqualified Frank for not wearing a safety helmet to allow a team of young Paras to win. Their unique tactic for clearing a few extra inches was to land head first.

The next time I saw the Paras was in Sierra Leone – in a warmer, but much less friendly, climate.

Anna came out to visit for a long weekend in January 1997. After a whisky-fuelled Burns' Night dinner we were walking down an icy slope on the way to my accommodation. We slipped and landed in a snow drift and lay there giggling with snow up our kilts, looking at the stars. On the spur of the moment, I asked Anna to marry me. She said yes but, with horrendous hangovers, we had to doublecheck in the morning that we both remembered what had happened.

We were married on 26 July 1997 in Abden House at the foot of a hill called Arthur's Seat in Edinburgh. Frank officiated. When I asked him to marry us and said we didn't plan to get hitched in a church, his eyes lit up. He maybe hoped he'd be officiating at the top of Ben Nevis, or jumping out of a plane. Anna and I would have enjoyed this but I'm not sure my grandmother in her wheel-chair would have been so keen. In the end the venue we chose was a little less adventurous, but more romantic.

The night before the wedding Frank, Anna and I went for a long run together, rehearsing our wedding vows half-way up Arthur's Seat. I hoped there would be less heavy breathing during the ceremony itself and that Anna would look a bit less sweaty. Tactful as ever, I voiced this opinion and only narrowly escaped a good slapping. Frank, now demonstrating his SAS training, chased after me and held me down in an armlock, while Anna pushed my face in the mud. I couldn't believe I was being beaten up by the vicar and my wife-to-be the night before my wedding!

The wedding itself was fantastic. It pissed with rain, babies cried, I sang badly but not as badly as my father, and my best man, Alistair, who had been with us in the avalanche, tried to snog some bridesmaids – which he enjoyed but his girlfriend didn't. Our wedding cake was a snow-covered mountain, with two miniature climbers at the bottom. My head fell off as we cut the cake. Not one to worry too much about symbolism, Anna popped it in her mouth and ate it.

After an all-night ceilidh Anna and I decided to do without a limo, reckoning it would be more romantic to walk back to our hotel. As we wandered through the deserted streets of Edinburgh's Old Town, I felt I had married the loveliest girl in the world. She was wearing a backless dress that just failed to cover the small bump where she had broken her back and when I caught a glimpse of it, I had to pretend not to have a tear in my eye. This had definitely been the best day of my life.

We went to Venice for our honeymoon – well, we spent the first two days of our honeymoon in Venice. The Dolomites were only two hours' drive away, so we spent the rest of the holiday walking and climbing in the mountains. We started out in a five-star hotel, downgraded through four-, three-, two- and one-star hotels, then a mountain hut and ended up in the cosy surround-ings of my two-man tent. Even the best hotels would struggle to compete with the view you can enjoy from a tent pitched half-way up a remote mountainside. Still, we avoided bivvying out in the open – this was our honeymoon, after all.

Newly married, Anna and I managed to juggle our professional lives enough to be in the same place at the same time for a while. In 1998 I passed my promotion exams, earning myself the rank of major and a desk job in London. Although this was an interesting enough posting, it wasn't the most exciting. I went to work in a suit, struggled with IT systems, processed mountains of paperwork and only put on my uniform for special occasions. I ran a few marathons to keep myself fit and was fortunate when my boss allowed me a month away from my desk to take part in an expedition to climb Mount McKinley in Alaska, the coldest mountain in the world. When we summited at 9.45 one evening in May 1999, my thermometer read minus 46°C.

In January 2000 I took up the opportunity of working somewhere much warmer for six months as a Military Observer attached to the United Nations in tropical West Africa. Like all British officers before they work with the UN, I attended a week-long briefing package to find out what I needed to know about my destination, Sierra Leone. But my real training was everything I had done so far in the Marines. UN tours of duty are not always the most eventful, and little did I know just how much I was going to depend on the specialist skills I had acquired as a Mountain Leader.

CHAPTER THREE

IN THE LION'S DEN

Peacekeeping in Sierra Leone

*'When the lion and the elephant fight,
the grass will be crushed.'*
FODAY SANKOH, REBEL LEADER

Just outside Freetown, Sierra Leone's capital, there is a beach called River Number Two, where miles of gleaming white sand stretch out under palm trees. It looks so idyllic that the original 'Bounty' chocolate bar ads were filmed here, with the slogan 'A Taste of Paradise'. Yet now, only 20 metres away, is a rehabilitation centre for former child soldiers. These children bear terrible physical scars – apart from war wounds, most have been branded like cattle by their commanders. Their emotional scars can only be guessed at.

When Foday Sankoh, leader of Sierra Leone's Revolutionary United Front (RUF), tries to justify the turmoil and misery he has caused and talks about 'crushed grass', it's the people he's

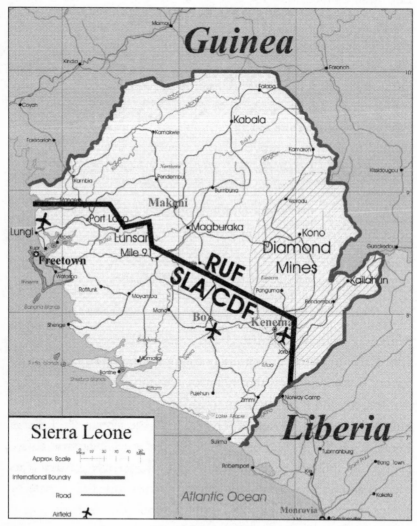

Map of Sierra Leone

referring to, and the desecration of the land itself. As a UN Observer, I was to bear witness to this.

Entering the war zone

European airlines don't like flying into war zones, so anyone wishing to travel to Sierra Leone has to fly to Conakry in neighbouring Guinea and catch a helicopter flight from there to Freetown. I duly spent a night in Conakry, which is not a pleasant place – hot, dirty, smelly, and full of people hassling you. I intervened when a young boy who was helping carry my bags at the airport was severely beaten by an older, rival 'porter'. I was shocked that I seemed to be the only person who even batted an eyelid at such brutal behaviour. An experienced aid-worker on the same flight told me I'd soon get used to it.

As we took off in the UN helicopter, I thought to myself: if peaceful Conakry is this unpleasant, how much worse is war-torn Freetown likely to be?

So when I peered out of the helicopter window as we approached the landing site in Freetown, I was pleasantly surprised to see how clean it was in comparison. About the only 'perk' of being the poorest country in the world is that you can't even afford the infrastructure needed for pollution. And the natural setting is stunning. On the Atlantic coast, unspoilt sandy beaches like River Number Two and mangrove swamps stretch for hundreds of miles, broken only by the natural harbour of the Sierra Leone River, the second biggest natural harbour in the world after Sydney. Freetown lies on the south side of the river estuary. The town was once known as the 'Athens of West Africa' and, despite the years of fighting, is still a beautiful place – at least from a distance. The lush, rolling hills around it are scattered with impressive white villas. In colonial days, Graham Greene sat on his veranda in one of these and wrote *The Heart of the Matter*. Sadly, the only Sierra Leoneans rich enough to live in places like this fifty years later are rebel commanders who have made a fortune through diamond smuggling and extortion. Graham Greene's old haunt is now a brothel where Liberian prostitutes can be picked up for a dollar a week.

The country is small by African standards, about the size of Ireland. It's surrounded by Guinea to the north and east and war-torn Liberia to the south. It got its name – which means 'Lion Mountains' – from early Portuguese explorers, who heard the roar of tropical thunderstorms booming out of the coastal hills on the Freetown peninsula. But Sierra Leone is not especially mountainous and its lions have long since been driven out by years of civil war. The RUF uses the 'Hungry Lion' as their symbol, but none of the rebels I was to meet had ever seen one.

Before deploying from the UK, I had attended a week of briefings that concentrated mainly on the risks of living and working in Sierra Leone. On the face of it, Sierra Leoneans should be well-off by African standards. They don't suffer from Mozambique's floods, Ethiopia's droughts, Algeria's religious conflict, Rwanda's ethnic hatred or Angola's legacy of unexploded landmines. In fact, until 1990, Sierra Leone was a stable, tolerant and prosperous country, a net exporter of food and blessed with rich mineral resources. After that, it plummeted to the bottom of the UN's Human Development Index. When I was there, it was officially the poorest country in the world, vying for this dubious honour with Afghanistan. In the year 2000, the average annual wage was less than $100 per person, and in RUF-controlled territory male life expectancy was as low as twenty-six. Half the population of about 4 million are effectively refugees or slaves. Most soldiers in the region have contracted HIV but expect to die young in fighting anyway, so don't much care. Here, malaria kills many more people than HIV/Aids, and so Aids is just one more deadly hazard to contend with.

How did this disaster happen? The main reason: the fight for diamonds. Sierra Leone has the world's third biggest reserves of diamonds, mostly found in the eastern part of the country. Diamonds have fuelled and financed a brutal twelve-year civil war, a war that has destroyed the infrastructure and quality of life for all but the most ruthless. When the Revolutionary United Front started the civil war in 1990, they might have had genuine grievances, but the war soon degenerated into a bloody scrap for control of the diamond mines.

The basic conflict has been between a succession of governments based in Freetown and the rebels of the Revolutionary United Front with a power base in the east of the country, armed and financed by Liberia in return for diamonds. What has complicated matters has been the on/off involvement of other interested parties, including the Sierra Leone Army – sometimes with the Government or as the Government, sometimes with the RUF and sometimes on both sides at once.

A Civilian Defence Force (or CDF) soon emerged to counter the savagery of the RUF and the ineptitude of the Sierra Leone Army. The CDF are mostly Kamajors (indigenous hunters) who make up for a lack of decent weapons or formal training with a generous dose of black magic. These Kamajors are, by local standards, the good guys, though some of their habits are a little unusual. Some believe, for example, that you become a stronger warrior from eating the heart of a respected enemy killed in battle, or that wearing jewellery made from the matted pubic hair of virgins can keep you healthy. However strange their habits may have seemed, I was later to be immensely glad of their support when they risked their lives to help me.

Sierra Leone's West African neighbours were also drawn into the civil war: the Nigerian-dominated ECOMOG forces on the Government side, Liberia with the RUF. ECOMOG, the economic community monitoring organization, is the military wing of ECOWAS – West Africa's version of the European Union. As mercenaries, nationalities from further afield have become involved, including Burkinabés (people from Burkina Faso), South Africans, Belgians, Ukrainians, and the British – though the UK-based organizations don't use the word 'mercenaries' these days, preferring to be known as 'private military companies'. The list goes on. Whatever spin they put on it, all these parties have had a vested interest in joining the conflict, lured ultimately by financial gain. I was even to meet mercenaries of the same nationality who were quite happy to go drinking together at the weekend, but during the week were working for opposing factions and presumably trying to kill each other. One pair of South Africans on opposite sides actually shared a house together in Freetown. They explained that they didn't mix work and leisure.

Incidentally, Britain has inadvertently provided the training for many of the leading protagonists in this brutal civil war. And not just the so-called good guys. Several renegade commanders have passed through the Royal Military Academy at Sandhurst, including Captain Valentine Strasser. When Strasser staged a military coup in 1992 at the age of just twenty-six, he became the world's youngest military dictator. Even ex-Army Corporal Foday Sankoh, the RUF leader, received training by the Royal Corps of Signals, though as a photographer.

Sierra Leone's civil war has been bloody, even by African standards. In January 1999, the President, Tejan Kabbah, a retired UN diplomat, was up for re-election. His campaign slogan was 'The future is in your hands'. Tragically, the RUF chose a macabre, literal interpretation of this slogan and countered it by systematically hacking off the hands of many thousands of people, both adults and children.

On 6 January 1999 the rebels smuggled weapons into Freetown hidden in a consignment of coffins, then infiltrated into the city, hiding in the crowds of people who had come to vote. A charity, Human Rights Watch, compiled evidence of the ensuing butchery and its conclusions make sobering reading.

The rebel occupation of Freetown was characterized by the systematic and widespread perpetration of all classes of gross human rights abuses against the civilian population. Civilians were gunned down within their houses, rounded up and massacred on the streets, thrown from the upper floors of buildings, used as human shields, and burned alive in cars and houses. They had their limbs hacked off with machetes, eyes gouged out with knives, hands smashed with hammers, and bodies burned with boiling water. Women and girls were systematically sexually abused, and children and young people abducted by the hundreds.

The rebels made little distinction between civilian and military targets. They repeatedly stated that they believed civilians should be punished for what they perceived to be their support for the existing government. Thus, the rebels waged war against the civilian population through the perpetration of human rights abuses. While there was some targeting of particular groups, such as Nigerians, police officers, journalists, and church workers, the vast majority of atrocities were committed by rebels who chose their victims apparently at random...

It is difficult to ascertain the level of seniority within the RUF at which the perpetration of human rights abuses was ordered, though the widespread participation in abuses suggests that they must have been authorized at a high level within the RUF's command structures. Victims and witnesses frequently overheard commanders on the ground give orders to perpetrate atrocities, and there are very few accounts of individual combatants or commanders trying to halt the abuses. When witnesses reported that individual combatants did object and try to halt the abuses, those objecting were often met with death threats from their fellow rebels.

The atrocities were often planned and premeditated. Victims and witnesses describe well-organized operations to round up civilians who were later executed, attacked with machetes, or raped. On several occasions rebels gave advance warning that atrocities were to be committed later.

Witnesses describe the existence of distinct units known for committing particular crimes, like the Burn House Unit, Cut Hands Commando, and Blood Shed Squad. Some of these squads had a trademark way of killing such as the Kill Man No Blood unit, whose method was to beat people to death without shedding blood, or the Born Naked Squad, who stripped their victims before killing them. The closer ECOMOG forces got to rebel positions, the more these squads were mobilized and sent on operation.

Upon gaining control of a neighbourhood or suburb, the rebels went on systematic looting raids, in which families were hit by wave after wave of rebels demanding money and valuables. Those who didn't have what the rebels demanded were often murdered. While rape and abduction were widespread throughout the offensive, the pace of the executions, amputations and burning of property picked up dramatically as the rebels were forced to withdraw. The abuses committed in the last several days of rebel occupation of any given neighbourhood were of staggering proportion.

Having systematically looted the capital, the rebels were forced out of Freetown by Nigerian peacekeepers and Kamajor militiamen.

In the aftermath of these atrocities, the people of Sierra Leone, with international support, decided that enough was enough. At Lomé in July 1999, a Peace Accord was signed between the Government and the RUF. Foday Sankoh, the RUF leader, was at that time on Death Row, guilty of mass murder and treason; he was released to become Vice President, and a blanket amnesty was given to all combatants. The UN was invited in by a Government of National Unity to oversee the Peace Process and a process of Disarmament, Demobilization and Reintegration (DDR). Under these processes, combatants from all factions, including the Army, would receive some training in civilian occupations, medical screening and a small amount of cash in return for handing over their weapons. The surviving victims of atrocities would receive nothing save the expectation of a more peaceful life.

I'm no lawyer but, even to me, some of the shortcomings of the Lomé Peace Accord were obvious. But if the people of Sierra Leone were big enough to forgive and forget, then who was I to decide otherwise?

The Peace Accord meant that when I arrived, in January 2000, there had been – more or less – a six-month ceasefire. After everything I had heard and read about the place, I was half-expecting to step off the helicopter straight into scenes of strife and violence. The reality was a little more mundane.

Working in the war zone

I spent my first week completing a tortuous 'joining routine' with the UN Mission in Sierra Leone, known as UNAMSIL. Never have I filled in so much paperwork for so little tangible benefit, but at least it gave me a week to discover the joys of Freetown and adjust to the rhythms of UN life.

As the ex-colonial power (granting independence in 1962), Britain is popular, if not universally loved, and you can see signs of its residual influence everywhere. English is the official language. The university, the Fourah Bay College in Freetown, was originally part of Durham University, and all the kids seem to support English football teams. Where they got them from I don't know, but in Makeni several rebels wore Manchester United football shirts. As a Chelsea fan, this did not endear them to me any more than their subsequent attempts to take me hostage or kill me!

Just a few days before arriving in Sierra Leone I'd been ice-climbing in Scotland, so I really noticed the heat and humidity. During the day the temperature went as high as 100°F (38°C), and even at night it didn't drop very much below 83°F or 28°C. It felt like being stuck on a crowded train in the London Underground on a hot summer's day while wearing thick winter clothes. The other thing that struck me was the smell – a pungent mixture of stale sweat, rotting fruit, fish and meat. Sierra Leone is a hot and sticky place but there is no running water, so bathing is a weekly, not daily, luxury and when I was there its civil infrastructure was almost non-existent. Discarded food remained where it was dropped: scraps lay by the side of the road until eaten by packs of disease-ridden dogs, rats or vultures. In comparison to 'developed' countries there was very little man-made litter – anything like strips of paper or polythene bags had salvage value. When I bought some oranges from a street vendor, I was amazed to discover that the polythene bag I bought to carry them in cost more than the oranges. No wonder people don't drop litter.

Sewage flowed in open storm drains by the sides of the roads, as I discovered after falling in one night on the way home from the bar...

In years gone by, West Africa was known as the 'white man's grave', as many a diplomat or businessman failed to survive a posting there. The heat and humidity provide ideal conditions for a host of tropical diseases such as malaria, typhoid and Lassa fever. While modern medicine offers rich Westerners reasonable protection, the locals are not so lucky and in the unsanitary conditions disease spreads easily. It was common to see orphaned kids scavenging from scraps of food on rubbish dumps, alongside the dogs and rats. But, as long as you were sensible, Freetown itself felt no more hazardous than any other large city. The biggest dangers to a visitor's health seemed to be from sunburn and cheap beer – but with a dusk-to-dawn curfew imposed in the capital it was hard even to get drunk.

Every one of UNAMSIL's twenty-four different nationalities seemed to have its own idea of working hours. The European nations preferred to take Sundays off while the Muslim nations took Fridays off. Every nation had the right to celebrate an annual 'national day' but many seemed to have adopted a monthly one. And a surprising number of nationalities claimed that a siesta was an integral part of their culture.

The highlight of the first week was my UN driving test. The roads had almost no traffic on them, but my instructor, a Jamaican guy called Trevor, still advised extreme caution: 'If there are people about, never drive faster than walking speed.' I asked why. He explained that after a local resident had been knocked down by a UN jeep and awarded $100 in compensation, half the population seemed to be trying to cash in. Locals had developed the unnerving habit of throwing themselves or their elderly relatives in front of UN vehicles, hoping to collect their bounty.

Life in Sierra Leone is cheap. And if you managed to avoid human obstacles, you still had to contend with Sierra Leonean dogs, which either lacked the common sense or energy to get out of the way of moving cars. Even at walking speed, disease-ridden dogs would refuse to drag themselves from underneath your wheels. If you couldn't drive round them, you had push them out of the way or drive over them.

I witnessed one ghoulish incident during an early morning run on the beach. As I ran, I saw a flock of vultures pecking out the eyes of a dead dog and gave them a wide berth. But as I returned along the beach with my legs beginning to tire, the vultures had flown off so I ran right past the dog. Suddenly, the 'dead' dog stood up and, with empty eye sockets, lurched towards me. My legs no longer felt so tired as I sprinted to avoid it; the thought of being savaged by a zombie dog was not a pleasant one.

Freetown was chaotic but friendly, its people optimistic that the UN would bring them prolonged peace and prosperity. The streets bustled with traders, the schools were full of smartly dressed pupils and, if you had a generator, you could even watch trashy US sitcoms or endless repeats of *Mr Bean* on national TV. But the relative normality of Freetown was only surface deep, hiding the grim reality of life in the interior of the country, especially in territory controlled by the RUF.

The rebels still controlled two-thirds of the country. Their military headquarters was in Makeni, a market town and the provincial capital of the mainly Muslim Northern province. I was assigned to a team of UN Military Observers (or UNMOs) based in Makeni itself. As Observers we were not allowed to bear arms. Our weapon was deemed to be the solidarity of representing the Rest of the World. I had doubts about the wisdom of being unarmed, but the UN does have Observers in many of the world's hotspots who survive largely unmolested, so who was I to argue?

In fact, our unarmed status was in many respects our best means of self-defence as nobody felt threatened by us. I lost count of the number of times I was searched at gunpoint by the RUF. If I'd carried a weapon openly, I'd have been treated as an enemy. If they had discovered a weapon hidden under my uniform or in my vehicle, I'd have been treated as a spy. Neither option was going to endear me to my RUF hosts. I took all the British badges off my uniform – the 'Commando daggers' and parachute wings that I wear on my uniforms in the UK were only likely to draw unwanted attention from the RUF.

I deployed to Makeni on the weekly UN resupply flight, an hour's journey in an ancient Russian MI-8 helicopter. This model was mass-produced by the Soviet Union and was the work-horse of its armed forces. It's the Lada of the helicopter world – cheap and cheerful and prone to breaking down. Since the end of the Cold War, the Russians have sold thousands of them around the world. You can buy one for less than the price of a top-of-the-range car.

We landed on an old football pitch in the next-door town of Magburaka, where I was met by my new UNMO team. Freetown was hot enough, but at least there was a sea-breeze. Here, inland, the heat was far more oppressive. When I got off the helicopter I felt a blast of hot air. I initially thought it was the heat of the exhaust, then realized this was the normal air temperature here. Just the strain of carrying my bags off the helicopter was enough to drench my clothes with sweat. I jumped into a 4x4 Toyota jeep with Mustafa, an Egyptian officer, for the twenty-minute trip to Makeni. He wound the windows up, turned the air-conditioning on, put Madonna's *Like a Virgin* on the car stereo and lit a ciga-rette. A group of kids had gathered at the helicopter landing site, to watch the weekly arrival. I was surprised when Mustafa simply accelerated towards them, sounding his horn loudly and forcing all the children to dive out of his way.

The main road between Magburaka and Makeni was surpris-ingly good quality tarmac. Built in the 1950s, it had not seen enough traffic over the years to do it much damage. Despite the occasional pot-hole, we zoomed along the narrow road at over 70 miles per hour, narrowly missing locals on foot or bicycle, carrying large loads. It struck me as arrogant to show such little regard for the local people, especially when Mustafa started beeping his horn as we overtook. In a crowded village, locals started running for cover. Pretending to be car-sick, I asked him to slow down a bit.

'Does everyone drive this fast?' I asked.

'No.'

Phew, I thought.

'The others are much faster, but I am getting better.'

From then on, I resolved that when I was in charge of a vehicle I would drive slowly with the windows down and say hello to people as I went by – an easy but effective way to start winning some hearts and minds. I had a constant battle with the rest of my team to slow down, but never managed to persuade them. My best friend in the team (until he was posted elsewhere after a couple of months) was a Bangladeshi officer called Mahbub. He explained that driving slowly would be seen as a sign of weakness by the locals, and we would lose respect if we did so. We agreed to differ.

I did continue to play the Madonna album, though. Music was a good way of defusing tension with groups of rebels.

We passed several roadblocks manned by bored-looking rebels but were waved straight through. At the last checkpoint before Makeni, I thought my eyes were deceiving me.

'Did I just see a chimpanzee manning that checkpoint?' I wondered if I was the victim of an elaborate hoax.

'Yes,' replied Mustafa.

'And was he holding an AK47?'

'Yes.'

'Can he fire it?'

'I don't know – there's a ceasefire, remember,' Mustafa answered, with no hint of sarcasm.

A few days later, I paid a visit to the checkpoint during an early-morning run. Sure enough, there was the chimpanzee. This time he was not holding a weapon. He had put it down so he could use both hands to smoke a cigarette. When he saw me approaching, he picked up his rifle and started snarling at me.

'Hey, *porto*,' the checkpoint commander shouted over to me (*porto* means 'white man' in Krio, the pidgin English spoken by the rebels). 'The sergeant major doesn't like you. He has no bullets but he might try to stab you.' The chimp's AK47 had a bayonet attached to it. I decided this was a good point to turn back.

The next time I saw the chimp he was smoking a joint. I never did find out whether he knew how to shoot.

The team site was in a walled compound on the outskirts of Makeni. On one side of the compound, there was a long, single-storey breeze-block house overlooking the main road, and there were two smaller buildings on the other side of the compound. The UN jeeps were parked in between the buildings out of sight of prying eyes. On the far side of the main road outside the compound was a well. This was the dry season and we had to top the well up once a week by water-tanker from Freetown.

I met my new colleagues. Our team of fourteen Observers had ten nationalities, eight languages, six religions and, for a while, a pet monkey called Oscar. The team leader was a charming Bolivian officer called Lieutenant Colonel de la Fuente. He did not speak good English, which put him in an unenviable position with the RUF, who would deliberately speak quickly to humiliate him. Colonel de la Fuente was transferred a couple of weeks later and replaced by a British Parachute Regiment colonel, Jim Skuse. We had an area of responsibility about the size of Northern Ireland and two main tasks: assessing the security situation and overseeing the Disarmament process.

As the new arrival, I was not greatly surprised to discover that all the bedrooms in the main house had been taken. Major Igor Kotov, a tough-looking Russian, showed me to my digs in one of the shacks on the far side of the compound. It had breeze-block walls, bars over the windows, a corrugated iron roof and a sturdy metal door that could be locked only from the outside. I asked Igor if this had been a storeroom.

'No. RUF prison. You sleep here. Very safe.' Igor was not a man to mince his words. The previous occupant of our house had been Dennis Mingo, aka 'Superman', an RUF commander with a feared and brutal reputation even by rebel standards. The RUF had captured Makeni from the Sierra Leone Army on Christmas Day 1998 and the rebel commanders had promptly requisitioned the best houses in town. I asked our landlord Musa who made the better tenants. Musa, displaying the tact and amiable nature that had been his best means of self-defence while working as a slave for Superman, smiled enigmatically but would not be drawn. I subsequently discovered that Mingo had earned his nickname as a result of his preferred method of killing – throwing his victims off tall buildings and telling them to 'fly like Superman'.

The room was filthy. I scrubbed the walls but was unable to remove some ominous dark red stains. A fresh lick of paint soon put the evidence of Superman's torture victims out of sight, if not out of mind.

The corrugated iron roof kept out the rain but meant the room stayed as hot as an oven, even at night. I was determined to acclimatize properly and didn't give in to the temptation to install a fan. Although this meant that for the first few days I was continuously drenched in sweat and too hot to sleep properly, it was a price worth paying. Once you're acclimatized, everyday life is much more comfortable. Unless they're playing football, local people don't sweat all day or complain about the heat, and I wanted to copy them. A principle of survival is to 'act like a local' and, although some of my colleagues thought my attitude a little strange, when things did go wrong being properly acclimatized was to prove a life-saver.

As an added 'bonus', my room was right next to the generator, which throbbed loudly like a clapped-out truck, though after a day or two I no longer minded the noise. Depending on the wind direction, the diesel fumes could be unpleasant but at least they kept the mosquitoes away.

Actually, it was easier to get to sleep with the generator running. When it broke or was switched off, I could hear the squealing, scurrying and scratching of the rats that lived in the roof space above me, which drove me to distraction. I tried rat poison, which was partially successful. It did kill one of the creatures but I never found the carcass. Believe me, the only thing worse than sharing your bedroom with a live rat is sharing a room with a dead, rotting one.

I came to know the habits of my rodent roommates quite well. Every three days they would clean out their nest, kicking droppings down on to my mosquito net. Scraping off the rat shit became a regular chore. Disturbingly, a British aid worker based nearby died on 23 March from Lassa fever. This is a disease that humans catch from breathing in the droplets of rat's urine that drip down from roof cavities. This prompted me to try an assortment of rat-catching techniques – smoking them out (no effect on the rats but my room reeked of smoke for weeks), and ripping the roof apart to look for them (the rats scurried away before I could catch them and thereafter the roof leaked). I even tried to buy a cat, but the only one I saw in Makeni was a scrawny, disease-ridden moggy not much bigger than the rats themselves and I didn't rate its chances.

I was initially appointed as the team's Military Information Officer. 'Military Information' is UN-speak for 'Intelligence', a word that has too many Cold War connotations and suggests that everybody is spying on each other. My role was not because, as the new man on the ground, I knew very much about the intelligence situation, but because with English as my first language I would find it easier to compile our daily situation reports (or sitreps). Some of the other team appointments seemed a little tongue in cheek. Juwono, an Indonesian army officer, was the Human Rights Officer, using skills he claimed to have 'learnt in East Timor'. Igor the Russian ran the bar at vast personal profit. A Cold War veteran and self-proclaimed Marxist-Leninist, he relished beating Western capitalists at their own game.

There were some almost irreconcilable differences. The African guys in the team tended to go womanizing every afternoon, which they saw as one of the perks of being a soldier. Unfortunately, the devout Muslims in the team just could not come to terms with this and refused to share a house with them. A compromise was reached – the African guys hired the house next door as a love shack and a notice was erected in the operations room: 'NO SMOKING OR WHORING IN THE OPS ROOM'.

Every member of the team had their own strengths and weaknesses but the bottom line was this: we all wore the same UN beret and badges on our uniforms and were there to act as the eyes and ears of the world community. Our diversity was our strength, despite the occasional misunderstanding.

The team was assisted in assessing the security situation and overseeing disarmament by a battalion of 500 lightly armed Kenyan infantry. They were armed in order to protect both their own camps and the disarmament camps. It was considered unlikely that the rebels would choose to disarm unless we had some means of protecting them – their fear of retribution from the local population was real and justified. The Kenyans were spread thinly with never more than company strength (100 men) in any one location. However, they were usually in smaller groups and we had just six men guarding our compound. In my opinion, the Kenyans were the best troops available to the UN in Sierra Leone at the time. It was therefore no coincidence that they had been given the hardest area in which to operate. In fact, I would not be here today were it not for their professionalism, discipline and bravery.

My standard routine involved getting up early to make the most of the coolest part of the day. I enjoyed my early-morning runs which, as well as keeping me fit, were the best way to explore the local area. You didn't have to go far off the beaten track to see how the RUF operated by harassing and intimidating the locals. Sometimes accompanied by Musa, I explored the backstreets and footpaths of Makeni and the surrounding fields and villages. Musa introduced me to the commanders of the numerous checkpoints on the roads and paths. He still enjoyed the patronage and protection of Superman, so I felt reasonably safe. Local kids would shout friendly abuse at us in the local language, Mende, as we ran and Musa would translate. I suspected their comments were not quite as generous as he made out. One group of children always shouted the same message as we passed them. Musa translated for me: 'Look how elegantly the white man runs!' This seemed too good to be true. And it was. I asked a neighbour for an accurate translation: 'Good morning, chicken legs!'

I could outrun Musa, but he was incredibly strong. I once challenged him to a press-ups competition and told him I would give him ten cents for every press-up he could beat me by. I managed seventy and felt very pleased with myself. Musa had scarcely warmed up as he passed my target, finally grinding to a halt after 380 but claiming he 'was disappointed not to reach 400'. He deserved his prize money.

After my daily run, I'd take a shower – hanging a water-filled plastic bag with holes in it off a tree branch – and shave out of a mess tin while listening to the World Service. It took nearly an hour after my run to cool down enough to stop sweating, so there was no need to hurry. I would then hand wash my running kit and my uniform from the day before. This upset some of my colleagues who thought it was demeaning for an officer to do his own laundry. It did not seem worth getting into an argument over but I found it therapeutic to do my own washing while listening to the radio. In the end, to avoid any hassle, I ended up hiding behind the shed with my bucket and soap suds, pretending that Musa was doing the dirty work. We paid Musa a generous wage on top of our rent money to act as our 'fixer' and also employed a cook and a couple of 'house-boys' to do the cleaning. One of these house-boys was a thirteen-year-old called Ibrahim, who had been forced to work as a slave after Superman had killed his parents. Musa had persuaded Superman to let him adopt Ibrahim as his 'brother' and we paid a local Islamic school to accept him as a pupil. He looked a bit out of place among his schoolmates, who were all seven or eight years old and half his size, but he was proud of his school uniform and worked hard.

After breakfast, the day's work began. We tried to get the bulk done in the morning while the rebels were still subdued. By early afternoon, most would be too fired up on drink or drugs to make much sense and their 'high spirits' made them even more unpredictable and dangerous than usual.

Our first major task was assessing the security situation. This involved patrolling on foot or by jeep and speaking to as many people as possible, both rebels and civilians, to find out what was going on. We also tried to 'sensitize' the local rebels by explaining why the UN were there and why disarmament would benefit them. In practice, this meant having many AK47s pointed in our faces while attempting to negotiate at the numerous rebel roadblocks. Most rebels had never come across neutral soldiers before – you were either with them or against them. It took weeks and weeks of effort and numerous close shaves to try to persuade them that we were against no one. As part of the Lomé Peace Accord, to which the rebels had signed up, the UN was supposed to have freedom of movement throughout the country. Despite this, most checkpoint commanders expected anybody who wanted safe passage through their position to bribe them. I refused to hand over money as this would have set a precedent. Each time I returned to the same checkpoint, the rebels would have expected more of the same, so instead I dished out Royal Marines paraphernalia such as pens and pencils that I'd brought out from the UK.

One of the hardest patrols we undertook was when we tried to reach the diamond mining town of Kono. Makeni was the RUF's military HQ, but their 'centre of gravity' was the town of Kono, 150 miles further east in the heart of the diamond mining region. As part of the Lomé Peace Accord, there was supposed to be a moratorium on the illegal mining and export of diamonds, so the RUF were unwilling to let the UN go there to discover what was really happening.

Kono was, technically, in another team's area of responsibility. But the Magburaka team had repeatedly found excuses not to go. With a weak team leader, they were not prepared to stick their necks out in any way or risk doing anything to disrupt their daily routine of sleeping and watching TV. They were happy to just sit back and collect their $100 UN pay every day and didn't want to jeopardize this happy arrangement. In the British military, disregarding orders results in a court martial. In the UN it is all too common. National sensitivities make it very difficult to sack or discipline any individual as there are inevitably accusations of national bias. That said, for all the UN's imperfections, I cannot think of a better alternative for international peacekeeping. I got into several drunken arguments with white South African mercenaries, defending the UN against accusations of incompetence.

Exasperated, the UN HQ asked our team to go instead. Colonel Jim led the patrol and I volunteered to accompany him in the lead vehicle. George, a Zambian, and Rizvi, a Pakistani, brought up the rear. On this occasion, we were obliged to take an armed escort of Kenyans along. They were a mixed blessing, as there were too few of them to win a battle with the RUF but enough to attract unwanted attention. Worse, their vehicles were hopelessly unreliable. Within minutes of breaking down (which happened every few miles) a large crowd of RUF would gather round to 'help'. Hardly the low-key, professional approach we were looking for.

To ensure a smooth passage through the numerous rebel road-blocks, Colonel Jim and I took two moderate RUF commanders along with us, Lieutenant Colonel Alfred Jimmy and Colonel Sherif. Both were well-educated, pragmatic men who saw the benefits of the Peace Process, if only because they fancied them-selves as budding politicians. But Jimmy and Sherif had earned their ranks through fighting, not politics, and as we advanced towards Kono, we passed through the sites of several battles where they had been in command.

The numerous burnt-out ECOMOG trucks and armoured cars were graphic evidence of RUF victories. They made grim scenes. Many of the human victims of these battles still lay where they had died, stripped of their uniforms by their killers, their skeletons picked clean by vultures. The RUF didn't bother burying their enemies.

Many of the skeletons we saw were headless, with the skulls displayed on nearby stakes. I asked Sherif whether the heads were severed before or after their owners died.

'Whichever,' he replied.

Professionally, I was intrigued to discover what I could about RUF tactics, and there was a morbid fascination in being shown the aftermath of massacres by the perpetrators themselves. An important part of UK officer training involves 'battlefield tours' to places such as the D-Day beaches in Normandy. Such tours are normally led by academics and, although interesting, the actual signs of fighting are few and far between and it takes some imagination to picture what it must have been like. Here, though, I was on the ultimate battlefield tour. Sherif took up the commentary: 'See that log over there? We put that across the road to stop the lead armoured car. And when the Nigerian soldiers got out to move it out the way, we fired an RPG [rocket-propelled grenade] from here, then machine-gunned the crew from behind that bush. You can see their heads in a pile over there!'

If this all seems a bit mad or absurd to the reader sitting reading this at home or on a commuter train, it seemed no less mad to me sitting next to Sherif. In the end, my curiosity outweighed my sense of revulsion and I quizzed him further about life as a rebel commander.

You had to be ruthless and cruel to make it into the senior ranks of the RUF. The lower ranks, however, were driven more by an extreme form of laddish bravado. Sherif admitted that he had quickly become numbed to the human suffering he and his comrades were causing and that, after a while, it became a game to outdo each other in terms of atrocities. He described how 'a friend of his' developed the technique of slicing off women's buttocks without killing them and this became his trademark. Thereafter, anyone who saw a woman without her usual female curves – or who couldn't sit down – knew that Sherif's 'friend' had been in town. Sadly, breast-cutting had already been invented and was by now an established practice.

Lurid anecdotes like this appalled me but gave an insight into rebel psychology. Although I found their attitude to violence sickening I could begin to see what made them tick. Indeed, some of their mentality was recognizable in the (usually male) anti-social behaviour that often masquerades as 'laddishness' in so-called civilized societies. Why do British men with good jobs and stable lives become football hooligans? Because it's fun being part of a gang and wreaking havoc. I've never been a football hooligan, but I have been in riots where most participants (both rioters and security forces) were clearly enjoying the buzz.

I think everyone has in them a small streak of sadistic voyeurism. How many of us watch motor-racing for the crashes and slow down on motorways to view the aftermath of a traffic accident?

I was aware of the significance of black magic in this part of the world, and asked Sherif about his experiences.

'There are things in Africa that you white men do not understand. Black magic may not work for you because you do not believe in it. For those who do believe, it is very powerful.'

He showed me an ambush position where a Nigerian soldier had fired a magazine of thirty rounds of ammo at him from a range of less than 20 metres. All the bullets had missed him. I tentatively suggested that this was more to do with the poor marksmanship of Nigerian soldiers than black magic, but Sherif was adamant.

I'd already discovered that magic charms, promising the wearer protection from bullets, were cheaply available in Freetown, but there are conditions. First, the wearer must believe absolutely that the charm will work. If he is shot and survives, the charm has worked. If he dies, it's not the charm's fault, he just didn't believe hard enough. The second condition is less philosophical: black magic apparently only works with bullets less than 0.5-inch calibre. This explains the popularity of heavy machine-guns and rocket-propelled grenades. And of course they're always good for posing with.

My conversation with Sherif now moved on to cannibalism. He explained that many fighters believed that if you ate the heart of a strong man then you would acquire his strength. Jim and I both rushed to point out that we were particularly weak individuals! Sherif did admit that he was not totally taken in by this philosophy but that eating the heart of your enemy was good for bonding and group morale. The RUF enjoyed playing up to their bloodthirsty reputation. All the factions tried to outdo each other and, worryingly, the RUF seemed to be the winners.

I asked as nonchalantly as I could, 'So, Sherif, have you ever eaten anyone?'

'Yeah.'

'Is it true the meat tastes like pork?'

'I wouldn't know,' he replied with implacable logic. 'I'm a Muslim.'

I asked Sherif how he had become a rebel. After leaving school with A-levels in English, History and Politics in 1987 (the same year I left school), he'd started a law degree at the Fourah Bay College in Freetown. However, during an attempted coup in 1990, he witnessed a terrible event. His father, a policeman, was on duty during the coup. Sherif watched as mutinous soldiers gouged out his father's eyes then poured battery acid into the empty sockets. Sherif joined the RUF soon afterwards. I could see how hard it would be to break the cycle of violence.

Sherif had become a cruel thug but was still capable of displays of kindness – on one occasion, I saw him give his lunch to a hungry beggar. I found him easy enough to get along with and wondered how I would have turned out if I had had his life.

For the first 50 miles or so of our patrol, the rebels manning checkpoints recognized Sherif and Jimmy and progress was straightforward enough. It was entertaining to watch the reactions of the rebels as we approached a checkpoint. They would walk up to the jeep, full of the bravado that an AK47 gives you, unaware that we had one of their commanders on the back seat.

When they saw our passengers they suddenly showed a lot more respect. But on one occasion a rebel stuck his rifle right into Sherif's face, without noticing who he was. Sherif flipped. I suspected that if Jim and I had not been there, Sherif would have had the boy shot.

Once outside their home turf, though, Sherif and Jimmy were no longer automatically recognized or respected, and they became a lot more twitchy. It took longer and longer to negotiate our way through each checkpoint and we all began to feel a long way from safety. The scenes of desolation became increasingly desperate – we entered an area where both sides in the civil war had operated a 'scorched earth' policy. The damage to the infrastructure was bad enough – bomb craters in the road that nobody had bothered to fill in, burnt-out villages, unharvested crops left to rot in the fields – but it was the attitude of the survivors we met that was especially unnerving. Most civilians had fled the area, preferring life in the squalor of a refugee camp to life among the rebels. The people who stayed behind were desperately malnourished and had the gaunt, faraway look I had seen in footage of concentration camp victims. Even in rebel-held Makeni, everybody smiled and laughed. Here, everyone just sat and stared into space. I asked some of them why they didn't start rebuilding their villages or at least harvest their crops.

'What's the point? Whatever we grow, the rebels will take it all.'

Most disturbingly, there were no young women to be seen. Those who had not fled had been rounded up and taken to Kono as sex slaves.

At each checkpoint we tried to explain why we were there. The rebels had been told that the UN was allied to the Government of Tejan Kabbah and was therefore their enemy. President Kabbah was, after all, an ex-UN diplomat and good friends with the UN Secretary General, Kofi Annan. It was difficult to convince them

otherwise. Progress got harder and harder as we drew closer
to Kono.

With just five miles to go, we were stopped again. The checkpoint commander here was called Major Psycho, aged all of
fifteen. I remember his distinctive red beret, with a bullet hole
through each temple. He was nothing more – and nothing less –
than a dangerous nutter. The Kenyan escort was forced to stay at
the checkpoint while Jim and I were 'invited' to drive to a nearby
village called Yengema to continue our discussions. Perhaps over-
optimistically, we decided to go. There, we were told it would be
impossible to continue to Kono that day and that we could spend
the night with them there and continue the next day. Given the
increasingly hostile atmosphere, this was the last place in the
world I wanted to spend the night. Jim agreed with me but
Psycho was now refusing to let us leave. Even Sherif and Jimmy
were frightened. At one stage, Jimmy produced a pistol he had
hidden down his trousers, and started brandishing it like a wild
man, threatening Psycho and his hoods. We were fast losing
control of the situation.

Ironically, our RUF escorts had now become our best allies and
were arguing more strongly on behalf of the UN than we had ever
managed. This was like a reverse-scenario 'Stockholm syndrome' –
where a threatened victim undergoes a psychological shift in favour
of their enemy – but it didn't really help. We were being 'asked' by
a psychopath with a gun to stay 'as his guests' and it was hard to
turn him down. To all intents and purposes we were now hostages.
Two unarmed Brits among a couple of hundred armed and angry
rebels with a chip on their shoulder. At times like this, I questioned
what the hell I was doing in Sierra Leone.

Back at the checkpoint, the Kenyans were having more success
with their negotiations. They had convinced the rebels that
'the two white men don't know what they're doing but they're

harmless' (I guess they had a point), and asked to come down to the village to sort things out the African way. Their arrival helped to calm things down, but it took another three hours of delicate negotiations to extract ourselves.

Jim and I both agreed we had pushed it too far. Even if we had been with our armed Kenyan escort, we were still 250 miles inside RUF territory and had passed through nearly eighty checkpoints to get this far. Fighting our way out would have been impossible. We drove through the night back to Makeni and never did make it to Kono. Before we were able to try again, the ceasefire had ended.

Not all patrols were so eventful, but I could see why the Magburaka team had been less than enthusiastic.

Disarming the rebels

Our second major task was overseeing the disarmament process when, or rather if, it started. The RUF were blatantly stalling for time, more or less observing the ceasefire so that aid agencies would operate in their territory and yet refusing to hand in any weapons. Some slow progress, however, was being made. Led by a charismatic Irishman called Fergus, a team from the UK Department for International Development (DfID) had persuaded the RUF commanders to let them start building a number of disarmament camps in the rebel heartlands. Our nearest one was 10 miles to the south of Makeni. The plan was that RUF fighters would live in these camps once they had disarmed. They would be fed, given medical attention, receive $300 and some basic training in skills such as farming or building. Not a bad deal for ex-combatants, but they needed to be looked after and shown the benefits of peace if they were not to drift back into fighting. Most rebels were too young to remember life before the civil war. As part of the process, child soldiers would be separated from the adult combatants and every effort made to reunite them with surviving members of their families. By the beginning of April, construction of the first DDR camps in RUF territory was almost complete.

The Disarmament, Demobilisation and Reintegration (DDR) process was going well in other parts of the country so we were able to visit other UNMO teams to see what the practical difficulties were. There were many. One of the major problems was determining exactly who was a combatant – the rules were clear on paper but not always easy to follow in practice. To be considered an ex-combatant, you had to hand in a weapon, but not any old weapon. For example, the UN did not consider you a combatant if you tried to disarm with just a hand grenade. This was because you could buy a hand grenade on the black market for $10, claim to be a combatant, then receive $300 for handing it in. One local woman who tried this ploy met a sticky end. When she was told she would not receive $300, she pulled the pin.

There were about 2,000 rebel fighters in the immediate vicinity of Makeni and maybe 10,000 in our whole Area of Responsibility. In our pre-deployment briefings back in the UK we had been warned to expect to encounter child soldiers, but it was still a shock to witness the reality of there being many more child fighters than adults. I reckoned the average age of an RUF soldier in Makeni was twelve or thirteen years old. Some were much younger. Every day, for example, two five-year-olds walked past our house, with rifles longer than they were, on their way to man their checkpoint. Both claimed to have killed their own parents and had a bush rank of RSM (Regimental Sergeant Major – in Britain, an RSM is typically forty-five years old). Later I saw them among a group that had summarily executed Kenyan peacekeepers and would try to do the same to us. These boys' daily routine consisted of extorting money or food at gunpoint from civilians and smoking or injecting drugs.

Interacting with child soldiers was problematic, both morally and practically. On the one hand, you realized they were children and that their wrongdoings were not really their fault. On the other hand, their very ignorance of normal morality made them particularly dangerous and rebel commanders were quick to exploit this. RUF recruitment was brutal but effective. A typical method was simply to attack a village, kill or maim the adults and abduct the children. To ensure loyalty, the RUF would then force their new recruits to take drugs and carry out an atrocity against their own family or community. Once they were orphaned, the RUF would then become the children's surrogate family. It was hard to hold a rational conversation with a child combatant but their stories were depressingly similar. I guess all kids can be cruel – in Britain, they enjoy running around with toy guns, playing 'war'. In Sierra Leone, the guns are real.

The little boy who gave the following testimony was twelve years old. He had been a rebel for eight years, and had scar tissue on his chest, spelling out the letters 'RUF' (another common measure to prevent child soldiers from running away.) This kid was lucky and had been rescued by a Catholic charity called CARITAS.

'I was captured in front of my father's house,' he said. 'They took me with them. Then they gave me drugs. After they gave me drugs, I started killing. I killed a lot of people, I don't know how many. While I was shooting, I had no idea how many people I was killing. I chopped off hands. I killed. But I wasn't myself when I was doing it. They would have killed me if I'd refused.'

After a while, it became hard to view rebel child soldiers as anything but savage little hooligans with no sense of right or wrong or value for life (other people's or their own). Yet they were armed with high velocity rifles and normally high as kites on cannabis, cocaine, or palm wine – often all three.

Cannabis grew everywhere and was many times cheaper than tobacco, so it was no great surprise that everybody smoked it. Similarly, 'palm wine' was plentiful and helped the RUF soldiers pass the time of day as they manned their checkpoints. Palm wine is an alcoholic sap that is tapped straight from the palm trees growing throughout this part of West Africa. It ferments while still in the tree, and is ready to drink as soon as it's harvested. It's about the same strength as beer but gives a hangover more like you've been drinking methylated spirits.

I had the dubious pleasure of sharing palm wine with the local rebels on a couple of occasions, most memorably when our unexpected arrival at a rebel outpost prevented the summary execution of a local villager, accused of witchcraft. Although we had no mandate to interfere with civil matters such as this, our very presence as Military Observers would often help to defuse tension. On the pretext of comparing military discipline in my country and theirs, I asked to be allowed to hang around. I was hoping to be able to do something to save the defendant, who had been tied up, badly beaten, his shoulders dislocated and arms broken before being suspended by his broken arms from the branches of a tree. Small talk soon evaporated and I decided the best way to gain influence with the rebels was by joining them for a drink. I've always enjoyed a drink or two, and I had the advantage over the rebels that I was physically much bigger than them and they were all half-cut to start with. (In addition, Igor the Russian had done his bit to toughen up us 'weak, Western Europeans' with some late-night vodka sessions.)

Palm wine is straw-coloured, warm and frothy. It even tastes like piss. The drunken rebels were passing round a dirty plastic mug of the stuff and I joined them for a drink. The mug was refilled from a bucket. Several mugs later, the rebels had decided I was their new best friend. I politely declined their offers to consume any more potent substances or share their women. They agreed to hand their prisoner over to the local village headman, whom I trusted would give the accused a fairer hearing. The headman later told me that the 'witch' was a local farmer who had fallen out with his eldest son. The son had denounced his own father to the rebels, hoping they would execute him, allowing the son to inherit the family farm.

Trying to work in the midst of some of these people was difficult, to put it mildly, but we really felt we were making a difference. After my first month with the team, I sent an e-mail home voicing my optimism. Not wanting to worry my loved ones, I tried to concentrate on the lighter side of life among the RUF.

20 Feb 00

All goes well in a hot and hanging-around-waiting-for-things-to-start-happening sort of way. I am deployed as a UN Military Observer in a place called Makeni, 150 km NE of Freetown. The team consists of 14 UNMOs from 10 different nations, so there is plenty of opportunity for misunderstanding and confusion. As always, the 'dangers' of a particular country or environment are exaggerated in the pre-deployment briefings. That said, there are a lot of people around here with fewer limbs than is traditional and this area is openly controlled by the RUF (Revolutionary United Front). Their leaders are more or less going along with the Peace Process but this message does not necessarily filter down to the 'troops' on the ground.

The average age of the RUF is mid-teenager. It's all a bit Lord of the Flies-like. Promotion is a result of successful rebel action (killing) – I've yet to meet anyone who's less than a self-promoted captain. Generally, as long as you are firm with them you can do what/go where you want, but (sorry for sounding middle aged) they're so drugged up/generally mental that they don't often know their own names, let alone that there's a Peace Process.

The following is a typical conversation:

Me: Hello, what's your name?

Rebel: I am Dead Body.

Me: Pleased to meet you, Mr Body.

Rebel: Staff Captain Dead Body!

Me: Sorry, Staff Captain. How old are you?

Rebel: I am twelve years old.

Me: How long have you been a rebel?

Rebel: Fifteen years.

Me: Ahh.

Rebel: Give me money. Give me drugs.

Me :   We can't give you anything today, but if you can guarantee the safety of UN personnel then we can ask aid agencies to come to this area where they can help everyone in the area... blah blah blah.

Rebel: You bring two million bags of rice tomorrow.

Me: ?'}@#$%$!

(Next day, same checkpoint, same rebel)

Me: Hello, Staff Captain Dead Body, how are you today?

Rebel: I am Major Sylvester Stallone.

Me :   Pleased to meet you, I am Major Rambo. *(Irony has a low pick-up rate, but doesn't stop me trying, though I was subsequently to discover that Major Rambo was a common nom-de-guerre so maybe I made a bad choice!)* How did you get those wounds? *(Fresh lacerations obvious on arms)*

Rebel: You have something for me? *(Drugs, food or money)*

Me: Not today, how did you get these cuts?

Rebel: Drugs. *(Due to a lack of needles, the best way to 'inject' is to cut open a flap of skin and simply insert the drug.)*

Me: Where did you get your drugs from?

Rebel: From my gun. *(This sounds odd)*

Me: How?

Rebel: I take the powder from my bullets, and put it under my skin. *(Gunpowder, I know, is an irritant)*

Me: Why do you take drugs?

Rebel: Drugs make you strong.

etc, etc, it's all a bit surreal... You remind yourself they've not known anything else and that they're only kids, but a temper tantrum when you've got a grenade launcher is not quite the same as a temper tantrum without a grenade launcher (from the perspective of the unarmed observer...)

The RUF are slaves to fashion. Sun glasses and flat tops, fair enough, but I'm not so sure about their clothes – 'Leonardo di Caprio' T-shirts seem to be their current favourite.

There is supposed to be a DDR (Disarmament, Demobilization and Reintegration) process going on. It has yet to start in this area. The RUF leadership claims to back DDR, but does not match its words with actions. This is frustrating as there seems to be a feeling of optimism and genuine desire for peace at grass roots level – expectations are high, and every day that goes by with no DDR is one step closer to a general recurrence of widespread violence. The RUF foot soldiers receive no pay. Their only remuneration comes from the spoils of war so we are, perhaps, living on borrowed time. As there is no DDR to oversee, we busy ourselves with patrolling and interacting with the local community – my frisbee throwing skills go from strength to strength. I am now known as Mr 'Are you ready' by the local horde of kids who come round to watch every evening. They are experts at fetching dropped frisbees. Every so often, I throw the frisbee into the seething mass of kids ('Are you ready, kids?' – hence the nickname). It normally ends in a mass stampede with some children being trampled underfoot, but they seem to love it, especially when the frisbee hits someone in the face.

My fellow UNMOs range from excellent, through nice but ineffectual, to lazy, useless money grabbing bastards whose only reason for being here is financial. The UN gives us a generous 'Mission Subsistence Allowance' (= money). That said, the guys from the poorest nations get more money every day from the UN than they do from their own government in a month, so you can't blame them. English is the official UN language here, but more importantly, the only common language with the rebels. Most of my colleagues speak reasonable English, but the combination of poor quality radio communications and bureaucratic levels of report writing mean that as a Brit you are much in demand.

We have a generator but no running water and the accommodation is fairly sparse. Food is repetitive but healthy enough, and there is ample opportunity for entertainment. This afternoon we are going to the local 'discotheque' to watch a football match (the final of the Africa Cup of Nations) on a satellite TV as guests of an RUF brigadier (he's a Liberian mercenary with a soft spot for George Weah, who plays for Chelsea, so I stick to talking football, not politics). He looted the TV and generator from Freetown last year. The RUF are supporting Nigeria. Bizarrely, many of the rebels wear the uniforms of Nigerian soldiers they have killed during the civil war, but they don't seem bothered by the double standards...

There is, apparently, a rifle shooting competition afterwards. I assume we're spectators or competitors rather than the targets.

We also have a monkey called Oscar, whose freedom we bought from some local kids (he lived with a collar and chain and had a permanently pissed off expression). We expected he'd do a runner but he now lives in a tree by the house, visits regularly and eats lots of bananas (as do I). He spends a lot of time chasing the children and they spend equal amounts of time chasing him. We have told the kids that if they throw stones at him (Sierra Leonean kids are very good stone throwers) or eat him we will eat them. This seems to have had the desired effect.

On Saturday nights, we set the TV up outside the house, and several hundred kids crowd round to watch a film – Robert de Niro movies seem to be their favourite. I tried showing them the Teletubbies, but the audience got bored and started stoning the telly. Oh well, I tried.

Communications here are not good – contact with the outside world is via satellite phone at the cheeky rate of $6 per minute. Hopefully someone will have forwarded this to you, but send me an e-mail and I should be able to read it at some stage.

Regards,

Phil

Unfortunately, Oscar was not to last much longer. Monkey meat is popular in Sierra Leone (I only tried it once, with salad and pitta bread. Served as a kebab, it was delicious). Some local hunters had shot Oscar's parents, but Oscar had been too small to eat and a group of kids had kept him as a pet. They kept him chained up and used to taunt him cruelly, so the animal-loving Europeans in my team decided to buy his freedom. We gave the kids a couple of dollars and they let Oscar go, but to our surprise he stuck around and took up residence in a local tree.

Oscar, perhaps lacking a monkey's normal fear of humans, was too friendly for his own good. We found his antics amusing – running into the house, stealing bananas, chasing chickens, chasing the neighbours' kids – but our neighbours didn't and this was to have serious consequences. Eventually, Oscar went too far when he started ripping palm leaves off our neighbours' roof. They threw stones at Oscar to stop him and he scampered back to his tree. Oscar had become addicted to damaging the neighbours' roof and, when the stoning stopped, he attacked it with renewed vigour. That evening, he disappeared.

I tasked one of our house-boys, Ibrahim, to do some detective work. The next day he brought grim news. Oscar had paid the ultimate price for vandalism and ended up in the cooking pot. It wasn't worth falling out with the neighbours so we said nothing. For obvious reasons, animal welfare is fairly low down most people's priorities in rebel-held Makeni.

Monitoring the ceasefire

I also held the position of chairman of a Ceasefire Monitoring Committee (or CMC) in a town called Kabala, two hours' drive north of Makeni. Kabala was still held by the Sierra Leonean Army and I went there every Thursday for a weekly meeting. The CMC was a neutral forum in which alleged ceasefire violations could be discussed. Each warring faction sent a representative to the weekly meeting: the RUF, the Sierra Leone Army, the Kamajors and the Armed Forces Revolutionary Council (or AFRC). Meetings had a tendency to deteriorate into shouting matches, with accusations and counter accusations flying but never physical blows. The deal was, if there was no physical violence during the meeting I'd buy everyone lunch afterwards. This seemed to have the desired effect. I also issued all my committee members with clipboards and stationery (including Royal Marines' pens and pencils, which I'd scrounged off the Royal Marines Recruiting Team back in the UK). I reckoned that if I treated them like politicians, they might start acting like them – I prepared a formal agenda before each meeting and wrote up the minutes afterwards.

One of the issues that arose concerned a splinter group of the AFRC, known as the Savage Group. Commanded by the self-styled 'Colonel Savage', the 500-strong group had been allied to both the Sierra Leone Army and the RUF at various stages. It had now managed to fall out with both its erstwhile allies at the same time and they were using my meeting to hatch a plot to make the Savage problem 'go away'.

I pointed out that, as the Chairman of the CMC, I could not condone a ceasefire violation, at which point the RUF rep, genuinely trying to be helpful, suggested that the problem could be solved without firing a shot. I asked him to elaborate. 'Well, we could club them all to death.'

The Committee minutes recorded:

Item 12: Any Other Business
Clubbing to Death of the Savage Group. The Chairman thanked the RUF Representative for his offer, but suggested that though 'clubbing to death' was not mentioned explicitly in the text of the Lomé Peace Accord, it was nevertheless against the spirit of the agreement.

The RUF, however, were still keen to take matters into their own hands and in the end we felt morally obliged to intervene. Over the next few days, we started receiving unconfirmed RUF reports of Savage Group attacks against their positions. Whether true or not, it was obvious the reports would give the RUF the justification to counter-attack without being seen as the aggressors. We asked the RUF if they had any evidence to back their allegations. The next day, they brought two injured men to the house with fresh gunshot wounds. I suspected these two 'RUF soldiers' were really prisoners from the Savage Group, as they seemed more worried about their minders than their injuries.

To prevent a massacre, I deployed with Colonel Jim and six other UNMOs to Kabala. We hoped that if we could disarm the Savage Group, we would be allowed to escort them through RUF territory to a demobilization camp in a safer part of the country, near Freetown. It would not be easy to persuade Savage and Co to hand over their weapons in the middle of a battle. There was no great subtlety to the plan we devised: we sent a message to Savage pointing out that if he co-operated with us we could arrange safe passage for him and his followers. If he refused, he would soon run out of ammunition and the RUF would kill him. His group of fighters were now stuck in a village near Kabala called Buenga between the Sierra Leone Army, who refused to help them, and the RUF, who intended to kill them. They had nowhere else to run to but, for two days, Savage and his men fought on.

We sent a series of teams forward to negotiate but Savage still refused to co-operate. On the third day it was my turn to go forward. I drove as far as the last Sierra Leone Army checkpoint, then walked across No Man's Land into the village. The Savage Group had been living in the bush for nearly two years and looked like a medieval army. The dishevelled fighters were accompanied by an assortment of 'camp followers': young women they had abducted as sex slaves, older women as cooks and children forced to carry ammunition or forage for food.

I was taken to Savage himself, a striking individual with a goatee beard, wrap-around sunglasses and a Tu-Pac T-shirt. He was directing the battle from an armchair, surrounded by bodyguards and a powerful hi-fi system blaring out American rap music. He was trying to play it cool, though he was obviously very nervous and was chain smoking. I too was nervous and tried to beat him at his own game of playing it cool. I told him bluntly that I was his last chance. I was prepared to stay for an hour but, once I left, that would be it. Feigning nonchalance, I put my own sunglasses on, took off my shirt and lay down to sunbathe (I had arranged to meet up with Anna in Gambia the following week, so needed to top up my tan...).

We continued this pretence for some minutes. The stalemate was broken when an RPG exploded nearby. This unnerved me, but the timing was perfect. Savage immediately told me his men would disarm and I returned to Kabala to help prepare a makeshift disarmament centre.

We worked late into the night to disarm about 350 people of their AK47s, machine-guns, RPGs and mortars. They had almost no ammunition, though, which perhaps explained why they had been unable to fight on.

Also, for each weapon handed in, there were two or three camp followers. Technically, these pitiful hangers-on were not entitled to be treated as ex-combatants, but we couldn't just abandon them to their fate with the RUF approaching, so we agreed to offer them safe passage out of the area as well.

Now that the Savage Group had disarmed, the Sierra Leone Army was prepared to let them enter the relative safety of Kabala. This would only be a temporary measure as the nearest formal demobilization camp was 300 miles away across RUF territory. So a convoy of Indian and Kenyan trucks with an armed escort was dispatched from Freetown to provide the transport we needed, taking nearly three days to reach us.

I enjoyed my enforced sojourn in Kabala as we waited for the trucks to arrive. This town had never fallen to the RUF so we got an inkling of what the country must have been like before the civil war. It was a bustling market town surrounded by stunning hills – impressive granite spires that rose sharply out of the jungle. I decided to lead a small group of ex-combatants on an ascent up one of these peaks. My main motivation was the aesthetic appeal of climbing a beautiful mountain, and as a bonus I found it satis-fying to show the lads that there was more to life than fighting.

The last hundred feet beneath the summit involved easy rock-climbing, and I was pleasantly surprised to see that my motley crew of fellow climbers seemed to be enjoying themselves as much as I was. For a few moments we were on the same wavelength, united by the bond of a shared challenge. On the one technical move to overcome a small overhang, I lowered my belt for the others to use as a handhold. As I helped them up the rock face, they were just a group of kids enjoying an adventure. Sadly, they reverted to type when we got back down to Kabala, where they got their fun from banditry.

I asked them to suggest a name for our new peak.

'Savage Mountain,' they proposed after some discussion.

'You can call it that if you like, but the second highest moun-tain in the world, K2, is already known as the Savage Mountain,' I told them.

More deliberation.

'OK, then. How about Virgin Blood Ripper Peak?'

I had to concede that it was unlikely another mountain would already have this name.

When the trucks arrived, it was a real challenge trying to impose some sort of order on the thousand or so people we were trying to move. Half the population of Kabala were now claiming to be ex-combatants, wanting to cadge a free lift to Freetown. Men, women, children, goats, chickens and even a small cow squeezed themselves on to the trucks.

There was a separate arrangement for Savage and his immediate family. The UN had agreed to send a helicopter to pick them up as we didn't believe the RUF would have resisted the temptation to do them in, had we taken them through their territory by road. Some in the UN thought Savage deserved nothing more than to be finished off by his enemies (and I agreed with them). But if we'd failed to give Savage the safe passage we had promised him, the UN's credibility and trustworthiness would have been severely dented. The message would then have gone around that the UN couldn't protect anybody and it would have become impossible to persuade other rebel commanders to disarm.

Furthermore, Savage had a young wife, a stunning girl he married after killing her first husband. I knew the RUF had 'special plans' for her even if they could not get at Savage himself. We gave Savage and his wife a lift to the helicopter landing site in our car and on the way the ungrateful bastard stole my sunglasses off the back seat. In the end, it amused me to think that such an image-conscious individual coveted my £2.99 Woolworths specs.

With the trucks loaded and ready to go, I saw an old man pleading with one of the Kenyan soldiers. I went to investigate. The man's daughter had been abducted and was being held on the truck by a group of ex-combatants. He pointed her out to me and I climbed on to the back of the truck. The young girl was being raped by two militiamen. I dragged them off her and passed her down to her father. We were then able to start the journey back through RUF territory with our human cargo.

At every town or village along the 250-mile trip, we had to pass through a series of RUF checkpoints. Before the main convoy of Kenyan trucks reached a checkpoint, a team of UNMOs drove ahead to warn the RUF what was happening and to pre-empt trouble. I drove forward to a checkpoint commanded by a twelve-year-old rebel called RSM Killer, and explained what was going on. He had been told by his commanders to co-operate, but he was not at all happy with the arrangements. I persuaded him to lower the rope that acted as the barrier at the roadblock. As the Kenyan convoy approached, he ordered his men to stand aside and everything seemed in control.

The first couple of trucks drove by unchallenged. Then Killer suddenly recognized an old adversary on the back of one of the trucks.

He started shouting wildly, 'That man, he attack my men!' He ordered his men to pull the rope back across the road, but it was too late for the next truck to stop. It ploughed straight into the checkpoint. The rope caught on the front of the truck, which drove on. Killer's checkpoint was torn to pieces. He went berserk, his anger now directed at me. He unslung his AK47. I considered grabbing it, then realized there were another ten weapons pointing at me, so thought better of it. In the distance I could see some armed Kenyans deploying from one of their trucks.

Killer was standing five feet in front of me, with his rifle pointing in my face and his finger curled around the trigger.

If a fire-fight started now, I was dead.

I tried to speak calmly but with authority in my voice. I was, after all, dealing with a twelve-year-old. 'RSM, two days ago the Savage Group were your enemies. I have disarmed them. I am not your enemy. Put your gun down, and we can all live to fight another day.'

Killer did not look totally convinced, but I had introduced an element of doubt. To my relief, the Kenyans slung their rifles over their shoulders and continued approaching us, armed only with broad grins. The moment of danger had passed and yet as I climbed back into my jeep I could feel myself shaking. It had been too close for comfort.

The convoy pushed on slowly. I suspected that every time we stopped for food, fuel or vehicle repairs we lost or gained a few passengers. One of the new additions was a baby, whose mother had given birth at 40 mph, crowded on the back of a truck with fifty or sixty people.

It was a relief to finally off-load our human cargo in a demobilization camp at Lungi, near the International Airport.

I had no reason to suspect I would see any of the Savage Group again. Some of them, however, decided to join another militia, the West Side Boys. It was this group of bandits that took some British soldiers hostage a few months later, in September 2000. By this time, I had finished my tour of Sierra Leone and was back in the UK, where the hostage-taking was a big news story. I didn't know any of the British hostages, but I did know several of the hostage-takers. I felt no regret when I heard that not all of Savage's men had survived the battle with British Special Forces when the hostages were rescued. I wonder who's wearing my sunglasses now...

The next week I was due some leave, so jumped on a plane to nearby Gambia for a week of pampering with Anna in a five-star hotel. It felt strange being in such luxury, less than two hours' travel from Sierra Leone. Gambia is a beautiful country, though nothing compared to Sierra Leone. It struck me, once again, what a tragedy the place had become. If people would just stop fighting for a few years, they could start attracting tourists instead of soldiers. I tried this argument on many rebels, explaining that they'd be much better off inviting rich foreigners into their country and ripping them off instead of fighting against them.

I've never been a great one for lying by a pool but, for the first time on holiday in my life, I was happy to do little else apart from eating, drinking and just being together. Anna had brought my wedding ring out with her from the UK, as taking expensive jewellery to Sierra Leone would not have been sensible, and it felt every bit as special putting it on as it did the day we were wed. Our week flashed by, and before I knew it I was taking my ring off again and saying farewell to Anna.

Flying back to Sierra Leone proved more exciting than I'd anticipated. The only airline flying between Gambia and Freetown was a dodgy set-up called West Coast Airlines, who had one knackered old Russian aeroplane and two knackered old Russian pilots, who had to be paged to the flight in the duty free shop. Unfortunately everyone flying that day (including me) had bribed the ground crew to be allowed to take extra luggage and/or extra passengers on board the aircraft. By the time I got on, there were no seats left unoccupied so I had to sit in the aisle, surrounded by the luggage overflow that couldn't be fitted in the hold. The plane struggled to take off with the extra weight and, despite the pilots' best efforts, never reached more than about 1,000 feet above the ground. Half an hour into the flight, steam started filling the cabin. I began to see why the pilots needed to drink so much. It was a relief to touch down back in Sierra Leone.

With only a couple of weeks until my thirtieth birthday, Anna had sent me back to Sierra Leone with a few token presents. Working on the theory that I should only take stuff I was prepared to lose, these included a new pair of Woolworths sunglasses, several music tapes, a *Father Ted* video and a small can of Heinz baked beans.

Seeing Anna made me miss her even more than usual, but I felt re-invigorated and was looking forward to pitting my wits against the hardcore RUF once again. So far, our achievements in Makeni had included disarming the Savage Group and 350 child soldiers released by the RUF to the Catholic Charity CARITAS, as a good will gesture. But we had not yet disarmed a single mainstream rebel.

By April 2000, nearly 25,000 ex-combatants (from all warring factions except the RUF) had entered the DDR process throughout the country. Sierra Leone was now being hailed as a long-awaited UN success story, following the ignominy of Rwanda, Somalia, Angola and other disasters. But in the RUF strongholds, disarmament had yet to start. Colonel Jim now appointed me as the team's Disarmament Officer and I felt honoured to be given the responsibility – Makeni was seen as the key to UN success. If the RUF in Makeni could be persuaded to disarm, the rest of their number would follow. Or so we hoped.

CHAPTER FOUR

HOW TO START A CIVIL WAR

'We learn from history that we do not learn from history.'
GEORG WILHELM F. HEGEL

During the last few days of April, things started to go wrong. After months of painfully slow negotiation – and stalling by the RUF – we had at last finished the construction of a Disarmament, Demobilization and Reintegration camp. The rebels would not allow us to site the camp in Makeni itself, so eventually we reached a compromise and established one 10 miles south of Makeni, near a main road but removed from habitation. We had also persuaded the rebels to allow us to establish a number of reception centres where combatants wanting to disarm would physically hand over their weapons.

The DDR process was this: an armed combatant would turn up at a reception centre, hand over his weapon and be issued with a set of identity papers. From there, the now ex-combatant would be taken to a DDR camp for medical screening and rehabilitation. The reception centres had to be separate from the DDR camps, to pre-empt the problems of rival factions fighting each other when some were armed and others weren't. In other parts of the country the UN built permanent reception centres, but in Makeni we decided this would be too provocative and any buildings would just end up being trashed by the rebels. So instead we set up a temporary camp and called it a reception centre. That way, we could dismantle the camp at the end of the day and relocate it overnight.

The DDR camps, on the other hand, were permanent fixtures as each one had to house up to a thousand ex-combatants with facilities for cooking, washing, administration and medical treatment. Several wells also had to be dug at each camp.

A waiting game

Our DDR camp and the first reception centre formally opened on 20 April and we dutifully started manning the sites even though, at this stage, there were no ex-combatants to use them. We hoped the rebels would begin to accept that the DDR camps posed no threat to them, and we actively encouraged people to come and have a look round.

As the team's Disarmament Officer, it was my job to oversee the reception centre in Makeni itself and to issue documentation to any combatants choosing to disarm. On the first day the DDR camp opened, I helped the Kenyans set up the reception centre first thing in the morning, while the rebels were still asleep or eating breakfast. We arranged tents, tables, chairs, sandbags, sign-posts and a sheltered 'waiting area' where any disarming rebels could enjoy a cup of tea and a biscuit before being transported, minus weapons, to the DDR camp itself.

I chatted to the Kenyan soldiers as we waited, sharing endless cups of tea. As well as using British Army Land Rovers, the Kenyan Army had also adopted the British Army habit of drinking copious amounts of sweet, lukewarm, milky tea, so I felt at home. They were all entertaining story-tellers and I enjoyed their tales of male bravado, as they boasted how they had all killed lions bare-handed during basic training. We were not expecting there to be many rebel 'customers' that day. So when we saw a load of rebels approaching in a pick-up truck, led by a hardliner called Colonel Augustine Bao, the RUF's Chief of Security, I told the Kenyans to be on their guard.

Colonel Bao jumped out of his truck. His eyes were bloodshot and I could smell the alcohol on his breath. He was clearly very angry. I tried to sound light-hearted: 'Colonel Bao, good to see you. I didn't think we'd be seeing you for a while yet. Would you like a cup of tea?'

He was not amused, and launched into a tirade of threats and abuse with which we had recently become familiar.

'THE HUNGRY LION ROARS AND WHEN THE BLOOD FLOWS LIKE RIVERS THE WORLD WILL REMEMBER THE NAME OF BAO. EVEN YOUR ANCESTORS WILL REGRET THE DAY YOU INVADED MY COUNTRY AND ABUSED THE TRUST OF THE LIBERATORS OF SIERRA LEONE, THE REVOLUTIONARY UNITED FRONT. POWER TO THE PEOPLE! WEALTH TO THE PEOPLE! ARMS TO THE PEOPLE. SANKOH IS OUR LEADER...' and so on and so on.

This was heavy going for nine o'clock in the morning, even by Bao's standards. I nodded politely and resisted the temptation to tell him what a wanker I thought he was. I hoped he was just trying to show off to his subordinates. To my relief, Colonel Jim showed up after a few minutes. The only person Bao seemed to dislike more than me was Jim, so at least I was out of the firing line for a while. Bao eventually ran out of steam and went off to bother someone else.

Despite incidents like this, we hoped the rebels' bark was worse than their bite. Indeed, once the news spread that money, food, medical screening – and ultimately the chance of a better future – would be available if the rebels chose to disarm, there was considerable enthusiasm among their rank and file.

For a week, we set up our desks every day and waited for our first customers. None came, so I took the opportunity to finish the book I was reading, Nelson Mandela's autobiography. It was always useful to steer a conversation with a rebel agitator on to a neutral topic, and even among the rebels it was hard to find anybody who didn't respect Mandela. So *Long Walk to Freedom* made useful, as well as stimulating, background reading.

After all our efforts to persuade the rebels to allow us to build the camp, and the hard work of constructing it, it was rather an anti-climax that nobody was using it. But I had been feeling rough for a few days and was glad to have some enforced inactivity. I caught up with some letter writing and, on 21 April, started writing a note to Anna:

21 April. Well, disarmament in Makeni has finally started – at least on paper. In practice, nobody has showed up yet. We wait…

A couple of moments of humour and danger yesterday. The RUF sent a heavily armed mob to the reception centre, claiming they were victims of persecution by the world in general and the UN in particular. Lots of excited ranting and raving (more bark than bite) until one over-enthusiastic RUF youth misheard one of the Kenyans saying 'Roger, out' on his radio. He thought the Kenyan had said 'Flush them out' and in response, forty armed rebels encircled our position. They eventually got bored after an hour or two and went off to bother someone else.

Unfortunately, those combatants who are prepared to disarm (the majority) are too scared of the violent minority (most of the middle-ranking commanders) who are, effectively, picketing the reception centre. We shall see...

I'm feeling a bit rough at the moment. Maybe it's just the combination of the muggy weather and too much sitting around, doing nothing.

22 April. No change. For some reason, I've got a splitting headache. Today's highlight was a visit from the UNAMSIL Deputy Force Commander, a Nigerian brigadier. My frisbee was sitting on the desk next to my radio and he thought it was a satellite dish.

23 April. Still waiting. My head's really hurting now. Probably too much sleep! And my backside is sore from sitting on it for too long...

The RUF political leadership also seemed in favour of disarmament. The Revolutionary United Front had by now conveniently renamed itself the Revolutionary United Front Party. Furthermore, under the terms of the Lomé Peace Accord, the RUF had three cabinet ministers in the Government of National Unity and their leader, Foday Sankoh, was now Sierra Leone's Vice-President. Sankoh had also been given the post of 'Chairman of the Commission for Mineral Resources' (in other words, he controlled the diamond mining). So, with the overall RUF leadership enjoying the life of fat-cat politicians in Freetown, they actually had a vested interest in a peaceful future.

The RUF military commanders on the ground had less motivation to co-operate. As rebel fighters, they lived as warlords, with the power of life and death in the areas they controlled and the prettiest girls as bush wives. As uneducated ex-combatants, they would be nobodies, but with many enemies. Worse, they would be nobodies with many enemies and no guns. The RUF's delaying tactics were simple but frustratingly effective and we all knew why they were stalling. They controlled the diamond mining areas and it was still the dry season. Diamond mining becomes almost impossible during the tropical rainstorms of the wet season that starts in June. So, every day that the RUF maintained their military control over the diamond mining areas meant more money for their leaders.

A typical delaying tactic was refusing to allow UN movement through a particular area without the written permission of a local commander. It was conveniently ignored that, under the Peace Accord, the UN was supposed to have complete freedom of movement. This was fine, until you asked where the local commander was.

'Di commandah not here. Come tomorrow.'

The next day: 'You missed di commandah. He was here yesterday.' And so on.

On one memorable occasion, I actually managed to track down the commander and acquire the relevant document, only to find when I reached the unco-operative checkpoint that nobody there could read – so I was still unable to pass by. Another common tactic was for a rebel commander to make impossible demands, then accuse us of bias against the RUF when we couldn't meet them. At one stage, for example, the rebels refused to co-operate further unless Foday Sankoh was appointed as Ambassador to Britain.

Our best weapon during such negotiations was an Indian officer in our team, S-P. He could talk for hours and had a stubbornness that meant he would never back down, even on the most trivial of points. When it suited him, he could be the most pedantic man in West Africa. For S-P, a week of pointless argument at a checkpoint was a real pleasure. Many rebels would eventually back down rather than face a lecture on the small print of an obscure UN declaration made several decades previously.

Even though there was a comic element to many of our dealings with rebels, our exchanges were always underpinned by menace. The bottom line was this: these were dangerous, unpredictable people who were prepared to kill us. Negotiations did not take place on neutral ground and there were no legal or diplomatic niceties. We were in the rebel heartland, and while negotiating we typically had forty or fifty henchmen pointing guns in our faces, doing their best to intimidate us, often successfully. I found it particularly unsettling that many rebels wore military uniforms taken from the bodies of soldiers they had killed in battle.

I gained moral courage from the knowledge that I was representing the 'Rest of the World'. The UN may not be an efficient organization or good at fighting wars, but its solidarity can be a remarkably effective weapon. On one occasion a Chinese officer, Major Xu, and I attended a routine meeting in the RUF headquarters. After the meeting, we were 'invited' (that is, ordered by an armed rebel commander and his bodyguards) to stay for a 'political discussion'. The atmosphere turned nasty, with Xu and I getting increasingly worried. An RUF 'political adviser' was ranting and raving about numerous alleged abuses of power by the UN, and claimed there was a 'white, Western imperialist conspiracy to destroy the peace-loving people of the RUF'.

Xu, from the People's Republic of China, caught my eye and whispered: 'Phil, let me deal with this.'

He then launched into a diatribe of his own against Western imperialism, with a passion that completely stole the rebels' thunder. The rebel agitator totally lost his momentum and we were able to slip out. Xu's final comment to the assembled rebels as we left: 'And don't forget, there are more soldiers in my army than there are people in your country!'

As we drove back to our house, Xu couldn't stop grinning and explained, 'For the first time, I see why they make us learn this stuff!'

It was an eye-opener to work alongside officers like Xu, share a common cause with them and live with them through the same fear and hardship. A decade previously, they might have been my enemies.

Dealing with the RUF was hard work both physically and mentally, and we were supposed to take a few days off every month to recharge our batteries. I had certainly needed my time away from it all in Gambia. But my team leader, Colonel Jim, had not wanted to leave Makeni until our DDR camp was up and running. He had not had a day off since January and looked drained, so we persuaded him to take some long-overdue leave. When the DDR camp opened on 20 April, he finally took a break, joking as he left, 'Don't start any civil wars until I get back.' With hindsight, this looked decidedly like tempting fate.

Certain rebel commanders, particularly Colonel Bao, had started to direct veiled threats at Jim and me, accusing us of being personally responsible for assorted British 'crimes' against the RUF. Our alleged crimes included colonialism, exploitation and tacit support for mercenary organizations, including the British company, Sandline International and a South African set-up, Executive Outcomes. Both organizations had either directly or indirectly been involved in successful military action against the RUF.

Sandline was a British company run by a retired British Army officer, Lieutenant Colonel Tim Spicer. In 1998, the company had technically breached a UN arms embargo by providing logistical and military support to the Government of President Tejan Kabbah, traditional adversary of the RUF. Sandline had also been involved in attempts to train the Civilian Defence Force. Both these activities were done with the tacit agreement of the British

Government. In RUF eyes, this meant the British had taken sides against them and this was reflected in their attitudes to us personally.

Indeed, Bao regarded the whole of the UN as nothing more than lackeys for President Tejan Kabbah. Kabbah had spent most of his career as a UN diplomat, as had his old friend, Kofi Annan. So the RUF considered UNAMSIL to be totally pro-Kabbah and 100 per cent anti-RUF.

Bao reserved a special loathing for Britain. He had lived for a while in both London and Glasgow and never lost an opportunity to tell us about the abuse he had suffered there. This may have been the case but, when I asked him for examples, the best he could come up with was the 'crime against humanity' committed when he was asked to turn his music down while driving through Peckham in South London. Hardly worth going to war over, I thought.

Britain did have several military and political advisers working with the Sierra Leonean government, including a retired senior British policeman, Keith Biddle, as head of the Sierra Leonean police. This just added weight to the RUF's conviction that the British were planning the downfall of the RUF, and they openly accused any Brits in the UN of being spies or agitators against them. They assumed our affiliation to the UN was nothing more than cover. I sympathized to a certain extent. Just as during the Cold War NATO was suspicious of countries that employed Soviet advisers, now the RUF was suspicious of a government that employed British advisers. If things went wrong, Bao and his cronies would not be able to get their hands on the British advisers – but Jim and I made easy targets.

Colonel Jim appointed Major Ganase, a Malaysian, as his deputy while he was away and asked me to help keep things on track. It would have been one conspiracy theory too far to have put me in charge.

On the day Jim left, however, I had another preoccupation. What had started as a dull headache and general lethargy was getting progressively worse. After a few days, the pain became so intense it was hard to think about anything else. Someone suggested I might have malaria, but I thought I probably just had bad flu. Malaria is a very unpleasant disease, which kills more people than Aids, but because there are no anti-malaria drugs available almost everybody has it and they just have to get on with life. When others in the team claimed to be suffering malarial attacks, I had not always been sympathetic. Most of the guys from Third World countries already had malaria before they arrived in Sierra Leone. For them it just wasn't a big deal – they took it easy for a couple of days, but didn't make the same fuss a Westerner would. Malaria only killed you if you were very young, old or pregnant, none of which applied to these men.

Conveniently, some 'malaria sufferers' only seemed to suffer attacks during the morning, when there was work to be done. By the afternoon and certainly by the evening, the symptoms would miraculously recede... until the next morning.

I had been religiously taking my weekly Larium anti-malaria pills and was adamant it couldn't be malaria. Larium, however, is only 95 per cent effective and I was destined to be one of the unlucky 5 per cent. I struggled on for a couple of days and went through the motions of going to work, but my symptoms were becoming worse – my headache felt like every hangover I'd ever had rolled into one. The racking pain made me feel sick and I was finding it hard to eat. When my body's temperature regulation packed up and I was reduced to lying miserably on a camp bed under a tree, I knew it was something more serious. A colleague took me to the Kenyan Battalion HQ to see their medical officer, who did some tests before confirming I had malaria. He pumped me full of drugs, and cheerfully told me I had the sort of malaria that either goes away quickly – and stays away – or kills you. 'So just take it easy for a couple of days,' he suggested.

I asked whether I should come back and see him again. 'Not much point,' he observed, with typical Kenyan pragmatism.

I spent the rest of the day being violently sick (a side effect of the medicine) but then started to feel much better. Clearly the medicine was having an effect, but also I had found a colleague who was even worse off than me. (It was like when you have a mild hangover and then meet a mate who's got an even worse one – suddenly your own predicament becomes quite funny.) Andy Samsonoff, another British UNMO who had recently joined the Magburaka team down the road, had just been released from hospital after a bout of typhoid. We compared medical notes and, as Andy dryly pointed out, at least I was only losing bodily fluids from one end of my body. It's always reassuring when there's someone feeling rougher than you.

On several occasions, small groups of rebels had come either to the reception centre or our team house to find out more about the deal they were being offered as part of the DDR process. On the face of it, this was good news. Initially, however, I suggested they go away and wait a few more days, until they received formal orders from their commanders to start disarming. I did not have much respect for the rebel commanders, but by-passing the chain of command is a bad idea in any military organization. Considering the low opinion that rebel commanders such as Bao already had of me, I was not keen to add 'incitement to mutiny' to their list of grievances. In any case, the government of Sierra Leone was planning to open six new DDR camps simultaneously across the country on 1 May: two for the RUF, two for the CDF and two for ex-Sierra Leone Army soldiers. On the same day the Sierra Leone Army itself would also return its weapons to its armouries in a show of solidarity. We guessed the RUF at large would be unlikely to disarm before then.

First – and last – customers

On 29 April, my thirtieth birthday, ten rebels approached me and asked to disarm. I hoped they would set a precedent for others to follow, but still thought it unwise to proceed until the local commanders gave their approval. I was not the only one with such concerns. These were shared by the Kenyan commanding officer, the next-door Magburaka UNMO team and Fergus from DfID, who knew the rebels better than anyone. Fergus was the site manager for construction of the DDR camp. He was a big, red-haired Irishman who could out-talk, out-smoke and out-drink almost anyone. A canny operator, he could play the anti-British card to great effect with the rebel commanders, and they had a soft spot for him.

The UN headquarters, however, did not see things as we all did. They considered it a risk worth taking to start disarming people in Makeni. Their reasoning was that the senior RUF leadership, including Sankoh, were in Freetown where they could be held accountable for the actions of their subordinates.

I suspected we in Makeni better understood the likely reaction of the local RUF commanders, and our formal written report that day was blunt: 'If we proceed as instructed, we risk provoking a violent reaction from the RUF without the military capacity to contain it.'

Our protestations were overridden and that afternoon I dutifully disarmed the ten rebels and issued them with their new ID papers. They were apprehensive and understandably so. Most of them had had to smuggle their weapons past RUF checkpoints and would have been executed had they been caught. Some of their methods of concealing weapons were imaginative, if ill-conceived. One arrived at the reception centre carrying a mattress on his head with an AK47 assault rifle hidden inside it. What reason he might have had for carrying a mattress into a UN position was not clear. Another group showed a little more ingenuity by hiding their weapons underneath a cartload of pineapples, which they then sold to us.

As these individuals were now ex-combatants, it became the UN's responsibility to protect them. We knew the local commanders would be upset, but hoped their anger would not turn violent. I have wondered, looking back, whether it would have been better for all concerned not to have started the disarmament then. But things would inevitably have come to a head at some stage. And if we weren't disarming rebels, what the hell were we doing there at all?

For my part, I was still feeling pretty rough from my malaria and a little homesick. The cards and gifts I had received for my birthday just made me miss my wife and friends. At least I had the satisfaction of knowing that disarmament in the rebel heartland had started. As I manned my desk in the reception centre for the final time, I noted in a letter home that 'if this leads to large-scale RUF disarmament, it'll be a pretty cool birthday present'. I never had the chance to post this letter – it was soon stolen by the rebels along with all my other belongings.

During the morning of 30 April, the Kenyans took the ten ex-combatants by truck to the DDR camp for registration and medical screening. In due course they would then receive payment of what the UN calls Transitional Safety Allowance, a sum of money to smooth the transition from combatant status to being a useful member of society. This was, in plain language, a $300 cash bribe. To my way of thinking, though, it was a small price to take deadly weapons out of circulation.

It was, of course, possible that the ten had been sent with the connivance of the RUF commanders, simply to provoke confrontation. But, as the officer who personally disarmed them, I was convinced they were genuine. Their fear certainly was.

We had tried to keep the disarmament as low key as possible – there was no point in publicly humiliating the local commanders. They knew well enough what was happening, and that afternoon, Colonel Bao, another hardliner called Colonel Kallon and several hundred rebels turned up at the DDR camp. They quickly surrounded the camp and the Kenyan platoon guarding it.

Siege

I had been on duty at the DDR camp during the morning, and a few minutes before the rebel mob arrived, I had returned to the team house in Makeni for lunch. For me, this mundane fact turned out to have been a life-saving twist of fate. I had actually passed Colonel Bao as I left the DDR camp and waved cheerily to him as I drove past. He scowled and shouted at me, but as he scowled and shouted at me every time he saw me, I thought nothing of it. Little did I know, as I nonchalantly ate pasta with my teammates from the morning shift, that the afternoon shift was being taken hostage.

There was an armed stand-off. Then as negotiations broke down, the rebels seized Major Ganase, our Malaysian acting team leader, and a number of Kenyans. Bao was incensed that his men had disobeyed his orders by disarming. Unable to punish the ten 'deserters', who had unsurprisingly legged it into the bush, he had decided to take brutal revenge on his UN tormentors instead.

As lightly armed peacekeepers, the UN mission in Sierra Leone depended on the consent of the warring factions. Within a matter of minutes, this consent had vanished and the RUF had a new enemy: the UN itself.

At the DDR camp, the remaining Kenyans and another UNMO (a Bangladeshi called Salah Uddin) spent the night on a knife-edge, surrounded and heavily outnumbered. Back in

Makeni, we knew things were going wrong from the initial situation reports sent on the radio. The flow of information ended abruptly, though, when the rebels seized the UN vehicles that were fitted with radios. In an attempt to find out what was going on, an increasingly worried UN HQ in Freetown ordered us to send another negotiating team to meet with the rebel commanders. I jumped in a jeep and was about to drive down to the rebels' HQ when a message came through from the Ops Room that I was wanted on the telephone. So my place was taken by a Norwegian officer. Accompanied by a Gambian lieutenant colonel, he went to find out was happening. Neither man returned. Fate had been on my side once again.

As the Norwegian was being snatched, he managed to press 'Transmit' on a radio he had hidden in his day-sack. We listened in horror as he and his companion were badly beaten up, stripped naked, trussed up with wire and sexually assaulted. When the rebels found the hidden radio they went mad. I don't know what they were doing at this stage but the two men's screams became even more desperate and they were begging for mercy. The screaming ended with a burst of automatic fire and we assumed the worst, but we later discovered the rebels had been playing mind games. Our colleagues had been 'lucky': they were not killed, but were to endure three weeks of hell. The Norwegian officer, a white man, was staked out naked in the tropical sun for twelve hours a day and was badly burnt. The Gambian lost a leg. Both had been repeatedly sexually molested, mainly by boys too young to understand sex, yet old enough to enjoy the sense of power it gave them. They were eventually released in a deal brokered by Liberia.

The Kenyans, bravely, also sent parties to negotiate with the rebels. They too did not return.

I felt particularly vulnerable – as a white Westerner, I would be likely to receive 'special treatment' from the rebels, and the RUF saw Britain as the root of all evils in Sierra Leone. Moreover, as a Commando, my slaying would be good for rebel street cred. The rebels had let slip via friendly civilians that it was their intention to 'do a Somalia'. (This referred to the debacle in October 1993 when dead US soldiers were dragged naked through the streets of Mogadishu, following a bungled US military intervention against a Somalian warlord, General Aidid. It was all captured on camera and broadcast live on CNN. This single, shocking event had such an impact on US public opinion that it effectively prevented any future US military involvement in Africa.) And just to cap it all, it was my signature on the disarmament forms of the rebels that had disarmed. I didn't rate my chances in a kangaroo court. In Conduct after Capture training you are taught to remain the 'grey man'. In rebel eyes, I could hardly be more colourful.

Of our team of fourteen, four were now missing, including Ganase, the acting team leader. Four others were on leave or back in Freetown, including Colonel Jim and Igor. Six of us remained.

That night, the rebels reinforced their positions on the routes out of the town and closed the roads. Even the aid agencies were being turned back when they tried to leave town – if Fergus couldn't talk his way out of this one, then no one could. We were now effectively trapped. Reports from other parts of the country made depressing listening. Hostages had been taken in numerous locations, including British Army Major Andy Harrison, who coincidentally was my next-door neighbour back in London. Meanwhile, Foday Sankoh was cranking up the propaganda machine, claiming the UN had attacked his men and forced them to disarm.

More and more rebels were now arriving in the town from nearby villages, and their excitement was tangible. We could hear intermittent gunfire from the town centre (always an indication of high spirits) as well as chanting and singing. Under more friendly circumstances, the rebels had been happy to give us a demonstration performance of their war-chants. Now, we were hearing them being used for their original purpose. Groups of rebels on foot or in pick-up trucks continually patrolled past our house, firing occasional bursts of gunfire to test our reaction. We bolted the doors and windows and I prepared a 'grab-bag' of emergency gear – food, water and a satellite phone – in case we had to make a run for it.

No one in the UN HQ in Freetown seemed to be taking our deteriorating security situation seriously. At this stage they were still unwilling to believe anything was amiss. It was exasperating, to put it mildly, to be told by UN HQ over the radio that 'everything was calm' and we should stop making a fuss. The duty officer in the Ops room in Freetown was Uruguayan, a lovely guy with terrible English. I explained that the RUF was shooting at us.

'Shooting,' he said. 'Who is shooting?'

'The RUF!' I shouted back.

'Please, spell RUF. I no spell RUF.'

This was not the time for English lessons. It was therefore strangely satisfying when, a few seconds later, there was a burst of automatic gunfire at my end of the line. My sceptical colleague on the other end of the radio heard the shots and finally grasped the gravity of the situation.

Bizarrely, however, even some of the five UNMOs still with me were refusing to acknowledge that we were in serious trouble. One of them asked me whether we would go on patrol the following morning as he wanted to buy some cigarettes on the way through town! Incredulous, I told him he could go if he wanted but pointed out that nobody leaving the house in the last twenty-four hours had come back. This attitude seemed to me to be a chronic case of ostrich syndrome: pretending nothing is wrong. I know people have different coping mechanisms for handling dangerous situations but this was not, in my view, a good strategy for survival.

I didn't want to escalate the situation, and told the six Kenyan armed guards to keep a low profile. They should return fire only if we actually came under 'effective enemy fire' (that is, if one of us was struck by a bullet or clearly about to be shot). The RUF could easily have brought a lynch mob of heavily armed rebels to storm our house, and I didn't want to provoke them or give them the excuse that we had 'attacked' them. I hoped this was just a show of high spirits and that everything would calm down in the morning. But the omens were not looking good.

The thirty-strong platoon of Kenyans back at the DDR camp had managed to assemble a working radio. Just before midnight, we heard them send a message to their commanding officer: they were still surrounded. The rebels were repeating their threats to attack if the ten 'deserters' were not handed over. Morally and legally, the UN had a duty to protect all ex-combatants who had disarmed in good faith, but these ex-combatants had long gone.

A surreal interlude occurred when RUF Colonel Sherif and his deputy, Lieutenant Colonel Alfred Jimmy, came to the house and asked to speak to me. I had come to know these guys quite well from the Ceasefire Monitoring Committee. And it was they who had been on patrol with us when we attempted to reach Kono a couple of months before. I trusted them enough to let them come into our house for a chat, despite the truck of heavily armed men they had brought with them.

Sherif was about my age, well educated, with an elder brother and sister in America. One was a lawyer and the other a doctor, and I had once asked him what he told them he did. With a wry smile, he had replied: 'Student leader. Calling myself a "rebel warlord" would scare my sister's kids.'

Sherif had genuinely benefited from the Peace Process and, as a member of the Ceasefire Monitoring Committee, he received a reasonable wage from the Government. He also saw himself as a budding politician so I wanted to hear what he had to say. In addition, I knew he had fallen out with Colonel Bao, who was holding my colleagues hostage. In fact, Sherif himself had only recently been released from the RUF prison where he had been held for three weeks, after Bao had accused him of embezzling RUF funds. I suspected the charges had been fabricated by Bao, who saw Sherif as a threat and didn't like his co-operating with the UN. I had visited Sherif in prison several times with food and water and had persuaded his guards to loosen the ropes tying him up. I may even have saved him from summary execution, though not torture, by pointing out to Bao that executing members of the Ceasefire Monitoring Committee was not the most conciliatory of gestures. Sankoh had finally ordered Bao to release Sherif.

Standing in our living room now, Sherif was looking worried. He told me there had been 'a terrible mistake and misunderstanding'. *That's a bloody understatement.* He told me that Bao and Kallon had become loose cannons and that it was not RUF policy to take UN personnel hostage. To protect himself, Bao had told Sankoh that the UN had attacked his men and forced them to disarm at gunpoint.

I asked Sherif if there was anything he could do to defuse things. He thought he might be able to persuade Sankoh that Bao and Kallon had been lying to him, so I let him use our satphone to call his leader. Sherif eventually spoke to Sankoh himself, but his protestations were in vain. Sankoh preferred to believe what the hardliners were telling him.

Even if Sherif and Jimmy had been sidelined by the other rebel commanders, I still thought it worthwhile staying in their good books, so I offered them a beer. I was too preoccupied to make small talk, so suggested we watch a video. Unfortunately the only videos the team had were violent war movies – *Rambo I, II* and *III* and *Terminator*. This did not seem the ideal moment to glamorize violence, especially with trigger-happy bodyguards trying to peer in through the windows. So instead, I dug out the *Father Ted* video that Anna had given me as a birthday present. I don't think my RUF companions got many of the jokes but it seemed to help calm things down a bit. Before Sherif left, he warned us that we should leave the town. I asked him how. He shrugged his shoulders. Did he know of any plans to attack us? He was evasive, but as he walked out of the door, he turned and looked me in the eye. 'Tomorrow, I think. Watch out for Bao. He has special plans for you.'

I didn't like the sound of 'special plans'. I decided to play the 'stupid white man' card to find out more.

'You mean he's going to look after me as an honoured guest?' I prompted.

'No, I mean he's going to eat you.'

Ah.

As conversation stoppers go, this was hard to beat. Sherif made his excuses, wished me good luck and left. This was the last time I ever saw Sherif and to this day I don't know what became of him.

I spent a long, nervous and sleepless night on radio watch, unable to think of much apart from being Bao's lunch.

The next day, 1 May, the ceasefire came to a spectacular end at the DDR camp. Shortly after first light a huge mob of rebels forced their way into the camp, on the pretext of 'liberating' their ten colleagues who had been 'forced' to disarm. While 'searching' the camp, they looted everything and set the buildings on fire. Within minutes they had destroyed what had taken four months to build. The Kenyan platoon and Salah Uddin, the Bangladeshi, took up a hasty defensive position among their trucks. Colonel Bao now demanded that the Kenyans hand over Salah Uddin. They refused, and the rebels attacked. The Kenyan platoon, by now outnumbered by about twenty to one, stood little chance. We heard the fire-fight, then the Kenyan radio operator's final message: 'We are being overrun.'

Then silence, and we assumed the worst.

Friendly civilians now came to warn us that we were to be next.

Several weeks before, I had been tasked to draft an evacuation plan for my team in the event of renewed hostilities between the warring factions. Due to traditional UN bureaucracy, the evacuation plan had yet to be formally approved but at least it meant we had talked through the options. I had tried to anticipate all likely scenarios, underestimating just how quickly the rebels might turn on us. We had hoped that, as unarmed Military Observers, the worst scenario was for us to get caught in the cross-fire between two warring factions. Now, however, we were fast becoming one of the warring factions. And although on paper the Kenyans were a strong force (a battalion, about 500 strong), they were spread out thinly over a vast area.

We had just six armed men guarding our house. The nearest Kenyan company position (normally 100 strong), 'A' Company, was only 800 metres from our house, but half of its men were at the DDR camp 10 miles away. 'D' Company and the Battalion HQ were on the other side of the town. 'B' Company and most of 'C' Company were over 25 miles away in Magburaka. The rest of 'C' Company were 125 miles away in Kabala.

During the preceding weeks, the RUF had refused to allow the Kenyans to stockpile extra food and equipment. We had assumed this was just the rebels being awkward, but it was beginning to look as if their motivation and planning had been more sinister. If the RUF chose to block the roads, the Kenyans would quickly run out of food, water and ammunition. Hardly the best preparation for a siege.

In the evacuation plan, I had considered that if we had to abandon our house, we should try to reach 'A' Company's position. However, I knew the house was being watched and that it would be hard to slip out undetected. We needed to create a diversion, and quickly. It wouldn't take long for Colonel Bao and his lynch mob to reach us from the DDR camp.

An idea struck me. A Canadian park ranger once told me how to survive a grizzly bear attack: just take off your backpack and calmly walk away. The bear will be more interested in eating your sandwiches than in eating you. I'd never had the chance to try it with a grizzly bear, but reckoned the same principle might apply to the rebels. So, leaving some expensive-looking kit unguarded at the front of the house, we slipped out the back. To my relief it worked, as the rebels who should have intercepted us were too busy stealing our belongings to bother giving chase. We lost our TV, video and fridge but not our lives. Adrenalin pumping, we legged it towards the Kenyan company position. Ten minutes after we abandoned the house, the rest of the rampaging RUF mob arrived, fired up from their victory at the DDR camp. We had moved just in time.

CHAPTER FIVE

SURROUNDED

'Courage is resistance to fear, mastery of fear – not absence of fear.'
MARK TWAIN

Running as fast as we could, we headed for 'A' Company, the nearest group of Kenyans. They sent out a patrol in an armoured car to escort us into their compound. This was a nice gesture, but the car broke down and we ended up having to push it back to their position.

It was a great relief to make it into the defended compound and, for a moment, we felt safe. But our new predicament was only marginally better than our last one. 'A' Company's position was a small compound, 100 by 150 metres, surrounded by a 2-metre mud-brick wall. The seventy Kenyan soldiers there were armed with powerful G3 rifles (7.62mm semi-automatics made by Heckler and Koch) but had only 100 rounds of ammunition each. Their company commander was missing, along with thirty men – the platoon that had been on duty at the DDR camp.

I noticed a group of vultures sitting in a nearby tree. They appeared to be watching us intently. It felt like they knew something we didn't and could smell imminent death. I hoped it was just my imagination running wild.

The compound was an old Catholic mission, consisting of a small chapel and three derelict buildings. Apart from the chapel, which was still in a good state of repair, the roofs of all the buildings had either collapsed or been burnt. When the Kenyan soldiers had moved into this position three months previously, they had pitched their tents inside the otherwise uninhabitable buildings. Canvas had served them well in keeping out the elements but would clearly offer no protection from bullets or exploding shell fragments. The soldiers were spread thinly around the perimeter wall in two-man trenches, with machine-guns at three of the four corners.

Digging in

The company second-in-command, Captain Moses Korir, had taken over and was coping admirably with the stress of having lost his boss and one in three of his men. I offered what assistance I could – moral support and technical advice – and we did as much as possible to improve the position. Our resources were limited, though. We had very little food, water or medical supplies, no barbed wire or sandbags, and almost non-existent fields of fire (the areas our weapons could cover with rifle or machine-gun fire). The mud-brick wall was a mixed blessing. Although it made it harder for the rebels to see in, it also made it near impossible to see out. Initially, the Kenyans were reduced to sticking their heads up over the wall. With their combat helmets painted bright blue (the UN colour) this made them ideal targets. From the rebel perspective, shooting Kenyans must have felt like playing an arcade game. So, instead, we cut some holes in the wall, enabling the Kenyan soldiers to stay in the relative safety of their trenches. It would now be the rebels sticking their heads above the parapet and us taking pot shots.

Furthermore, the compound was completely surrounded by houses and trees, making it very easy for rebels to approach right up to the perimeter. Ironically, the UN HQ itself had earlier refused the Kenyans permission to improve their own defences, as barbed wire and sandbags were considered 'too aggressive'. Nothing about our UN status was designed to help us win a battle in our newly adopted role as combatants. While our helmets were bright blue, our vehicles were painted bright white, and our posture was designed to be unthreatening and approachable.

With the Kenyans, I had to tread a very careful path. Their commander appreciated my support, but I didn't want to interfere with their chain of command. If I started pulling rank then so would my fellow UNMOs, some of whom out-ranked me, and the result could have been anarchy. As far as I was concerned, our unarmed Observer status was now academic. Some of my colleagues, however, thought otherwise and still considered their best means of self-preservation was to dissociate themselves from the armed Kenyans. In any event, I threw my lot in with the soldiers and helped them improve their defences. We managed to site their three GPMGs (general purpose machine-guns – a battle-proven, 7.62mm man-portable weapon) more effectively, and clear some vegetation to improve the fields of fire.

On the bright side, from my point of view, the Magburaka team of UNMOs was also seeking refuge in the compound, including some other Brits: Lieutenant Commander Paul Rowland, Major Dave Lingard and (my recent fellow invalid) Major Andy Samsonoff. They were all relative newcomers to the team, drafted in to boost the team's effectiveness.

Paul was one of the most highly trained officers in the Royal Navy. Unfortunately, his speciality was nuclear engineering... He was also a talented orienteer and very fit. Like me, he was tall and skinny and all the locals were convinced we were brothers. They saw him as mildly eccentric, as he had a policy of walking every-where with a large black umbrella. It kept the rain off him in the wet season, the sun off him in the dry season and ensured he looked faintly ridiculous in all seasons.

Dave was only an honorary Brit (a dubious honour in the circumstances), as he was really a New Zealand Army Signals offi-cer. Unfortunately for him, though, the rebels didn't appreciate that New Zealand was separate from the United Kingdom. From their perspective, Dave looked like a Brit, spoke like a Brit, and wore the same uniform as a Brit, though his boots were slightly different. He had soon realized that playing the 'non-aligned Kiwi' card would not work with the RUF, so had little option but to join us.

Andy, a Light Infantry officer, was normally a fit, strong guy, but he was still run-down from the after-effects of his illness. Only a few days before, he and I had tentatively tried some gentle weight training together, fed up with feeling shit from our typhoid and malaria respectively. It had turned into an informal competi-tion to test which disease was more debilitating. Typhoid 'won', when Andy passed out, badly dehydrated. At least he had proved his point.

Andy had not been in the Makeni area for long. For the previ-ous three months he had been working in Moyamba, a relatively safe, pro-government part of the country. Thoroughly bored, he had hassled our boss in Freetown to send him to a more 'interest-ing' area. We now congratulated him on his timing.

Sitting in the compound, the four of us had a quick confab and all reached the same conclusion: it would be better to do some-thing positive than simply do nothing and wait for the worst to happen. Some of the other UNMOs had now become fatalistic and were suffering from terror-induced lethargy. They were just sitting around, staring into space, waiting for the end. One of them told me our fate was 'in God's hands now'. Well, it might have been, but there was a lot we could do to help ourselves just in case God was busy somewhere else. I snapped at some of them on a couple of occasions and told them to have a bit of pride in their countries as they were setting a bad example to the Kenyans. Luckily, however, the acting Kenyan company commander and the company sergeant major both showed a lot more resolve and the Kenyan contingent remained remarkably upbeat.

As a Royal Marines Commando, I was fortunate to enjoy considerable respect from the Kenyans. Most of them had trained alongside British soldiers on exercise in Kenya, where the British Army maintains a training base near Nairobi. The Kenyan Army uses British tactics and equipment so, professionally, we saw eye to eye. Their official language is English, but we all knew the rebels were listening to our radio transmissions on UN radios they had stolen from us, so the Kenyans used tribal languages instead when speaking on the radio. It might only have been mutual bluff and bravado, but friendly rivalry certainly helped ensure the Kenyans stayed professional and their morale high.

Light-heartedly, I suggested to my 'lion-wrestling' friends from the reception centre that now was a good time to demonstrate their prowess at extreme acts of bravery and I would be 'right behind them' if they now chose to take on the RUF. They returned the compliment but said that as a Commando I should lead from the front and they would be right behind me. We compromised and sensibly stayed exactly where we were. Their attitude was very positive: 'For every one of us we'll take ten of them.' They were convinced that I must have regularly experienced situations like this during Commando training. It would have been counter-productive to have shattered the illusion, so I kept my thoughts to myself. But I smiled inwardly as I remembered how, in my last UK job, I once found myself completing a risk assessment for use of the office photocopier. I wondered what a health and safety adviser would have said about our current predicament.

Military historians and psychologists have repeatedly noted that well-trained and well-led soldiers are often more scared of letting down their colleagues than of injury and death. I'd always been rather sceptical and wondered whether it would really work that way in practice, but I began to see what they meant. None of us, either Kenyans or Brits, really considered the UN mission important enough to die for, but it would have been inconceivable to let each other down by going to pieces or giving up. The robust attitude of the Kenyans was a lifesaver. Without their professionalism and courage, I don't think any of us would have made it.

As night fell, the rebels started to attack. Under cover of darkness, they first encircled our position, then began rhythmic drumming and chanting. I crawled up to the wall and everywhere I looked there appeared to be a solid mass of rebels. I didn't recognize the languages I heard. They had stopped speaking Krio, the common language, and started chanting in local tribal languages – those used in animistic religions that involve spirit and ancestor worship. I tried not to think too hard about Sherif's final words to me, warning me about Bao's special plans. The rebels were trying to terrorize us and they succeeded. My throat was dry and I felt my bowels twitch. I did my best to stay calm outwardly, but inwardly I was terrified. I wondered what it would feel like to die and hoped it would be swift. I hoped I could keep my dignity if it was not. I cannot describe the impotence I felt without a weapon in my hands.

I found myself a stand-to position in the front Kenyan trench and hoped that if any of my trench mates was killed I could pick up his rifle and keep shooting. The Brit UNMOs did likewise, while the others huddled together in the chapel, pathetically trying to convince themselves they could simply declare their unarmed Observer status when the rebels overran the position. I didn't share their optimism. In the dark the rebels would, at the very least, shoot first and ask questions later. Andy, Paul, Dave and I agreed to stick together whatever happened.

I had no idea how many rebels were attacking us – most likely several hundred but, in the darkness, it seemed like thousands. West African gun battles involve a lot of shooting but not a lot of hitting. The initial firefight was short and sharp. The distinctive crack and thump of incoming rifle fire is disconcerting, but we could hear the noise of bullets cutting at supersonic speed through the air above our heads, so we knew that the rebels were aiming high. I guessed they must have been shooting over the wall so, as long as we kept our heads down, we were relatively safe. The Kenyans kept their nerve and, in contrast to their poorly trained adversaries, proved to be good shots. As the rebels started to sustain casualties, they seemed less keen to put themselves in the danger zone and the attack began to peter out.

The rebels then appeared to choose the easier option of starving us out. A sporadic gunfight continued throughout the night and on and off for the next four days. With the close proximity of the rebels and incoming fire, sleep and rest were impossible. I tried lying down on the concrete floor of the chapel, shutting my eyes and trying to nod off, but I soon realized I wasn't really resting and would be better off keeping myself busy. So I spent my time walking or crawling round the position, encouraging the Kenyan soldiers and trying to ascertain the rebels' positions, numbers and tactics.

I was crouching in an isolated trench with two Kenyans on the far side of the compound shortly before first light, when I heard something landing in the bushes nearby. I crawled over to investigate. I couldn't initially see what it was in the darkness so I picked it up. It was a freshly severed human hand. I decided not to tell the others, but confided in the Kenyan sergeant major. He told me that I was not the only one to come across severed body parts that night, but he had told his men to keep it to themselves so as not to create panic.

I also sat for hours on end with my Sony shortwave radio pressed against my ear, listening to the World Service or one of the military command nets. My radio had a scanner on it so I was able to tune it to the frequency being used by the RUF. It was difficult to make out everything they said as they spoke in Krio and used a lot of codewords, but I could get a gist of what was going on.

For that first night, I kept my Kevlar body armour and combat helmet on as I crawled around, but discarded them in the morning when I realized how much they were making me sweat. Water was going to be scarce, and I knew that dehydration would be as big a threat as gunfire. Makeni is the hottest part of Sierra Leone and May is the hottest month of the year. With the dry season coming to an end, the combination of heat and humidity was crippling. Under the midday sun, the temperature was well over 100 degrees and even at night rarely dropped beneath 90. I was glad I had stubbornly refused the luxury of air-conditioning in the preceding months.

There was a well in one corner of the compound but, like the well outside our house, it needed filling once a week by water tanker. We estimated how much water was left in the well and started rationing straight away. Each man could drink no more than one litre per day – much less than we would need in the extreme heat but better than nothing, and it would keep us going for three or four days. We hoped this would be enough time for someone to come and help us out. I remembered the recommended intake of fluid as laid out in the Staff Officer's Handbook for hot, tropical conditions: 8–9 litres a day.

Just after first light, something remarkable happened that would stiffen everyone's resolve. A Kenyan sentry started to get excited when he heard someone outside the compound, shouting in Swahili. Then, as we watched, a Kenyan soldier, carrying a badly injured colleague, ran through the rebel cordon and into the compound. The rebels were clearly expecting the cordon to prevent people leaving the compound, not entering it. The man, Sergeant Stephen Nyamohanga, and his colleague were from the platoon attacked at the DDR camp. The platoon had stood its ground and fought but took heavy casualties. With their ammunition almost spent, the platoon commander had ordered his men to attempt a fighting withdrawal into the jungle. Sergeant Nyamohanga didn't know how far they had got. But as their position was being overrun, he bravely chose to stay behind with an injured corporal. The corporal had been shot through the thigh and had his right arm almost ripped off by an RPG. Nyamohanga somehow managed to stop the man bleeding to death and to hide from the rebels until dusk. Overnight, he carried his mate nearly 15 miles through rebel-held territory to reach Makeni, before breaking in through the cordon.

Both men survived. After witnessing an act of heroism like this, nobody in our compound was going to give up without a fight.

For the first two days of the siege, the surrounding town was in anarchy, with rebels running riot, looting, raping and pillaging. Hearing this was bad enough, but being powerless to stop it was far worse. The rebels started using acts of atrocity as bait, to try to lure us out of the relative safety of the compound. Their first ploy was rape. The screams of their victims normally went on all night, but sometimes ended abruptly with a gunshot. Some of the Kenyan soldiers had struck up relationships with local girls and they must have found it even harder to listen to the distressed – and distressing – cries.

I thought the surrounding anarchy might offer the distraction needed to attempt to escape. I asked the UN HQ for permission to attempt to lead a breakout, but was refused. My immediate boss in the UN was coincidentally another Royal Marine, Colonel Peter Babbington MC. A tough, no-nonsense individual, he had won his Military Cross as a company commander in the Falklands War. I knew he wouldn't be put off making tough decisions if needed, and he was a source of immense strength. On one occasion, I was talking to him on the satphone as an attack started and it was looking like the rebels were about to break into the compound. In desperation, I asked him what to do.

'Stand and fight!' was his firm response.

'But, sir, we don't have any weapons,' I whined.

'Don't fuck about, man. Stand and fight anyway!' he commanded.

If the colonel was telling us to stay where we were, I knew it would be for a good reason. A massive diplomatic effort was under way. President Kabbah, other West African heads of state and even UN Secretary General Kofi Annan were lobbying Foday Sankoh hard to order his men to stop. Incredibly, though, Sankoh was still denying that the RUF had done anything wrong and was publicly dismissing reports of UN casualties and hostage-takings as unsubstantiated government propaganda. It was exasperating to listen to his denials being broadcast on the World Service, but there was nothing we could do about it.

Rescue attempt

While the diplomats were trying to defuse the situation, a battalion of Zambian UN troops was tasked to relieve our siege. Their orders had been ridiculously vague and they were poorly equipped. All they were told was to drive 100 miles into the rebel heartland and link up with the Kenyans. I suspected it would not be quite so simple. The Zambian battalion had only recently arrived in the country, so perhaps they underestimated the RUF's military capability. They certainly overestimated the RUF's trustworthiness. I had a horrible feeling that sending in the Zambians would just escalate the situation and make a diplomatic solution impossible. We would become caught, proverbially and physically, in the crossfire.

Once again, our advice on the ground was ignored. Colonel Jim had, in the meantime, arrived back in Freetown after his ten-day leave in the UK. I spoke to him at length and he agreed with my assessment but he, too, failed to change the minds of the UN planners. So the Zambians started towards Makeni, with 500 soldiers and twenty-five armoured cars. On paper, this was a strong and well-armed unit. But in years of civil war, the RUF had learnt how to ambush armoured columns. The road to Makeni, though made of tarmac, was narrow with jungle on both sides. So, unable to move off the road, only the front vehicle in the column could engage targets ahead. In effect, the firepower of twenty-five armoured cars was reduced to one. If the rebels could physically block the road, the column would not be able to turn round, and would get stuck like a lobster caught in a lobster pot. To confuse things further, the Zambians had terrible communications. Those at the front of the column could not even talk to their colleagues at the back, let alone the outside world.

We listened to the Zambians' progress on the UN command net. This was an insecure radio net, meaning anybody who had a suitable radio could listen in, including the RUF. The Zambians' advance started well enough. When they entered RUF territory and reached the first checkpoints, at a town called Lunsar, they were waved straight through, and reported that the rebels there were actually friendly. I knew it would not be that easy. My suspicions grew when the Kenyan 'D' Company, on the north side of Makeni, reported that they had seen several trucks of armed rebels moving west on a road parallel to the main Lunsar–Makeni road. From there it would be easy to swing south to reach the main road. If I had been planning to ambush the Zambians, this would have been my route.

Finally, the Zambians were stopped at a village called Makoth, just 20 kilometres west of Makeni, and reported that they were negotiating with the checkpoint commander. Eventually, a 'compromise' was reached. The rebels were claiming that it had all been 'a terrible misunderstanding' (a phrase I had heard before) and invited the Zambian commanding officer and his entourage to drive into Makeni to discuss 'arrangements' with the local commanders. The rebels politely asked the Zambians to send only a small group, 'so as not to scare the locals'. We heard the Zambian vehicles driving past our position and tried to shout a warning to them. But our compound was set well back from the main road, and the Zambians couldn't hear us over the noise of their vehicles. We tried to raise them on the radio but they could use their radios only when their vehicles were stationary. Oblivious to their probable fate, the Zambians trundled by.

Weeks later, we found out what had happened. The Zambian CO and his three armoured cars drove right into the rebel HQ and the gates were shut behind them. Suddenly, a huge mob rushed out of the surrounding buildings and clambered on to the vehicles. The Zambians were pulled from their vehicles, stripped and tied up.

Back at the main convoy, after three hours had passed, the Zambian second-in-command decided to lead another recce party to Makeni. Just as before, the rebels were co-operative so long as the Zambians only sent a small group. I was chatting to Paul when we heard the sound of more armoured cars approaching on the main road and we made a snap decision to try to warn them. We grabbed a group of Kenyans and ran out of the compound towards the road. I was about to flag down the approaching convoy when

Sierra Leone. A beautiful and fertile place, but in 2000 it was officially the poorest country in the world and in some areas male life expectancy was only twenty-six.

One of my tasks in Sierra Leone was disarming child soldiers. The average age of the rebel combatants was twelve.

On patrol, telling local rebels about the disarmament process. Pointing a camera at unfriendly rebels was often the best way to win them over.

Musa, my Sierra Leonean running partner, and Milos,
a Croatian colleague, on a Sunday afternoon walk.

Kamajor militiamen and Sierra Leone Army soldiers –
in Sierra Leonean terms these were the good guys.

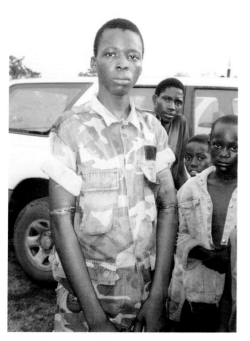

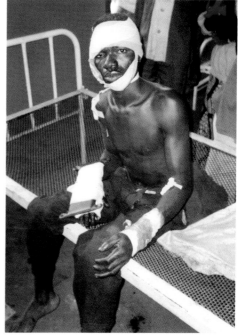

*A prisoner after his release from the RUF,
his arms badly scarred from being
tied up with barbed wire.*

*The rebels who had tried to hack off this man's
limbs were too drunk and stoned to manage
it the first time. Only our timely arrival
prevented them from finishing off the job.*

*This man was due to be summarily executed,
but I persuaded his captors to try an
alternative punishment by making him stand
on his head – uncomfortable, but not lethal.*

*Corporal Opuk from the Kenyan Army.
If it weren't for the professionalism,
dedication and bravery of the
Kenyans I would not be here today.*

Dennis Mingo, aka 'Superman', a nasty piece of work even by rebel standards. He had earned his nickname by throwing people off high buildings and telling them to 'fly like Superman'.

Disarming the rebels could be a dangerous process. This poor guy was shot in the testicles after a fight broke out in the disarmament centre.

Bored during the ceasefire, these rebels amused themselves with a black magic dance. On other occasions their black magic was much more sinister.

Foday Sankoh, leader of the RUF, at a disarmament centre. Before the ceasefire ended 25,000 weapons were handed in.

My fellow escapees (l to r), Lieutenant Commander Paul Rowland, Major David Lingard, me and Major Andy Samsonoff, on day one of the siege – before the water ran out.

Andy (left) and me on the run. I hadn't slept for over a week and had been hallucinating badly all night.

Using sign language to ascertain which nearby villages were in rebel hands. I hoped that by wearing my UN baseball cap, I would look as unthreatening as possible.

Waiting while a farmer filled our water bottles from his well. Never had a drink tasted quite so good.

Negotiating with friendly villagers. The chap in the middle – Alusayne, agreed to act as our guide despite sporting an open machete wound and a bad dose of malaria.

In the relative safety of a Kamajor village. Ibrahim (front), their commander, positioned his warriors in a protective circle around us, armed only with machetes and black magic, and told us to sleep.

Relaxing with Anna after escaping from Sierra Leone.
Topically, we chose a climbing trip to East Africa.

My teacher friend Usman, who had offered to smuggle us out of the compound dressed as holy men.

I'd just had my thirtieth birthday and was feeling fitter and stronger than ever. But three weeks after this photo was taken I was rushed to hospital paralysed from the waist down.

I noticed that the lead vehicle was swarming with rebels. The Zambians were nowhere to be seen. My heart sank as I realized what was happening. We only just made it back into the compound before the rebels cut us off.

The main Zambian column had no idea what was going on. They had lost their CO and second-in-command and all their radios, so they stayed where they were. Unable to lure any more Zambians into their trap, the RUF now tried a new tactic. They forced the Zambian CO to sign a letter, ordering his men to advance towards Makeni in small groups. He initially refused, even when tortured. The rebels then took one of the Zambian soldiers and skinned him alive. The CO now signed.

The rebels delivered the letter to the main body of the Zambians, who were relieved to receive formal orders. So, yet again, the column split into smaller groups and headed for Makeni. And yet again they were systematically ambushed and taken prisoner.

Back in our compound, we watched, incredulous but help-less, as truck after truck of Zambian prisoners was driven past our position. For a while I joined some of my colleagues in their gloomy introspection. I felt I was trapped in a farce – if it wasn't so serious, it would have been funny. Morale sank. We were now on our own.

Even more confusing was the fact that the RUF stripped all the Zambian prisoners and put on their uniforms. They failed to trick us, but it was horrible to be shooting at people who might have been our allies. The rebels were experts at using human shields, and often forced civilians or groups of prisoners to stand in front of them as they came near our compound.

Sadly, the RUF were then able to deceive some UN troops. Dressed as Zambians, and driving in Zambian vehicles, the RUF advanced towards Freetown. Having driven unopposed up to a UN checkpoint, it was easy for them to surprise and overpower the

UN troops and take them prisoner or execute them. With poor UN communications, not all outposts were warned off in time and the Nigerian units to our west lost several positions in this way.

Not all the Zambians were taken prisoner. One sergeant managed to escape. He hid in a tree for forty-eight hours, then stripped off to his underwear and walked to safety. Every time he had to pass through a rebel checkpoint, he pretended to be a madman to avoid answering any questions.

On more than one occasion I remember wishing I were black so I could try something similar. As a six-foot-four gangly white man, I was unlikely to persuade even the most drugged-up rebel that I was a local. But a friend of mine called Usman still thought it might work. Usman was a teacher and had helped me to organize a football tournament among some local teams of schoolkids back in February. I had given Usman a pair of shoes to say thank you and we had become good friends. I had seen him loitering around outside the compound and wanted to talk to him, but feared the rebels would punish him if they caught him helping us in any way. On the pretext of selling us cigarettes (I had become a newly converted chain smoker in an attempt to calm my nerves), Usman persuaded the rebels to let him enter our compound during a lull in the battle. Amazingly, even some of the rebels were happy to trade with us between battles, and on one surreal occasion we had managed to buy a crate of Coca-Cola from the same people who were trying to kill us!

Endearingly, Usman told me he had a 'cunning plan' to smuggle Andy, Paul, Dave and me out of Makeni. The conversation went something like this:

Usman: We shall pretend to be refugees.
Me: But Usman, I think the rebels will realize we're not locals.
Usman: Don't worry, I will lend you some clothes.

Me (*beginning to spot the weaknesses in Usman's scheme*):
> But Usman, we're not Sierra Leoneans – the rebels will realize straight away.

Usman: I have thought of that, there is no need to talk. I will accompany you and tell the rebels that you are holy men who have taken a vow of silence.

Me: But Usman, we don't look like Africans.

Usman: I know. Your hair is different. But don't worry, I will shave your heads.

Me (*enjoying the conversation, but beginning to lose my patience*):
> BUT WE'RE NOT BLACK, USMAN!

Usman: Oh yes. (*He ponders for a while.*) In that case you will have to wear a large hat.

I hope Usman is a better teacher than he is escape manager. But maybe his logic was that the rebels would be laughing too hard to capture us, if they had seen the four of us disguised as bald, mute 'Africans' wearing huge hats. In any case, I knew Usman's wife was heavily pregnant and told him to go home and look after her instead of trying to help us.

Some of the Zambians were executed. I don't know why. Probably just for fun. Having skinned one prisoner alive, the rebels threw his bloodstained uniform into our compound with a message attached: 'Surrender, or we'll do the same to you.'

The rebels also started using the captured Zambian weapons against us – not always successfully. Their enthusiasm often failed to overcome their lack of skill and they managed some spectacular cock-ups. On one occasion, I watched as a group of rebels set up a captured mortar directly underneath a tree. The predictable result when they fired it was gratifying. The mortar bomb inevitably struck the branches above their heads and exploded, killing them instantly.

Another, even bloodier, own goal was the result of an argument between two rival RUF commanders over who should get to drive a captured UN jeep. The argument deteriorated into a gunfight and several rebels were killed. Better still, the winners then proceeded on a lap of honour in their trophy vehicle. Overloaded and driven at breakneck speed, the jeep failed to negotiate a corner and ploughed into a tree. Not all the passengers survived. Then, perhaps because they couldn't take out their anger on us, the rebels carried out a series of atrocities on the civilians in the houses next to our compound.

The screw tightens

Over the next three days we held out, with a constant feeling that we were only seconds from a violent death. Being constantly frightened is physically very tiring, as the adrenalin makes your heart beat quickly so you use considerable nervous energy even if you're just sitting around. As we grew hungrier and thirstier, we grew weaker but our resolve didn't falter. If one of us was feeling low, someone else would perk us up.

I racked my brains trying to devise an escape plan, or at least work out how to try to save myself if the rebels overran the position. I contemplated putting on my running gear, sunglasses and Walkman and going for my normal early-morning run. Perhaps, if I acted as if nothing was wrong, the bluff might work and I could casually jog through the rebel cordon. The rebels would just assume that the mad Brit was going for his normal morning run and would be back in half an hour. When I reached the point where I usually turned around, I would just keep going. I also considered trying to sneak out on my own at night. I knew I would be able to move more quickly and quietly on my own than with my companions. It would also be easier to keep a low profile and sneak past the rebels. But there was no way I could have abandoned my mates and the advantages of being in a team were always going to outweigh the advantages of being alone. Still, it was tempting, and I could feel the demons in my mind nagging at me.

If the rebels broke into the compound, I wondered whether it would be possible to hide somewhere. I thought about digging a hole in the ground and burying myself in it, but the ground was too hard. The best hiding place would have been inside the pit-latrine. I'm sure the rebels would have checked even there. However, it was 10 feet deep and with earth walls softened by human waste, I could have tunnelled into the side wall of the shit-filled pit and prepared a hiding place there. If the rebels were overrunning the position, I could hide myself underground, wait for several hours or even days until the rebels had left, before sneaking out again.

Looking back, I am amazed I was even thinking about such madcap schemes, but when you're desperate, you'll consider almost anything. In Jewish ghettos during the Second World War, people fought to be allowed into pit-latrines, so desperate were they to hide.

Of course, there were moments of humour. On the third day, for example, the Kenyans decided to cook their remaining food. When the cry went up that dinner was served, the Kenyans, almost to a man, rushed to the mess tent. I started shouting at them not to leave all their posts at the same time, but their sergeant major took me aside and calmed me down. 'Don't worry,' he said, 'this is Africa. The rebels will be eating too and won't attack until later.' Luckily, he was right.

Fergus and his colleagues from DfID had also taken refuge in the same compound. They had an alternative coping strategy – huge quantities of marijuana. I was more than a little jealous as they sat in their jeep, stoned out of their heads, giggling maniacally as the bullets flew overhead.

On the third day of the siege, we received more bad news on

the satphone: Foday Sankoh's bodyguards had shot twenty-five unarmed civilians at a rally in Freetown. In the ensuing chaos, Sankoh himself had escaped into the bush. Diplomacy had failed.

On the same day General Issah, the RUF military field commander who lived in Makeni, personally tightened up the rebel cordon around our compound and imposed a curfew on civilian and rebel movement at night. This would make any attempt to escape considerably harder. Ironically, the advice now came through from Colonel Babbington: 'Attempt to escape.'

I felt bitter that we had been refused permission to attempt an escape when I thought we had a good chance of making it, yet were now being encouraged to do just that when the circumstances were less favourable.

I had a long, soul-searching conversation with Colonel Babbington. I didn't rate our chances too highly of making it out alive if we tried to break out through the cordon, and told him so. He still reckoned we should try.

'Sir, if I told you I thought we had a 20 per cent chance of making it through the cordon, what would your advice be?'

'Go for it!'

The inferred message was sobering. Shit, I thought. He thinks we're all going to be butchered. Colonel Bao knew by this stage that the UK was considering a military response to help out the UN. The RUF's anti-British persecution complex was bad enough already. If British troops started arriving in Sierra Leone and fighting against the rebels, any pretence at British neutrality was going to disappear. The rebels would not be able to do much about that, but they could direct their anger at us. Although the UK might be able to save UNAMSIL from completely collapsing, we were likely to be the sacrificial lambs. And like many retreating armies in war, the RUF's worst atrocities had always been when they were about to lose militarily.

Back in January 1999, the Nigerian-dominated ECOMOG forces had successfully driven the RUF out of Freetown. Before the RUF retreated, however, they had captured a number of ECOMOG soldiers. The final act of the rebels before they fled was to get take their frustration out on the prisoners and most were executed. Human Rights Watch recorded some harrowing examples of RUF brutality, as in this account by 48-year-old Aaron, 17 April 1999:

On January 9, I saw an ECOMOG prisoner, bloody, stripped naked and with a rope around his waist and his private parts, being led up Pademba Road by a group of rebels. They were pushing him and ordering civilians to touch his privates. When they reached a rebel checkpoint, they brought out another ECOMOG soldier who was also naked and looked like he'd been horribly beaten up. Then they lay both of them on the ground and some of the rebels started kicking and beating them. Then, a few of them took a machete and started cutting off the head of the second soldier. It took them about ten minutes and when they were finished, they started dancing around and brought it around to show the other soldier. I felt sick.

By this time there was a lot of gunfire and it seemed like the rebels were going really mad. They pushed the other prisoner down and grabbed a long stick and started shoving it up his backside: sodomizing him. They kept doing it for about thirty minutes. The soldier was screaming and crying and eventually just passed out. And then they shot him and just left him in the gutter. He was very bloody and everyone thought he was dead. But, several hours later he regained consciousness and called people to come and help him.

Another unpleasant thought struck me. Perhaps the UN military commander in Freetown, an Indian general, would actually benefit if a few Brits were killed. Reports of the death of a few Third World soldiers hardly even make the inside pages of Western newspapers. But a few white men would be front-page news. Rich Western nations might then feel guilty enough to send some troops to help him out.

I wondered if consideration was being given to sending in British troops to come and rescue us. But this would have been signing the death warrants of the hundreds of hostages being held by the RUF. Who could condone sacrificing the lives of 500 Africans to save four Brits?

We were definitely on our own.

I kept my thoughts to myself. I'm sure the others had enough demons of their own to deal with. Even though the chances of getting out alive seemed low, the chances if we stayed seemed even lower.

I had repeatedly asked the Kenyans for a rifle but there were not enough to go round, even for the Kenyan soldiers, so my requests were turned down. We determined to try to escape that night, but then bottled out. We just couldn't commit ourselves to leaving the relative safety of the compound and running, unarmed, towards the heavily armed rebels. Maybe if we stayed where we were, we would be able to prolong our lives, even if for just a few hours.

Tensions continued to rise the following day when a rebel 'delegation' sent a message to the Kenyans that their safety would be guaranteed if they handed over the British UNMOs. 'Brother Africans, we have no fight with you. Hand over the white men and you can go free. Refuse, and we will kill you all.' The Kenyan sergeant major took me to one side and quietly told me the bad news. Again, I decided not to tell the others. The Kenyans had already proved that they were prepared to fight and die to protect

Military Observers but I felt that, morally, this put unreasonable pressure on them. I knew that we, as British officers, would have to escape or die trying.

I also knew that once the food and water were completely gone, our reserves of strength would rapidly diminish. It would have to be tonight or never. The Kenyans reckoned they could go a few more days on iron rations. Half of them were Masai tribesman, for whom drought and famine were almost a way of life, but I doubted that we Europeans could hold out much longer. By making a break for it now, we would be maximizing what little chance we had.

All the while, I had a nagging doubt about the Kenyans. If I had been their commander, would I have been prepared to sacrifice my own men to save the life of others? In practice, the rebels were unlikely to honour any promises they made – and the Kenyans knew this – so Captain Korir refused to negotiate.

I prayed for rain but nature was not on our side. In the distance I could see thunderclouds and sometimes even lightning but Makeni was enjoying 'perfect' weather. The clouds stayed agonizngly far away and I felt the full moon and stars were mocking us.

Again, I approached the company sergeant major for a rifle, but to arm us he would have had to have disarmed one of his men. In fact, not even all the Kenyans were armed, as several of the survivors from the DDR camp had lost their rifles as they fled. I did not press the point and, in any case, I could hardly claim to be a marksman on a weapon that I had not trained on. (The G3 rifles pack one hell of a punch, especially at the short range we were engaging the rebels at. A 7.62mm bullet at a range of 20 metres is travelling at nearly three times the speed of sound and causes huge damage as it rips through flesh.)

The Kenyans stayed professional, held their nerve throughout the siege, and showed good 'fire discipline'. In other words, they resisted the temptation to fire at shadows in the darkness or let off bursts of automatic fire, which is all too easy to do if panic sets in. With only 100 rounds per man and no chance of resupply, it was crucial not to waste ammunition. Accurate shooting early on had saved us, the rebels apparently deciding that it would be easier to starve us out. And as they were having such success elsewhere against troops that were putting up less of a fight, they could afford to wait.

The rebels were a scary bunch but their military tactics lacked subtlety. I did wonder, though, just how long it would be before they realized that, with one of their heavy machine-guns set up on a nearby hill, they could fire down on to our position and obliterate us. The mud-brick walls of the compound would scarcely have slowed down heavy-calibre bullets, let alone stopped them and we had no weapons to match the range of their heavy machine-guns.

Our UK bosses would have backed us if we'd chosen to steal weapons from the Kenyans but I thought it a bad idea, both morally and practically. It would have been easy enough to steal Captain Korir's pistol from him when I saw him sleeping at his desk in the Ops room, but I could not do it. And it would have been easier still to have stolen a rifle off one of the badly injured Kenyans lying on his bed in the sick-bay. But, again, I couldn't bring myself to do this. I would be depriving him of his only means of self-defence if the rebels were able to overrun our position. At least we would have some chance of running away, but the wounded would have none.

And of course there was the practical point that if the Kenyans had caught us stealing off them, it might have persuaded them that we were not worth protecting after all and that we should be handed over to the RUF, or maybe even shot by the Kenyans.

The rebels had already boasted that it was their intention to 'do a Somalia', when dead US soldiers were dragged naked through the streets of Mogadishu. The RUF, understandably perhaps, saw Great Britain as the major threat to their control of Sierra Leone and were attempting much the same thing. Commanders like Colonel Bao knew the power of the media and had regularly been interviewed by channels such as the BBC World Service. A frightening thought crossed my mind. If we were captured and tortured, Bao was certainly capable of broadcasting our screams to the media by satellite phone. I tried to keep macabre thoughts like this out of my head, but, under siege for days, there was ample opportunity for my imagination to run wild. I saw a rebel outside the gate, whom I knew had earned his nickname Captain 'Eye-Gouger'. How would I cope if he turned on me?

It is easier to be brave when there is no time to think; but we had very little to do but think. I can see why extended exposure to danger and death can drive people mad.

Although the rebels didn't like me, as a Commando I knew they respected me, but this was hardly good news. I now knew enough about black magic to consider that being eaten was a very real possibility if caught. In a funny sort of way I saw this as a compliment, having learnt that their most prized trophies were the hearts of warriors they feared, but I was quite keen not to add 'victim of cannibalism' to my CV!

When I look back, I realize I had been fishing for precise orders from the chain of command: 'Major Ashby, you are to steal a weapon and attempt to escape.' This approach would have made it easier for me, but it never happened. 'Strong advice' was the best we got. I can understand why: if we were going to lose our lives, it would be better for everyone that we did it on our own initiative.

We decided not to tell the Kenyans officially what we intended to do as I thought they would try to stop us. I suspect the sergeant major knew what our intentions were, but he kept his silence. As a group, we decided that it would be tonight or never. Again we prayed for rain. As subtly as possible, to maintain OpSec (operational security – the 'need to know' principle), we checked and rechecked our kit, talked through numerous actions, rehearsed hand-signals and did our best to rest. We gave our UK chain of command our proposed E & E route but not the UN. We expected the compound to fall to the RUF and did not want to risk our UN colleagues being forced to say where we intended to go.

Our escape plan was simple. I had identified a possible blindspot at the north-west corner of the compound. We would climb over the wall at this point, attempt to run through the cordon, make our way out of the town and into the jungle, then head for Mile 91, the nearest UN-held town. Mile 91 was about 50 miles away as the crow flies, most of this distance in rebel-held territory. The jungle in this part of Sierra Leone had been cleared in places for agriculture, and there were numerous small villages and farms and lots of people. Many would be civilians, but the RUF would have personnel in most of the settlements. This meant that that it would be impossible to move during the day if we wanted to remain undetected. We would move only at night and lie low during daylight.

It would be like walking from London to Brighton in total darkness – with almost no food or drink, through thick vegetation in what would feel like a sauna, doing our best to avoid the locals. For every step forward, we would have to take several in the wrong direction. Fifty miles as the crow flies could easily become 150 miles on the ground. I reckoned it might take us a week. I knew from previous experience (such as running out of food in Spitsbergen) that I could keep going with empty batteries, and I hoped my colleagues would also be able to rise to the challenge.

I confided in Fergus and felt guilty that we were abandoning him. As Fergus candidly observed, though, we were more of the problem than the solution. Fergus had decided he would risk his luck the following day with the rebels and try to talk or bribe his way out. I didn't envy him, and asked if his group would prefer to try their luck with us. He didn't think they would be strong enough physically to cope, so turned down the offer. We wished each other luck.

Having already abandoned most of our kit, our admin was depressingly easy. We would take:

- one litre of water each (saved for the occasion)
- a few scraps of bread and my small tin of baked beans (we were too thirsty to eat much food even had we had it – adrenalin would have to see us through)
- 1:500,000 map – one-tenth of the scale of a standard UK Ordnance Survey map (1 cm on the map represented 5 km on the ground)
- a compass
- Andy's hand-held GPS (Global Positioning System)
- a small first-aid kit
- hand-held water filters, plus a supply of iodine and chlorine-based purifying tablets

Paul was adamant he would take his camera. This was not as frivolous as it might appear. The rebels loved posing and showing off. If we were captured, it was possible that by taking photos of them and promising to send them copies, they might let us go rather than kill us. More realistically, though, a camera would be a good way of breaking the ice with anybody we met, whether friendly or not. And it did work. On more than one occasion, the simple act of getting the camera out was enough to turn potentially hostile villagers into our best friends.

In addition, I would carry the satphone. Satphones are about the same size and shape as a laptop computer. Like a laptop, they are not very tough and the batteries tend to run out at inopportune moments. I made sure I had one fully charged battery, and we considered carrying a back-up just in case. In the end, we decided not to – our best means of self-preservation was likely to be outrunning any pursuers and we did not want to be weighed down. The rebels would only be carrying rifles or machetes and, in flip-flops or barefoot, they would be quick on their feet.

Last calls

I used the satphone to pass details of our intended Escape and Evasion route to Colonel Jim, our absent team leader, who was stuck in Freetown. He gave a few well-chosen words of encouragement. For the first time in my life, I was feeling the 'loneliness of command' but it was reassuring to know that, even many miles away, colleagues we knew and trusted would be doing all they could to help us out. We agreed that we would send regular sitreps on the satphone if we made it out of the compound. I asked whether there were any other British forces that might be able to come and help us. At this stage there were none.

Jim then bluntly told me that he thought Freetown might be about to fall to the RUF, who were advancing rapidly towards the capital. The Nigerian forces were in disarray and appeared to be trying to broker a unilateral peace deal with the RUF to save themselves. The Jordanians (including a Company of Special Forces) had abandoned their positions, made their way to the port and were trying to hire a freighter to evacuate. The only thing 'Special' about their 'Special Forces' appeared to be their ability to run away more quickly than everyone else. The Zambians had been killed or captured. The Kenyans were doing their best but, if they chose to sue for peace, it would have effectively been signing our death warrant.

As the sun set, I made three more calls back to the UK. First, to my parents. I spoke to my dad, and thanked him for being such a great father. I wanted to speak to my mother but didn't, so as not to worry her. I asked Dad not to tell her what was happening until he knew we were either safe or dead. My father told me he loved me and wished me luck. Maybe it was the way he said it, but it triggered something in me and I briefly went to pieces. I was struggling to get the words out and failed to hold back the tears. I was glad nobody saw me – I don't think at that particular moment I'd have inspired much confidence.

Next I phoned a fellow Bootneck, Dan Bailey – my old training Batch-mate who had dropped the climbing rope from the Devon sea-stack. I told him my preferred funeral arrangements. I didn't mind where I was buried, but asked for some rousing hymns and a happy send-off. I also asked him to make sure Anna was OK if we didn't make it. Dan pointed out I had started speaking like a corny Hollywood war movie, so we went on to discuss the football scores.

Lastly, a fifteen-minute conversation with Anna. I tried to sound upbeat but had to admit that it might be goodbye. She tried to make helpful suggestions: 'Get some sleep before you try anything... Can't you steal a gun off someone?... Is there anyone I should call...?' It took me a while to explain why none of these was possible and that we would soon be on the run. I couldn't think of enough ways to tell her how much I loved her and was missing her and it was hard to hang up. Our final message to each other was the same: 'Take care of yourself. I love you.'

I felt relieved to have spoken to her. I don't know what it feels like to die but I'm sure that in the split second before oblivion you know what's happening and, for me, it would have been unbearable not to have said farewell.

Having said it, I felt a weight had been taken off my shoulders. It was easier to concentrate solely on the situation in hand: escape.

CHAPTER SIX

ON THE RUN

'The jungle is neutral.'
LIEUTENANT COLONEL F. SPENCER CHAPMAN, 1949,
ON FIGHTING AGAINST THE JAPANESE IN THE MALAY
PENINSULA DURING THE SECOND WORLD WAR

While we remained in Makeni, the odds were stacked against us. However, I felt I had done the best jungle training there was and knew as much as anyone about how to escape from an enemy and evade pursuit. So if we could make it into the jungle, I reckoned we had a reasonable chance of getting to safety. But first, we had to break out through the rebel cordon.

I had set H-hour for three a.m. If you stay up all night (without chemical assistance, that is) you feel at your lowest ebb about four o'clock in the morning. We had to take advantage of this. Adrenalin was making us feel wide awake, despite our own lack of sleep, but I hoped many of the rebels surrounding us would be groggy enough to give us a chance of sneaking past them. If we waited until four o'clock, though, we would have less than two hours before daybreak to make it out of the town and into the relative safety of the jungle. This would not give us enough time.

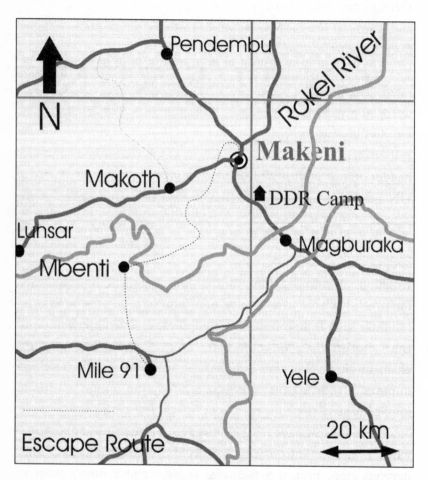

Map of Makeni

Three o'clock would have to do. I was also hoping that by this time of night many of the rebels, if they weren't actively attacking us, would have sneaked off in the darkness to see their bush wives.

With half an hour to go, we checked our kit and talked through our escape plan one final time. I made everyone jump up and down to check their kit didn't rattle. We then used charcoal from a fire to blacken our faces. Dave had recently been paid and had $1,000 in cash. We split this between us in case we were separated. The most secure means of carrying it was to swallow it. I wrapped my share of the money in a condom I had in my survival kit. Swallowing the packet with a dry throat and no water was a real challenge. I eventually managed. Finally, we ripped the UN badges off our uniforms. These bright blue badges are a symbol of UN neutrality and are supposed to guarantee the safety of the person who wears them, but all they were going to do for us was to make us show up more easily in the dark. As we removed the badges, we were abandoning our last symbol of neutrality. We would no longer be Observers. From now on, despite being unarmed, we were combatants.

Dave and I shared a last cigarette, to calm our nerves, and then another one. He observed wryly that we'd both become chain smokers. But with possible life expectancy down to thirty minutes, I didn't worry too much about the long-term health implications.

There was time for one last incident – amusing in retrospect – when I sneaked into a secluded corner of the compound for a nervous crap. Fear is a powerful laxative and I didn't want to embarrass myself later. Unfortunately, the pit-latrine was between one of the Kenyan trenches and a rebel position – not the safest place to be crawling around in the dark. So I found a bush to squat behind instead. I heard rustling nearby and, for a moment, thought a rebel infiltrator was about to catch me with my pants down. Trousers round my ankles, I did my best to escape, only to bump straight into the intruder, who turned out to be Paul, also with his trousers round his ankles.

At 2.45, we had no more preparations to make and there seemed little point in waiting any longer. I suggested we go early and the others agreed. As quietly as possible, we crept over to the north-west corner of the compound. I propped a chair against the wall, to make it easier to climb over. We had agreed not to tell Captain Korir, the Kenyan acting commander, what we were up to. He might have stopped us. So instead, I briefed the corporal whose men would cover us. He objected, and told us not to go anywhere until he had checked with his boss.

I did my best to sound confident: 'Corporal, I have been ordered by my government to attempt to escape. As you are Kenyan, I cannot order you to help. So I'm asking you as a brother in arms. We're going to try to make it through the cordon. If you see any movement from the rebel positions, please tell your men to give us covering fire.'

He said nothing, but I decided to interpret this as tacit agreement.

I whispered a few final words to the others. 'Good luck, guys. Stay close behind me.' Then I climbed over the wall and dropped into no-man's-land.

We had intended to have a twenty-second listening halt once we were all safely over the wall, but things started to go wrong straight away. I dropped off the wall, waited... and waited. Suddenly, one of the Kenyans, perhaps half-asleep, cocked his weapon and started shouting. Maybe he thought we were RUF. Clearly this was not the low-profile start we were after. I stayed where I was, and could see some rebels moving. I hoped they couldn't see me. I could sense their eyes straining in the darkness, trying to see what was causing the commotion.

I thought about climbing back over the wall. Maybe escape wasn't such a good idea – or we could just try later? But, in my heart, I knew it was now or never. As I crouched there in front of the wall, I felt horribly exposed. Every second felt like an hour and I willed the others to hurry up. But they were having problems of their own. On the 'safe' side of the wall, one of the Kenyans had pointed his rifle in Andy's face, and had threatened to shoot him if he climbed over the wall. Coolly, Andy decided to call his bluff. I then recognized the voice of the sentry I had sat next to for three hours earlier that night, and heard him put in a good word for us. It seemed to make the difference, and the others eventually managed to calm the soldier down.

Paul the submariner was next. Despite being frightened, I couldn't help smiling as he managed to snag his webbing belt on top of the wall. For a few seconds he dangled inelegantly with his legs kicking in the air before freeing his belt and lowering himself to the ground. Dave and Andy then clambered over as quietly as they could. In the still night air, though, even the slightest noise would signal our presence.

We were now irreversibly committed.

'Everyone OK? Right, follow me.'

No going back

From early-morning runs during the previous few months, I knew the backstreets and footpaths of Makeni well. In my head I had repeatedly rehearsed the first, crucial few hundred metres: *Left round the first building – right of the next one – across the yard – 20 metres to the line of trees – drop into low ground – across the field – head towards the old radio mast.* I had created a map in my head and now I had to follow it.

We had decided a fast walking pace would offer the best compromise of speed and stealth, but it was difficult to resist the temptation to run. I regretted this as I rounded the first building and ran face first into a barbed-wire fence, cutting my eye and mouth. I tasted blood. Out of the corner of my eye, I could make out someone moving at the nearest rebel position.

This is it, I thought. Keep going. Don't stop.

I tensed up, expecting incoming fire.

None came. Perhaps they thought we were a rebel patrol. Perhaps they thought we were armed and chose 'not to see us' in case we won the ensuing fire-fight. Perhaps we were just lucky and found a part of the cordon manned by rebels too slow or confused to react. Badly trained soldiers, if they are not told exactly what to do, very often do nothing. Maybe it was this that gave us the break we needed. For a split second, I looked into the nearest rebel's eyes, then glanced away and just kept going. My guardian angel must have been having a late night.

At every corner and behind every building as we wove through the town, I expected to run into a rebel ambush. Several times we saw rebel patrols but shied away from them before they could work out who we were. Everything seemed eerily quiet – the loudest noise was our own breathing. I could even hear my own heart beating. All my senses felt highly tuned and, with every step, my fear seemed to turn to exhilaration. I felt more alive than I ever had before and enjoyed a surge of primeval strength. Now totally committed, I was surprised to feel strangely calm. For a few moments, I felt almost invincible, both physically and psychologically. If a rebel tried to stop me now, I was sure I would kill him with my bare hands, even if he shot me.

The whole episode seemed unreal. I had to remind myself this was not a game or a training exercise. In training, your adversaries are your instructors. If you screw up, you're repri-manded but learn from the experience. Our adversaries now were less formidable than our instructors but, if they caught us, the penalty would be death.

I used an old radio mast on the outskirts of town to orientate myself in the darkness. Once we had passed it, I used a star in the night sky as a marker. We passed near to our old house. I wondered whether Superman had moved back in. If so, would he have guards there? Best not to hang around and find out. We pressed on, heading for agricultural land. The rebels were more likely to be near buildings or on paths and the crops would give us some cover. For 2 kilometres we headed north-west on a deception bearing (deliberately heading in the wrong direction), then swung south on to the correct bearing. I hoped this would be enough to confuse any RUF follow-up or search – I suspected they lacked the skills to track us properly.

The next major obstacle was the main road we had to cross. We had heard rebel patrols driving up and down the road throughout the night and had planned to stake it out before crossing. In the event, though, I literally stumbled on to it. One minute I was forcing my way through thick vegetation, the next I had fallen down a bank and on to the tarmac. I picked myself up, glanced both ways then legged it across, with the others close behind.

For the next hour, we scrambled around the side of a steep hill. By following difficult terrain, we hoped to avoid any people, friendly or otherwise. But it was hard going underfoot and we kept falling over. I hoped any rebels manning a nearby check-point might think the noise of us crashing through the under-growth was wild animals, but I doubt they would have mistaken the accompanying muffled groans and curses. Again, we saw rebel checkpoints before they saw us. Usually, they gave them-selves away by smoking, and we could see the glow of their ciga-rettes in the dark.

We nearly came a cropper when we inadvertently wandered straight into a village. A technique for navigating in the dark is to fix on a distant feature. I could make out the shape of some hills far away, and as they were more or less in the right direction I started walking towards them Suddenly, a dog started barking and men started shouting. My eyesight had fooled me – the hills were actually huts, and they were only metres, not miles, in front of me. We turned and ran.

My companions were already having problems keeping up. Walking over rough ground in the dark is a skill that takes lots of practice. Commando training and working as a Mountain Leader had given me plenty of this (though we had complained like bastards at the time), but the others were struggling. It was frustrating to be spending more and more time waiting for them to catch up. We had to keep moving fast to avoid any follow-up. Dave and a weakened Andy were finding it really tough. I told them to stay close behind me and asked Paul to bring up the rear.

I had no need of map or compass for the first few miles, as I was more or less following the route of my standard early-morning run. But after an hour or so we stopped for a map check and a quick sip of water. We were all drenched in sweat and craving a decent drink, but knew there would be no water to replace our meagre supplies for many miles. I made a quick assessment. Paul and I were feeling strong, but Andy and Dave were moving too slowly. Paul offered to carry Dave's pack and we took a drink from a communal water bottle. I told everyone to drink as much as they thought they needed. I only took a sip. I begrudged not drinking my fair share of the water, but our speed as a group was limited by the slowest man. So if I could help that man by giving him some of my share of the water, it would be doing us all a favour. In the clear light of day, this approach may seem logical. But at the time, I could hear the demons in my head again telling me I'd be better off on my own. I wondered what I'd do if I thought one of the team was too weak to continue. Could I abandon him in the bush, or leave him for the rebels to find? How would I face a colleague's friends and family if I'd abandoned him? How would I face my own?

I pushed these thoughts aside and we pressed on.

We reached the point at which I had always turned back on my morning runs. Now we were no longer on familiar ground, we would have to follow a compass bearing. Back in the compound, I had discarded my full-size compass in favour of a miniature one, which I had hidden in the hem of my shirt – 'just in case we are caught and searched' was my reasoning at the time. So I now unpicked the stitching of my shirt and extracted the compass. *Shit*. In the darkness, it was impossible to read. Normal military-issue compasses have a luminous dial on them for night-time navigation, but this one didn't. *Why hadn't I checked it?* I had a small flashlight on me, but if I had to use it every few metres to check my compass, it would be tantamount to telling the rebels, 'Yoohoo, we're over here!'

Embarrassed and worried by the potential consequences of my mistake, I asked if anyone had a compass I could borrow. I hate to think how many press-ups this cock-up would have cost me on my ML course… here, though, the penalty could be fatal.

To my immense relief, Paul had one and let me use it. Of course he didn't miss such a great opportunity to take the piss out of me. I didn't mind in the least – being rude to each other was good for morale. And anyway I deserved it.

We kept up a forced march pace as best we could through thick bush. With every step I knew we were getting further from the worst of the danger, and for a while I was actually enjoying myself. My mind started to wander, anticipating how good it would feel to be back in civilization. *Beer, sleep, a soft bed…*

A dull thud and a painful moan behind me brought me back to reality.

Dave had fallen. He got back up but was now starting to struggle badly. His rapid, shallow breathing was a sure sign of heat exhaustion. I remembered my first-aid training: 'Cover the casualty with a cool, wet cloth and administer fluid.' Simple – if we'd only had any. The best we could do was to take off our shirts and use them as fans to try to cool Dave down.

I thought of something else to try.

'Dave, have you got a sweat rag?' I whispered.

'Sure, mate, what for?'

'Give it here – I'll piss on it for you, and you can use it to cool your face.' I doubted there was enough fluid in my bladder but Dave wasn't to know this. He suddenly claimed to be feeling much better... We pressed on.

I was hoping we might stumble across some puddles or even a small stream that night, but it had not rained for a week and the ground was dry. The only local water sources were likely to be the wells in nearby villages. This close to Makeni, these villages would be rebel-controlled, so were no-go areas for us. We would have to survive through the heat of the day, then try to find water the next night.

With only thirty minutes before daybreak, I started looking out for a good spot to lie up.

We pushed on for another mile or so, along the side of some ploughed fields. This was relatively easy going but risky, as our tracks would be simple to follow. Not many locals wore size 11 Army-issue boots so it would be pretty obvious who had made them. We were doing our best to disguise our footprints in the mud, but I doubted it would fool even a half-decent tracker, so I kept my fingers crossed that our earlier deception plan had worked.

As a back-up, I took advantage of some rockier ground to make another abrupt change of direction. I hoped, once again, that anyone following our tracks would continue in a straight line over the rocks when our visible footprints ran out. We forced our way into the thickest clump of bushes we could find, pulling the branches back together behind us as we squeezed in. We managed to find a gap in among some thorn bushes with enough room for the four of us to lie down. Despite the discomfort, the thorns gave us added security. It was unlikely that anybody else would happen to be walking through thorn bushes, and removing barbs from our hands and knees would help pass the time.

This was a good lie-up position. As long as we kept still and quiet, no one would be able to see or hear us and it would be near-impossible for anybody to sneak up on us without us hearing them. Better still, there were some overhanging branches to give us a bit of shade. We psyched ourselves for a long, hot wait.

We lay on our backs in the pre-dawn and congratulated each other. We wondered what the other UNMOs would be saying back in Makeni. I had a horrible feeling we would never see them again. I took my shortwave radio out of my pocket, tuned it to the BBC World Service, and pressed it to my ear. The deteriorating situation in Sierra Leone was the first item on the news.

As our lie-up position was pretty secure, we risked taking our shirts off for a few minutes. We all had excruciating prickly heat, and the fresh air on our torsos felt like bliss. Short-lived though – the ants and mosquitoes soon forced us to put our tops back on. I lost count of the number of insects that bit me as I lay there. We did have insect repellent with us but couldn't risk putting it on. Anybody walking nearby would be able to smell it – in the jungle, you often smell people before you see or hear them. But despite the discomfort, all was going according to plan, and it was a good feeling. Kind of brazenly, Paul even took a photo. I began to feel more confident we might actually make it.

Inevitably, perhaps, pride was to come before a fall.

The longest day

I had told Colonel Jim in Freetown I would send him a sitrep as soon as possible if we made it out of Makeni. But I couldn't risk setting the satphone up before first light as a bright yellow light comes on when you switch it on. It was now getting light, however, and I was just taking the phone out of my pack when I heard voices nearby. My heart missed a beat. I assumed it was rebels following our tracks and quickly signalled to be ready to move if we were discovered. We had a prearranged drill for this. We would split up and run off in different directions as the rebels would not be able to chase us all, then try to make it back to an agreed rendezvous.

The voices got louder. Still louder. I couldn't believe we had come this far only to get caught now.

Have faith. You're well hidden. Don't lose your nerve.

The voices grew quieter again but didn't go away. Other voices joined in, then laughter and singing.

Our carefully chosen lie-up position turned out to be right next to a village.

We listened as the villagers started their daily routine. We were so close that we could hear the noise of water sloshing about in buckets from the well, and we could also hear rebel soldiers. We were in dire need of water. Yet, for all the good it did us, the well could have been on the other side of the world.

This is a nightmare. Dying of thirst in a desert is fair enough, but this is a fucking jungle! And there's a fucking well right next to us!

We lay there without moving, for an hour or so. It seemed we were well hidden from the village, so I decided to give the satphone another go. I dialled Colonel Jim's number in Freetown. He had sat up all night by the phone and answered immediately.

I whispered as quietly as I possibly could.

'Colonel, it's Phil. We're out of Makeni. I'm not in a good position to talk.'

'Speak up!' he boomed down the line.

'Please be very quiet.'

'I CAN'T HEAR YOU, IT MUST BE A BAD LINE,' he shouted.

This would have been funny if it was not so deadly serious.

'Please speak quietly. We're only 20 metres from rebels and hiding in a bush. We're all OK but very thirsty. We're 6 kilometres south-west of Makeni. We'll start moving again after dark. See you in a few days. Don't expect another call until tomorrow. This isn't a good place to stay and chat.'

He got the message, told me that Britain was 'responding to the crisis militarily', wished us luck and hung up.

It was a long, hot day. There was not much shade, so we had to take turns sitting in it. Had we been able to stand up, there would at least have been a slight breeze. But lying or sitting down, the thick undergrowth stopped the air from circulating and the heat there was stifling. We were almost on the equator and this was the hottest time of year. With the humidity, it felt as if we were in a sauna. It was so humid I kept thinking it was going to rain, but the rain never came. Nature seemed to be mocking us again. I tried to get some sleep but it was just too hot and uncomfortable. And, of course, staying awake seemed the best means of self-preservation. We still had one more litre of water between us, but I'd given strict instructions not to touch it until the next night. However little we had, we had to keep something in reserve.

I'd been chewing a small piece of chewing gum for several days. It had long since lost any flavour. I offered pieces of it to my companions but it was too small to split into more than one piece, so we passed the gum round, taking it in turns to chew it for an hour or so each.

With my little shortwave radio pressed against my ear, I was able to monitor some of the military radio frequencies being used by the UN and by the RUF, so I had a fair idea what was going on around the country. And every hour I tuned the radio to the BBC World Service, hoping there would be some good news.

Even in our bush, there was some light relief. It was a Saturday afternoon, when the BBC World Service broadcasts live football from the English Premiership. Today's featured match was Arsenal v Chelsea and, as a dedicated Chelsea fan, I couldn't resist the temptation to listen in. (The others thought I was dutifully moni-toring UN radio transmissions and I didn't put them right.) It was a close match but, with fifteen minutes to go, Arsenal scored the winning goal... I almost swore out loud.

(The press later picked up on this, and I was amused to receive a letter from Ken Bates, the Chairman of Chelsea Football Club, thanking me for my support under difficult circumstances.)

We had some other, less welcome, distractions. There were mango trees nearby and it was mango season. We could hear kids throwing stones into the trees to knock down fruit. Every so often, a rock would land in a bush nearby. I feared that if a mango fell near to where we were hidden, a child might crawl into the bushes to pick it up and inadvertently compromise us. I doubted the kid would be a rebel himself, but knew it was unlikely he would resist the temptation to tell his mates about the four white soldiers sitting in a nearby bush. The message would spread like wildfire and the rebels would find out. I kept my thoughts to myself, but hoped we would not have to 'silence' a small child, whose only crime was collecting fruit.

We could also hear farmers working in the nearby fields. I

didn't worry too much about this until I smelt smoke being blown towards us. Sierra Leonean subsistence farmers use 'slash and burn' methods to clear the jungle for agriculture, and the locals were burning back vegetation to increase the size of their fields. The only problem was, we were hiding in this vegetation. I started to feel like a wild animal being flushed out of the bush by hunters. To my relief, though, the wind gradually changed direction and blew the danger away from us.

The hours dragged by slowly. We were all desperately craving water, but nobody complained and we kept these thoughts to ourselves. I did my best to ignore the physical discomfort, and tried instead to concentrate on the challenges that still lay ahead of us. Feeling sorry for myself was not a luxury I could afford. I allowed myself to daydream, and tried to imagine what Anna was up to. At this particular moment, there was nowhere I would rather have been than curled up on a sofa with my wife and a cup of tea, watching mindless telly... I later discovered that she'd not been on the sofa with a cup of tea but sitting by the phone with something much stronger.

By six o'clock in the evening, the hottest part of the day had passed, but we'd been lying in the fierce tropical heat for over twelve hours without drinking. I took stock of our situation. As the crow flies, we were now about 6 kilometres from Makeni, but had used considerable energy and most of our water to get there. Our progress the next night was going to be even harder. Without water, we would not get much further. Dehydration had become as much the enemy as the RUF. Ideally, we would not leave our lie-up position until after midnight, when the locals would most likely be asleep. But with every hour that passed we would grow weaker and weaker. So we needed to take a calculated risk. I suggested to the others that we drink our final water bottle now and move as soon as it was dark. I hoped that drinking our remaining water in one go would give us the physical and psychological boost we needed to reach a fresh water source. Everybody agreed.

Our map showed a dotted blue line meaning 'river – seasonal' about 5 miles away from our lie-up position. Although it was still the dry season, there had been occasional rain in the preceding weeks and we hoped there would be some water in the river. The deal was this: if we pushed ourselves hard, we would make it to the river. If the river turned out to be dry, then we were screwed.

Another night

As soon as it was dark, I crept on my own out of our hiding place to recce a route past the village. I returned to pick up the others and we skirted round the north side of the village. We continued on a bearing towards the river but soon found ourselves in almost impenetrable vegetation, which blotted out the moonlight. In the pitch darkness, I was literally fighting my way forwards, flailing with both arms to rip holes through the dense foliage and using my head and shoulders to burrow through the almost solid wall of trees and shrubs. I asked the others to take turns in front but they seemed to lack the energy to break trail, so I crashed on, digging deep into my last reserves of strength. I was too knackered to feel much pain but was aware of small trickles of blood running down my arms from numerous cuts and scrapes, and my uniform was getting slowly shredded. I continually lost my footing but found I was so wedged in by branches I couldn't fall over. Our progress slowed to 100 metres an hour. The river we were aiming for was beginning to seem impossibly far away, let alone the safe haven, which was still over 50 miles away.

We reached a slight clearing, and collapsed in a heap. I could feel the group's negative vibes. In desperation, someone protested: 'Let's just fucking stop here.'

'And then what?' I countered.

He had no answer.

I was blunt: 'If we don't keep going we're going to die.'

I promised the others there would be water in the river, and that our strength would return once we drank. 'Just a few more miles. We can do it.'

I took my pack off, and wearily clambered up a tall tree to look out above the jungle canopy, searching for easier terrain in the distance. I couldn't see any, and slithered despondently back down again.

I tried to sound optimistic.

'Well, it can't get any worse,' I ventured. I decided to bluff. 'I think I can see a path just a bit ahead, and if it's going in the right direction we'll just follow it.' We all needed something to aim for. Avoiding paths is a cardinal rule of E & E, but we were going to have to start breaking the rules if we were to make any meaningful progress.

'Come on. Let's go.' My tongue and throat were so dry it was painful to talk. We pushed on.

Nature seemed against us, but luck was ultimately on our side and, sure enough, we stumbled across a half-decent path that had been cut through the vegetation. I couldn't worry too much about the risk, so just turned left on to the path and kept going.

As point man, I felt dangerously exposed and, for the umpteenth time, I wished I had a weapon. Physically, it was a relief to be on easier terrain but ironically we were now in greater danger. We knew the RUF controlled territory by establishing checkpoints on all the paths in an area, and it seemed just a matter of time before we bumped into one. I wondered what to do if we did. The bushes were too thick on either side of the path to run left or right, and we felt too weak to turn and run. I decided I would try to keep walking calmly up to the checkpoint, hoping the rebels on duty would think that I was one of them. At the last minute, I would rush them, and try to grab a weapon. It occurred to me that out of all the wildlife in the African jungle, the most dangerous animals were our fellow human beings.

In the event, it was academic as the gamble paid off. After about a mile on the path, we reached an area where the jungle had been slashed and burnt. I left the path, not wanting to tempt fate any more than I had to. The terrain now consisted of knee- and groin-high stubble and stakes, strewn with fallen tree trunks and branches. It was hard going underfoot but at least we could see where we were headed. We could now make out probable RUF positions and were able to detour round them unseen. Thank God the RUF were not better soldiers – all their sentries seemed to be sitting by fires or smoking cigarettes, so we could see them before they saw us.

My memory goes a bit hazy at this point. I realized that I had stopped sweating, but not because I had cooled down. There was just no more liquid left in me to sweat out. When heat exhaustion gets this far, it's known as heat stroke. And like a normal stroke, without treatment, the next stages are coma followed by death. Our mental faculties were going awry as, unable to regulate our body temperature by sweating, our brains were literally starting to stew.

Andy began to collapse more and more. I did my best to bully him to continue, but we all felt on our last legs. He kept begging, 'Just ten minutes. I need to rest.' I couldn't let him. I suspect that if he had lain down, he would never have got up again and I told him so.

'Andy, it's not far now to the water. You'll feel better once you've had a drink.' I was slurring my words.

'Just ten minutes,' he repeated.

I tried to sound angry. 'Get up! If you stay here, you're fucking well dead. You're not staying here on your own, so that means we're fucking dead as well, and I have no intention of dying so let's keep going.'

We staggered on. I'd felt like this before – on the rugby pitch, having banged my head, vaguely aware that I was about to pass out and wondering why people were looking at me oddly...

I wondered what to do if someone did lose consciousness. Back in the compound, we had agreed that if one of us was shot, we would be prepared to abandon him to save the other three. Did the same principle apply now? It would be the toughest decision of my life, but if one of my friends could go no further, could I order the others, and myself, to abandon him? I doubted we had the strength to carry him. Maybe we could drag him to a path and just leave him to his fate at the hands of the rebels? Maybe the kindest thing to do would be to administer a *coup de grâce* with a large rock? It was not a nice thought.

Andy toppled over again and seemed oblivious to our attempts to rouse him, Paul knelt down beside him then suddenly leapt back up again, saying: 'Andy, there's a large snake by your head.' Paul might have been bluffing, but if he was it was a moment of genius. Andy was up again, quick as a flash.

It took us four hours to cover the 5 miles to where we hoped the river would be. Every step was a huge effort, and all I could think about was water.

Using Paul's compass, I knew we were going in the right direction, but my only method of judging how far we had come was by counting my paces as I walked. (Not very accurate, when you're zig-zagging round obstacles in difficult terrain and in the dark.) But I had done a lot of navigating in difficult terrain over the years, by day and by night, and was confident I'd not cocked up. An element of doubt, however, was beginning to creep in. Could the map be wrong? Could I have knocked the dial of my compass and followed the wrong bearing? I called a halt, and we dropped wearily on to the ground. We had to take another calculated risk: Andy's pack contained a hand-held GPS (Global Positioning System). Like the satphone, though, a light came on when it was switched on, so using it in the dark was almost prohibitively dangerous. But this did seem a good time to check exactly where we were. We huddled round Andy, to try to shield the light, and he switched it on. It gave us the accurate fix we needed. Still a couple of hundred metres to go.

'Come on, let's do it.' I counted off the remaining paces. We reached a large ditch, banked by trees. We had arrived at the river.

It was dry.

We slumped back onto the ground, and sat there in silence, each man dealing with the disappointment as best he could. I lay back and looked at the stars above me, perhaps searching for divine inspiration.

And then we heard a noise. Quietly at first, then louder and louder as they warmed up their voices. Frogs! Croaking into the night sky.

'Where there's frogs there's got to be water!' I took a compass bearing on the frogs, and we headed towards them. Once we started moving, though, the frogs could hear us again and immediately stopped croaking. If we'd not stopped and sat there staring into space, we'd never have known they were there. I trusted my compass bearing, and, sure enough, almost walked right into the large muddy pool that was their home.

Even in the moonlight, I could make out a scum of insect larvae and algae on the surface of the water, and there was a powerful stench of mud and rotting vegetation. But, in my uncritical state, I reasoned that if it was good enough for frogs, it was good enough for us.

Paul and I had hand-held water filters with us, and we set to work. I scraped the pond's surface scum aside and we started pumping water into our bottles. The water was so full of silt that my pump soon broke. But as well as filtering the water, we added drops of iodine and triple the normal dose of chlorine-based purifying tablets to kill anything harmful. The resulting water tasted more like something you'd use to clean the sink than a refreshing drink, but it did the trick. Our plan was to make like camels, but we had to be careful. In our dehydrated state, if we drank too much too quickly, we could make ourselves ill, so we sat there for nearly two hours, drinking slowly, but forcing water down our throats until our stomachs felt bloated. I dreaded to think what might now be living in my guts and hoped any side-effects would wait until we reached safety. We were also able to wash down the few scraps of bread we had with us. As we rehydrated, so our strength returned.

Feeling a little better, we continued on as best we could. Frustratingly, for the first time in several days, it clouded over. When we had prayed for total darkness back in Makeni, we had got bright moonlight. Now we got the opposite. Yet, despite the cloud cover, it still didn't rain. In daylight, it might have been easy enough, but in this gloom it was impossible to progress without falling over. Every two or three paces I tripped over some obstacle hidden in the darkness, and seemed to use as much energy getting back on my feet as I did actually walking. I remember making a conscious effort to fall forwards each time as at least then I was making progress in the right direction. Our hands and legs burned with numerous scratches and cuts but we were thankful not to twist our ankles or fall, eye socket first, on to the numerous tree-stumps where the jungle had been burnt. Many of the tree stumps came up to waist height, and I lost count of the number of times we caught ourselves on them.

Andy, in particular, seemed to be having a hard time of it and had an uncanny knack of locating obstacles with his groin. It was easy to tell where Andy was in the dark – all you had to do was listen for the groans.

I walked with the compass in my hand, stopping every five paces to ensure I was still on the correct bearing. There were no visual points of reference such as the moon or stars or landmarks, so without a compass we'd literally have been walking round in circles. If you can't see where you're going, you invariably veer either left or right until you get back to where you started.

Every time we saw signs of habitation, we were forced to back-track and move off on a dogleg before continuing.

I enforced a strict regime. One hour walking, five minutes' rest. One hour walking, five minutes' rest. Over and over. The going was relentless. Yomping was not pleasant that night.

Dehydration was now not such a problem, but fatigue was. We were all just plain knackered. In particular, sleep deprivation was taking its toll. By this stage, I hadn't slept for a week, and my mind was playing all sorts of tricks. In the *Staff Officer's Handbook*, a reference book issued to British military officers, there is an annexe that gives guidance on the effects of sleep deprivation. After ninety-six hours without sleep, troops are said to be '100 per cent ineffective'. We had gone nearly twice this long without sleep. In training, the longest I'd not slept was three days, so at least I had some idea what to expect.

The jungle at night is a freaky place at the best of times, with strange shapes, shadows and noises everywhere. In our state, it felt like a bad trip. It was getting harder and harder to tell the difference between what was real and what was not. My hallucinations became more and more extreme. I saw rebels, friends, wild animals, and an assortment of ghosts. Wherever I looked, out of the corner of my eye, I saw small weaselly creatures peering at me from the shadows. I had to have several reality checks with my companions to work out what was real. If all four of us could see the same thing, then it was real. If only one or two of us could see it, then we ignored it.

On one occasion, for example, we had stopped briefly underneath a mango tree, and were crawling around, trying to find fruit on the ground. Out of the corner of my eye, I thought I could make out a large snake.

Me: 'Guys, I can see a 10-foot snake over there. But I don't think it's real.'

Paul: 'Uh oh, I was just thinking the same thing.'

Dave: 'And me.'

Andy: 'Shit.'

Me: 'Aren't snakes territorial? Let's get out of here.'

Before first light, we took another bearing on some croaking frogs and made our way back to the 'river', looking for a lie-up position close to water but hidden in a forested area. A map check revealed we were now about 15 kilometres from Makeni. Still less than a quarter of the distance we needed to travel. The water here was even more disgusting than before and I wondered whether drinking it would do us more harm than good. We drank anyway. This seemed like a good moment to produce the treat that I had been saving for a special occasion: the can of baked beans that Anna had given me for my birthday. I had taken the piss at the time, for the world's crappiest thirtieth birthday present, but right now it seemed a pretty inspired choice. We enjoyed our one mouthful of beans each and as a bonus used the can to scoop up water, avoiding as many of the insect larvae swimming in the fetid pond as possible.

We needed to reassess our options. From what Colonel Jim had told us by satphone the day before, we hoped that other

British forces would be arriving in the country. I reckoned we were now far enough from known rebel positions to make helicopter pick-up feasible. We agreed on this, and at first light set the satphone up.

I pressed the on/off button. Nothing happened. I tried again. Still nothing. I checked the battery connection, in case it had come loose. The connector looked OK.

Shit. It must be the battery. How to tell the others?

I guessed that the phone had switched itself on as I had struggled through the bush, and the battery had drained. I contemplated a 'D'you want the good news or the bad news?' approach, but decided this would be an unfair test of my colleagues' sense of humour.

'Guys, the satphone's knackered. We're walking to Mile 91.'

Without the satphone working, we could not call for extraction by helicopter. Psychologically, we had all made the mistake of convincing ourselves we'd made it. Now we knew we had not, morale hit rock bottom. Two nights' forced march had taken us less than a quarter of the distance we needed to cover. We were only likely to get slower as our bodies became more exhausted and our mental faculties were already beginning to go. Seizing the moment, Paul took a photo. We couldn't even force a grin for the camera. Emotionally, we were all spent. Temporarily, it was all too much to cope with. We just lay there, too tired to think, feeling nothing.

We must have fallen asleep, as the next thing I remember, two hours had passed and I was waking up with gentle rain falling on my face.

Change of tactics

I felt a little more human again. I woke the others up and we had another team talk. They thought that progress at night was simply too hard and that we should consider moving by day. I disagreed initially. It might take us a week, but we'd get there in the end. As long as we stayed near the river, we could drink every night. We might arrive a bit skinnier than before, but so what?

My friends did not share my optimism. Eventually, I conceded the point when it occurred to me that, if we took too long, there was a very real danger that our intended 'safe haven' might have fallen to the rebels. Reports on the World Service indicated the RUF were still advancing relentlessly towards Freetown. Where would we go then?

If we started moving by day, our tactics would have to change. We agreed we should gamble early on and attempt to enlist the help of friendly civilians. It would be impossible to avoid the local population during daylight hours, so why not find a guide who would know the jungle paths and be able to steer us clear of known RUF-controlled villages? This seemed a reasonable plan, and with nothing to gain by staying where we were, we continued on carefully in the general direction of Mile 91.

It was a great relief to be doing something positive again. We soon came to the edge of the forested area and stopped again to study the agricultural land in front of us. We could see a couple of mud huts and an old man lying by a fire. We watched for a few minutes. There was no one else around – a good sign. We could see the man was a farmer and he looked too old to be a rebel. Furthermore, if there were no young women nearby, I doubted there were any rebels. The RUF enjoyed their creature comforts, particularly bush wives.

We put on our UN baseball caps and approached the local farmer. He was very friendly but not much use to us – we lacked a common language and my sign language seemed to go over his head. So we just smiled a lot. I swapped a cigarette I was carrying for some water and a handful of nuts. We thanked him and moved on to the next farm.

The farmer here had a wife and kids. A few more cigarettes changed hands, then the family sat down on a bench in front of me and I tried my sign language again. It felt like playing charades. I read out some place names from the map. With each place name, if I knew the place was controlled by the RUF I gave a 'thumbs down' sign and frowned. 'Makeni' (*frown*), 'Magburaka' (*frown*), and so on. If I knew the place was not controlled by the RUF, then I gave a 'thumbs up' sign and smiled. 'Freetown' (*smile*), 'Kenema' (*smile*). They soon caught on. I read out the names of local villages and they gave me thumbs up or thumbs down. The nearest rebel-free village was called Yela, 4 or 5 miles away. One of the farmer's kids took us there.

We walked confidently into Yela, and asked to speak to the chief. If there were rebels there, we would try to bluff our way and claim to be a routine UN patrol. It was obvious, though, that this village hated the RUF – several villagers were missing limbs thanks to the rebels. The chief talked to us through a teenage interpreter called Alusayne, who spoke good English. He told us his village had suffered terribly at the hands of the RUF, stealing their possessions and abducting many of their women and children. We explained that we had not come to Sierra Leone to fight the RUF. Our motivation for being here was to help the Sierra Leonean people, but the RUF had turned on us and killed our colleagues. He told us that hospitality to visitors was an integral part of Sierra Leonean culture, and was dismayed at the RUF behaviour. I was struck that he seemed even more upset by the RUF's treatment of us as strangers than he was by the suffering of his own people. I asked the chief if there was a guide who could take us to Mile 91. Alusayne, the interpreter, volunteered. He felt confident that he knew how to lead us around rebel positions.

Although we couldn't be entirely sure that we wouldn't be led into a trap, we thought it unlikely.

We tipped the village chief generously and promised more of the same when we reached safety. Just in case, we also swore that, if they tricked us, we (or our countrymen) would arrange to have them killed and their village destroyed. How we were to achieve this, I don't know, but it seemed to do the trick. The chief might have thought that the best way to curry favour with the local RUF warlords was to hand us over to them. I had to convince this elder that, although we were defenceless, sending us to our deaths would not be without retribution.

Alusayne was as hard as nails. He was suffering an attack of malaria and had an open wound on his abdomen which was dressed with a poultice of leaves and bark. He dismissed the injury as 'a gift from the RUF', but didn't elaborate further. And, for some reason, he never stopped smiling. He had never seen a map before and his only concept of distance was how long it took to walk somewhere ('fourteen hours to Mile 91 if we go fast'). This was not a good place to hang around as rebel patrols 'visited' regularly to gather food, so we filled our water bottles, ate a couple of the most delicious mangoes I've ever tasted, then set off again. We still had a 40-mile walk through RUF-held jungle to crack.

Even in his flip-flops, Alusayne had only one pace (fast) and he didn't like stopping. He pointed out that news of four white soldiers being in the area would spread quickly and was keen to travel faster than the rumours did. We struggled to keep up. Every time we stopped for a drink, Alusayne rolled himself a small joint of cannabis. No wonder he smiled so much. I lost count, but reckoned he was smoking two large reefers every hour. Not bad going for a fourteen-year-old. He clearly knew all the bush paths like the back of his hand and which routes the rebels tended to use.

We still tried to avoid all habitation but, when this was impossible, we lay low while Alusayne scouted ahead. If we had to go through a village that was clear of rebels, at least we were able to fill our water bottles from the well. We also made sure we paid our respects to each village chief, leaving generous tips, knowing that other UN escapees might be following in our footsteps and would benefit from any goodwill we managed to generate.

I was impressed by the many locals who helped us, especially Alusayne. For minimal financial gain, they were putting themselves in huge amounts of danger. If we were caught, at least as Westerners we could be of some benefit to the RUF as hostages and might be kept alive. Alusayne would be summarily executed. I asked him why he was prepared to risk his life to help us. He took a drag on his cigarette and replied wistfully, 'Well, I had nothing else to do today.'

It got hotter and hotter as the day went on, but we stuck to a good fast pace, spurred on by the thought that every step was a step closer to safety. Yet there was no room for complacency. This was rebel territory and we still had to pass through their front line, where we could expect them to be more on their guard.

We passed through vast forests, where some of the trees were hundreds of years old, and lush agricultural land. We stopped at wells in tiny villages where lithe young girls smiled demurely as they offered us fruit. The scenery and the people were beautiful. I was almost beginning to enjoy myself again. Like many mountaineers, I regard the savagery and danger of the landscape as an integral part of its beauty. The world's highest mountains are appealing partly because they have claimed the lives of many would-be climbers. The same principle applied here. For me, as on so many occasions before, the tired legs, blistered feet and fear of death or capture made our surroundings even more absorbing. All my senses were primed to identify potential threats to my safety.

So, as a bonus, I found I picked up all kinds of detail I would normally miss, like the noise of birds singing in the distance and the sight of monkeys playing in the trees. Never had mangoes tasted so divine or water been so refreshing. Our feet were rubbed raw but once again I couldn't really feel sorry for myself as Andy had horrendous jock-rot and was walking like John Wayne. Even he had to see the funny side.

By two o'clock that afternoon, we had been walking virtually non-stop for twenty hours and our feet were in bits. I ordered a halt, to avoid exerting ourselves during the hottest part of the day, and we lay up for two hours in the shade of a tree. I grabbed some much-needed sleep, but woke suddenly when I felt someone kicking me in the ribs.

Rebels? No, only Andy.

'What d'you have to wake me up for?' I complained.

'You've started snoring. The rebels might hear you. Anyway, you're covered in ants. So are we and they bite.'

We took it turns to strip and pick the biting ants off each other. Our change of tactics was paying off. Moving by night without using paths, we could have stumbled around for weeks. But with the benefits of daylight and a guide, we covered nearly 40 kilometres before dusk, arriving at a Kamajor village called Mbenti.

Mbenti lay on the south bank of the Rokel River which, in this part of Sierra Leone, marked the historical boundary between RUF and CDF. But with the RUF advancing towards Freetown, we were not sure whether Mbenti would be friendly or not. The rebels might have captured it, or the CDF might resent the UN for having disarmed them and not the RUF.

While we hid, Alusayne asked some local farmers who assured him that Mbenti was still in CDF hands. On the map, the Rokel River looked a formidable obstacle. But Alusayne knew a spot where we were able to wade across. The river was about 200 metres wide at this point, but never more than waist deep and was wonderfully refreshing to our tired legs.

As the sun was setting, we wandered into Mbenti. It had been a long day. I suggested to Alusayne that he stay the night with us in Mbenti, before returning to his own village the next day, but he didn't want to hang around. I paid him generously – enough I hoped to pay for an operation for his wound and some extra for his village. I thanked him for one final time. Still smiling, he smoked one last joint, then headed off into the darkness, seemingly unperturbed at the thought of walking another 40 kilometres that night back to his own village.

Mbenti's chief was away in Freetown but, to our relief, the Kamajor commander, Ibrahim, promised to protect us. Ironically perhaps, his fighters had disarmed in good faith to the UN just two weeks before, leaving him with only an ancient hunting rifle, machetes, and black magic to protect his village from the rebels. The nearest RUF position was less than a mile away, on the far bank of the river. Ibrahim asked his wife to slaughter a chicken for us to eat, then positioned his warriors around us, and told us to sleep. That whole night was very weird. We were invited to sleep, surrounded by machete-wielding Kamajor hunters, who were quite happy to take on rebels armed with AK47s or machine guns. And as night fell, my hallucinations recommenced. I was just too wired to sleep properly – every now and then I'd drift off, only to wake a few moments later, confused by where I was, forgetting momentarily that the machete-wielding warriors were on my side.

Britain gets involved

Back home, the UK government had acted decisively to prevent the total collapse of UNAMSIL and pre-empt the mayhem that would ensue if the RUF captured Freetown. As we dined on chicken and rice with the Kamajors that evening, the advance elements of Britain's Joint Rapid Deployment Force were beginning to arrive in Sierra Leone. They included the 1st Battalion of the Parachute Regiment and 42 Commando Royal Marines. The force's initial task was to secure the airport and conduct a NEO (Non-combatant Evacuation Operation) – in other words, evacuating foreign nationals before the rebels reached Freetown. Their secondary task was to bolster UN resolve and provide a small body of highly trained professional soldiers, who were not afraid to stand up to the RUF.

At one stage, the rebels had reached as close as 20 kilometres from Freetown and panic had set in, both among the local population and the UN. As the UN had successfully managed to disarm many of the pro-Government militias such as the CDF, there was no one else to counter the rebels, who were advancing almost unopposed.

It was now thirty-six hours since we had last established communications with the outside world and, back in the UK, our next of kin had been told we were Missing in Action. 'Missing in Action' is all too often a euphemism for 'Killed in Action but we haven't found the body yet', so our loved ones had good reason to worry. Anna was calm and collected, helped by her best friend Mel who happened to be staying with her, but she was under no illusion about the dangers we had already escaped and how precarious our situation must now have been. She telephoned the Permanent Joint Headquarters in London (which would be co-ordinating any British military response to the crisis). The officer on duty confirmed that we had left the Makeni base three days before, 'presumed heading for Freetown', and that we were carrying a satellite telephone. When Anna asked whether we had tried to use the phone, the officer replied simply that we had not. She thought it best not to speculate why. Anna had faith in my survival instincts – she and I had come through one life-threatening situation before and several, less serious, adventurous episodes. Her attitude was 'He's fine until I've got evidence that he's not.'

Anna later told me she kept this up for three days, until the early hours of Monday morning just at the time when we were being watched over by the Kamajors. That night she could not sleep, distracted by disturbing images of me surrounded by a group of men wielding machetes, discussing my death, and for a few hours, she managed to convince herself I was already dead. Mel administered a large measure of whisky and calmed her down, but admitted she found her friend's uncharacteristic panic attack unnerving. She even wondered whether Anna 'knew' something she didn't.

Anna later dismissed this as an entirely rational response. 'I reckoned the chances of Phil surviving intact were about 90:10 in his favour. So, 90 per cent of the time I was calm and the rest of the time I was not.'

The timing of the episodes was surely a coincidence but I'm still less sceptical now of black magic than I was before. It didn't seem fair that Anna should have been most distressed at a time when we were relatively safe and comfortable.

Restless, I wandered back down to the river at first light to watch the sunrise. The Kamajors assured me there had been no sign of the rebels during the night, so I risked a quick dip, and rinsed my body and clothes in the cool river water. It was tempting to strip right off but I thought it would be pushing my luck so close to known rebel positions – the thought of E & E stark naked was not one I fancied.

Although we were now at the end of a dirt track, we were still 15 miles from Mile 91. We hoped the town was still occupied by a company of Guinean UN troops. Our feet were not in good condition, especially Dave's. He had lost most of the skin on the soles of his feet during our long hike the previous day. At hobbling pace, it was going to take at least another day to cover the remaining distance, so I asked Ibrahim if there was a vehicle we could hire. The only transport in the village was a bicycle with one pedal. He was prepared to lend it to me, but pointed out that the track to Mile 91 was regularly staked out by RUF patrols, and if I cycled (lopsidedly) into an ambush I was unlikely to escape. So instead we sent the village messenger forward on the village bicycle with a letter and my ID card, asking for a UN patrol to be sent to pick us up. The bicycle had lost its left pedal several years before, so the messenger had a very strong right leg...

If Mile 91 had fallen to the RUF, we were probably safer where we were with the CDF than on our own in the bush, especially now that word had leaked out that there were white soldiers on the loose.

While we waited for the messenger to return we ate, drank and tried to improvise a battery for the satphone. We scrounged as many torch batteries off the locals as we could lay our hands on. Paul wired them up in series and attached them to the phone. The batteries were not enough to power the satphone on their own but at least, in Paul, we had a genuine expert on the matter. (His speciality was actually charging submarine batteries using nuclear reactors, but the theory must be the same.) Paul suggested we try leaving the torch batteries connected to the satphone to 'trickle charge' for an hour or so.

We waited impatiently and tried again. 'Fingers crossed, everyone.' I hit the on/off button. The light came on and the display powered up. *Welcome to Inmarsat... Please enter your PIN code...* I tapped the code in furiously. *Searching for satellite... Connecting with satellite... Please dial number now...* I started dialling. *Battery low... Battery empty.* And with that, the phone switched off.

'Shit.'

Paul was optimistic. 'Well, the principle's right. Let's try again but leave it even longer this time.'

This time we would wait two hours for the phone to recharge. As we waited, Ibrahim called us over to a ramshackle hut used as the village school, to listen to the children sing. The rebels had sent a 'recruiting party' to the school the previous year. They had killed the previous teacher and abducted half the pupils as their new recruits. Sierra Leonean kids all seem to be talented singers and I found their song deeply moving.

> *'We are the children*
> *We are not soldiers*
> *We not do fighting*
> *We are the children...'*

I was embarrassed to feel a tear trickling down my cheek until I saw I was not the only member of our party who was affected.

Before we had time to try the phone again, the messenger returned with good news. ('The first for days – maybe it's a bad omen,' was Dave's laconic observation.) The Guineans still occupied Mile 91 and had promised to send out a patrol to escort us back to their position. We packed up our gear, rewarded the villagers with our remaining cash and I gave Ibrahim my penknife. In due course, a Guinean patrol arrived, we jumped into one of their pick-up trucks and stormed off towards Mile 91.

As we bumped along in the truck, I asked the patrol commander in my best pidgin French what was happening in their area. His reply was understated: they were having some 'slight problems of their own with the rebels'.

Here we go again – out of the frying pan into the fire. Stand by for another siege...

Mile 91 was still notionally in UN hands but it was now an isolated pocket, as the surrounding area had fallen to the RUF. Remobilizing Sierra Leone soldiers were piling into Mile 91, along with an assortment of pro-Government militias, including the infamous West Side Boys. There was a real danger that these militiamen would swap sides if they thought the RUF were winning. The Guinean commander expected imminent attack and tensions were high. To complicate matters, thousands of civilian refugees were beginning to seek refuge in the area, some of whom, inevitably, would have been RUF infiltrators. The Guinean explained that ambushes were common on this section of track. I asked him what his anti-ambush drills were.

'*Rouler plus vite*' ('Driving faster').

We passed several groups of armed militiamen. Either these groups were pro-Government or the Guinean commander's rally-driving anti-ambush technique worked well, and we made it to Mile 91 without having to stop.

Deliverance

The Guinean position at Mile 91 did not inspire confidence. In comparison, the Kenyan position now seemed like Fort Knox. They had a couple of machine-guns set up, overlooking the road they expected the rebels to approach down, but that was about it. No trenches, no look-outs, and no contingency plans. I tried to explain in French how to improve their defensive position, but my language skills let me down. I can buy food and read climbing guidebooks in French, but my O-level French classes had never taught me any military vocabulary.

The Guinean soldiers had only twenty rounds of ammunition each. Their company commander explained that if they were issued any more than this, they tended to sell it on the black market to the rebels. He added his theory as to why his unit were not issued with decent vehicles and equipment: we were only four hours' drive from the Guinean border. The Guinean government was concerned that if there was a fully trained and equipped unit that close to home, they might drive back to Guinea and attempt a coup.

We now managed more successfully to improvise a power supply for the satphone using a car battery, and it partially recharged. The battery display indicated 1 minute 20 seconds of talk time. I phoned the UN HQ in Freetown. No one answered. I let the phone ring for thirty seconds. Now I had only fifty seconds of battery life left.

Oh no. Freetown's fallen. What's happened to Jim? I half expected a rebel to answer the phone. Our spirits sank. We surmised (wrongly) that Freetown had fallen to the rebels and that the UN had completely surrendered or evacuated. *Who to phone next?* One of the last things I had done leaving the compound in Makeni was to wipe the satphone's memory. If you think you might be captured you 'sanitize' your kit. This means making sure you have no marked maps, address books, jewellery, love-letters or photos on you. If you are caught with any of these things, your interrogators can use them against you. Stupidly, I had committed to memory only Jim's number in Freetown. *Why hadn't I memorized a number for the Permanent Joint Headquarters in London?* Forty seconds of battery life. *Who do I trust to pass on a message? Who'll answer the phone quickly enough? Hurry up! Think!*

I phoned Anna.

She answered immediately.

'Hi. We're safe.' No time for what I really wanted to say to her. I told her where we were and what we were up to and trusted her to pass on the necessary information.

In reality, it had been academic who we spoke to as all calls on the phone were now being intercepted and monitored in the UK.

As I struggled with the satphone, Andy and Dave borrowed a Guinean radio and managed to speak to the UN HQ in Freetown. The UN had evacuated from their normal headquarters, but only as far as the Mammy Yoko hotel, a hotel complex on the very western tip of the Freetown peninsula. The Mammy Yoko was a considerably better position to defend than their original HQ in the city centre. Colonel Jim had relocated there and had a new phone number. We recharged the phone again, and managed to get through to him on his new number. To our amazement, he told us a British RAF helicopter was on its way to pick us up and would be there in fifteen minutes.

This seemed too good to be true, as the nearest airstrip was forty-five minutes' flying time away, but it turned out our previous abortive phone call back in Mbenti had been partially successful. We hadn't known it at the time, but the phone had connected briefly with the satellite, and UK electronic warfare 'assets' had managed to gain a fix on our position. They couldn't be 100 per cent sure it was us, but knew that somebody, on our intended E & E route, had switched our phone on and known its PIN code. This warranted putting a British helicopter on standby, ready to come and investigate.

In preparation for the helicopter pick-up, we used Andy's GPS to give an exact latitude and longitude of where we were standing and a suggested direction of approach for the helicopter. Finally, I spent a frenzied quarter of an hour before the helicopter arrived, cajoling and bribing with cigarettes as many trigger-happy factions as possible not to shoot at the helicopter. The local militiamen were used to UN helicopters, which were painted white, but a British one would be green, and might be regarded as hostile. I was concerned that if someone took a potshot at the helicopter, it would return fire, and we would be caught in the cross-fire.

With thirty seconds to go, there was nothing to indicate the imminent arrival of our pick-up. We had all experienced the frustration of waiting for helicopters before. An element of doubt crept in. *Maybe I had sent the wrong grid reference?* But with fifteen seconds to go, we heard the deep throb of a Chinook helicopter approaching. It arrived exactly on cue.

'D'you think they'll let me on as a Kiwi?' Dave asked, only half in jest.

Flying 50 feet above us at 150 mph, the Chinook passed directly over our heads (to check the landing sight was secure) then slammed on its brakes, turned and landed just 20 feet from where we were huddled. Huge clouds of dust billowed in the air, and the downwash from the Chinook's powerful rotor blades sent debris flying everywhere, including the helmets of several Guinean soldiers who had not bothered to fasten their chin straps. Some of the local militiamen looked as if they were witnessing a UFO landing. A second Chinook circled around above us, ready to give covering fire with its powerful chaingun in case there was a problem on the ground.

A burly British soldier stepped off the Chinook's tail ramp and beckoned me over. Above the roar of the engine noise, he shouted in my ear, 'Are you all OK?'

'Yes.'

'What is the name of your parents' first dog?' (This seemed odd.)

'You what?' I was confused.

'Your first dog. What was its name?' Before you go on an operational tour, you write down the answers to a number of simple identification questions that only you can answer. But it now seemed a little superfluous in the circumstances – four white men in British uniform surrounded by a sea of black Africans...

My mind promptly went blank, so I mumbled something to hide the fact that I couldn't remember the answer.

'Climb on board.'

We didn't need much encouragement.

The heavily armed soldiers on board were sweating profusely. They had come straight from a mountain training exercise in Scotland, and were still wearing cold weather gear. A couple of them were Marines and I'd even been on a climbing holiday with one of them. *Small world*, I thought to myself, grinning inanely.

The pick-up was carried out with clinical efficiency. The two Chinooks flew, hugging the ground, in tactical formation over the jungle back towards Freetown. There was a brief moment of excitement when the other helicopter suddenly discharged phosphorus flares as we flew over a village. Helicopters fire flares automatically if they detect a heat-seeking missile flying towards them. It was highly unlikely that a missile had been fired at us, though the rebels did have some SAM7s (Russian-made, shoulder-launched surface-to-air missiles). More likely, the helicopter's sensors mistook the heat of a cooking fire for the heat signature of a missile being launched.

Within an hour we were landing at the International Airport near Freetown, where the newly arriving British forces were a welcome sight.

CHAPTER SEVEN

AFTERMATH

'Talk softly and carry a large stick – you will go far.'
WEST AFRICAN PROVERB, FAMOUSLY QUOTED BY
THEODORE ROOSEVELT IN JANUARY 1900

Before we could relax or even wash, we had to undergo a 'hot debrief' straight away. It was important for us to stay in the same frame of mind, to maximize our recall. If we started relaxing, our memories would lose some of their sharp edges. Psychological debriefing and the touchy-feely bits could wait till later – in the short term, military matters took precedence.

Our debrief lasted well into the early hours. Who were the rebel leaders? Where did they live? How was their morale? How many soldiers did they have? What were their intentions? Where were the hostages being held? Did they have anti-aircraft weapons? How effective were their tactics? What sort of radios did they have?

The questions went on and on but it was immensely satisfying no longer to be constrained by being an unarmed Observer. Sure, I was not actively going into battle against the RUF, but inside information can be as powerful a weapon as military might. After four months living among the RUF, I knew them inside out. Did I feel guilty dishing the dirt on them? Absolutely not. I had worked hard to try to help the RUF break the cycle of violence in which they seemed to be stuck. If the RUF were not willing to give peace a chance under the generous terms they had been offered, I had no sympathy. The RUF had violated my neutrality and trust and had murdered my UN colleagues in cold blood, so I had no moral qualms about taking sides against them now. I hoped that information I gave to the British debriefing teams would find its way to the pilot of the Sierra Leone Army's only helicopter gunship, which would soon be paying a visit to some of the rebel commanders' homes in Makeni.

Hot debrief over, I peeled off my torn and bloodstained uniform and washed the dirt out of the cuts on my arms and legs. A little cleaner, but still in the same smelly uniform, I went for a stroll around the airport. The first unit to arrive in Sierra Leone was the 1st Battalion, the Parachute Regiment. From the two years I had spent working with the Paras, I knew many of the officers and NCOs and it was surreal to keep bumping into old friends. 1 Para had requisitioned the duty free shop as their Battalion Operations' Room. As I wandered by, I saw an old mate called Nick. Last time I had seen him was on the dance floor at a friend's wedding.

'All right, Nick?'

'Hi, Phil. How are you doing?'

'Not bad. Yourself?'

'Yeah, fine thanks. Good to see you.'

It was the archetypal conversation that blokes have with their mates no matter what is going on around them. This injection of normality should perhaps have brought me back down to earth but it only made my situation seem even more unreal.

It felt good now to be part of an organization that was able to bring some order to the chaos that was taking hold in Sierra

Leone. The United Kingdom had certainly not deployed a major task force just to save Andy, Paul and me. But I had known throughout my time in Sierra Leone that my actions would be backed by my country and this had given me the confidence to make difficult decisions. The timely arrival of the British forces was the best back-up I could have hoped for.

We scrounged some rations off the Paras, then tried to rest. I was still too wired to sleep properly and spent most of the night observing the build-up of the British troops or watching CNN in the airport VIP lounge. It was strangely liberating to be walking round with nothing except the clothes I stood up in, while everyone else was weighed down with weapons, radios and all the other paraphernalia of modern soldiering. In any case, I no longer had any ID, money or so much as a biro to carry around.

Against the busy backdrop of a major military build-up, Paul, Andy, Dave and I sat on the balcony of the airport lounge and chatted long into the night. We all agreed that we were mildly pissed off to have had everything stolen from us by a bunch of thugs. We had deliberately taken nothing of huge sentimental or material value with us. Still, Paul was a bit sad to have lost his umbrella and I minded losing my yellow frisbee, my address book and some tapes that friends had compiled for me. We laughed at the fact that doubtless there were now rebels dressed as Royal Marines Commandos, sleeping on my camp bed and listening to my dubious music collection.

In the morning, I visited the field hospital, to have my feet dressed properly, then jumped on board a Chinook with a company of Paras for the short flight across the estuary to Freetown itself. The Paras had established their HQ in the Mammy Yoko hotel, alongside the UN HQ, and I was keen to track down Colonel Jim to thank him for the tireless vigil he had kept for us. While the rest of the UN had been evacuating, Jim and another Brit called Mike had set up their communications kit in a shack by the hotel swimming pool and maintained a twenty-four-hour watch, awaiting our call.

I finally found Jim's new office, hidden in a quiet corner of the hotel. I knocked on the door and he called me in. Since he was simultaneously my boss, my teammate and my friend, I wasn't sure whether to salute, shake his hand or give him a hug. In the end, I did a bit of all three (unfortunately for Jim, as I'd been wearing the same clothes for over a week in the sweatiest place in the world).

Jim had now been given the task of running the 'Detainee Co-ordination Team'. 'Detainee' was UN-speak for 'hostage', a term that might imply a worse crisis than the UN cared to admit. Jim's task in the Detainee Team was an important one, which was a bonus for me as it meant he had been allocated a plush office with ensuite bathroom and shower facilities. He lent me a towel and razor and I immediately made the most of the facilities. What I didn't realize, as I was washing and shaving, was that Jim had convened a meeting in the adjoining room. I was a little surprised to wander out of the shower stark naked only to bump straight into a senior Iranian UN diplomat and a pair of British police hostage negotiators. But not as surprised as they were.

Afterwards, I was keen to find out what had happened to my UN colleagues and asked Jim what was going on. He explained that, although it looked like the UK forces were managing to stabilize the military situation around Freetown and the airport, the news from the rest of the country was not good. The RUF was still holding over 500 UN personnel hostage, including Parachute Regiment Major Andy Harrison, my next-door neighbour from back home in London. I was relieved that we had managed to escape, but there was not much cause for celebration while others were still missing. Jim was pessimistic about Andy's chances of making it out alive. We could only imagine what he was going through. We also thought of Andy's wife Carolyn, who had been told her husband was missing. Anna's wait was now over, but Carolyn's was to go on for weeks and weeks. In fact the two of them were to share more than the odd glass of wine, swapping macabre stories and keeping each others' spirits up.

Back in Freetown, the priority was stopping the RUF advance towards the capital. Not for the first time, it struck me as ironic that the UN had managed to disarm only the pro-Government militias. I wondered whether there would be any armed groups able to stop the RUF in their tracks before they reached Freetown. To hear the Sierra Leonean perspective on things, I tuned in my pocket radio and listened to the local news on Radio Democracy, the Government radio station.

'Here is an announcement from His Excellency, President Tejan Kabbah. All citizens of Freetown are asked to remain calm. There is no cause for panic. All loyal soldiers and militiamen are requested to report to the National Football Stadium for further orders...'

This seemed pretty good cause for panic to me. The locals had obviously lost all confidence in the UN and were mustering their own troops. Who would take control of the gathering ragtag mob of gunmen at the stadium? I could feel a coup coming on.

'...This announcement is brought to you courtesy of Bangura's Hardware Store, 118d Siaka Stevens Street, purveyors of Freetown's finest wood, cement and nails, open seven days a week.'

Sierra Leonean businesses obviously needed to make money whether there was a civil war on or not.

Trouble brewing

I tagged along with a patrol of Paras and we drove into the town centre to find out what was going on. Freetown was eerily quiet. There wasn't a civilian to be seen. The normally bustling markets were deserted and the shops were boarded up to prevent looting. The local population seemed terrified of what might be about to happen. Everyone had vivid memories of the mayhem and butchery that took place last time the rebels hit Freetown back in January 1999. The RUF had called this Operation Annihilate Every Living Thing. Were we now experiencing the lull before the next storm?

The only locals on the streets were groups of re-mobilizing soldiers and Kamajors. No one asked too many questions about where they were getting their weapons from. Freetown was supposed to be a UN-controlled 'de-militarized' zone but guns just seemed to be an integral part of the local infrastructure.

The arriving British soldiers were finding it hard to distinguish between rebels and friendly militias, none of whom wore official uniforms or badges. After months in the country, I was a little more street-wise and was asked to brief various groups of Brits, based on my local knowledge.

I explained the tell-tale features of different factions, some of which were easy to spot, others less so. For example:

Weapons: The RUF preferred AK47s; pro-Government militias tended to use British-made SLRs.

Hair: The current RUF fashion was for flat-tops; the Kamajors went for the scraggy 'bushman' look.

Clothes: The RUF in Freetown dressed like would-be members of an American rap band; the Kamajors stayed with the wild 'bushman' look.

Intoxication: The Kamajors were normally stoned, which made them a bit deranged and incomprehensible; the RUF were normally stoned and drunk, which made them even more deranged

and aggressive. It also gave them permanently
bloodshot eyes.

Attitude: The RUF strutted around like they owned the
place; the Kamajors wandered around in a daze.

If the men were really aggressive – and wore uniforms – they were
probably Nigerian peacekeepers. Some of the Nigerians, who had
been 'peacekeeping' in Sierra Leone for four or five years, now
resented the high-profile British presence and took it out on any
British soldier they came across. It never got beyond a lot of shouting and posturing, but it took some delicate negotiations to
remind everyone that we were all on the same side.

I also explained to the newly arrived British troops about the
groups of kids that would inevitably crowd round their positions.
Although some of these children might have been RUF spies, if
you were nice to them they became an excellent early-warning
system, as they knew exactly who everyone was. We weren't too
bothered if, in turn, they passed on what they saw to the RUF – it
was pretty obvious to everyone who the white soldiers with the
guns were. Anyway, short of rounding up all these crowds of kids,
beating them off with sticks (the traditional local method of crowd
control) or shooting at them, it was impossible to make them go
away. So it was as well to have them on your side.

The Paras had set up a roadblock on the main road that ran
parallel to the beach. I wandered down to their position and,
having got the briefing out of the way, asked them to keep a look-
out while I went for a quick dip in the ocean. Despite the bank of
armed men pointing their guns in my general direction as I swam,
this was the best relaxation I'd had for weeks.

Once they had secured the airport, 1 Para established a secure
cordon around the UN headquarters and began evacuating any
foreign (that is, non-Sierra Leonean) nationals who wanted to

leave the country. The British deployment was slick and professional, in contrast to the disjointedness and inefficiency of UNAMSIL. That said, it was hardly surprising that the UN was disjointed and inefficient. Many of the Western nations that were so quick to criticize the UN were remarkably unwilling to commit troops themselves to peacekeeping missions in Africa. In the diplomatic arena, the UN's multinational make-up is its clear strength. In a military situation, though, this lack of cohesion is a major weakness. Member nations have different languages, different military doctrines, often incompatible comms equipment and even diverging objectives. With so many disparate elements involved, the UN is never likely to be efficient as a military fighting force. Furthermore, in this particular situation, with so many hostages being held, the UNAMSIL Force Commander's hands were now tied. Any overt UN aggression against the RUF would possibly lead to the death of hundreds of hostages.

Within forty-eight hours, the British operation to evacuate non-combatants had been completed. Almost immediately there was pressure from the UK for the British forces to withdraw promptly from Sierra Leone and avoid 'mission creep' – getting sucked into somebody else's civil war as one of the warring factions. However, the UK forces could not abandon UNAMSIL until it had regained some kind of control. So far, a timely show of British force had been enough to persuade the RUF to halt their advance without physically coming to blows. The UK military presence, though not strong in numerical terms (never more than 1,000 troops on the ground in comparison to the UN's 12,000), did a lot to reassure both the UN and people of Sierra Leone that the RUF would not be able to capture Freetown. Not only were there 600 Paras guarding Sierra Leone's 'vital ground' (the airport, seaport and Freetown itself), but it was public knowledge that up to 1,000 Royal Marine Commandos would be arriving in

Sierra Leone in a couple of days. In addition a frigate, HMS *Chatham*, lurked just off the coast of Freetown where it was a visible and reassuring symbol of British power and commitment. If this wasn't enough, RAF and Royal Navy Harrier jump jets made regular sorties from HMS *Illustrious*, one of Britain's two aircraft carriers, which was loitering just over the horizon. These 'air-presence' sorties, overflying rebel strongholds and troop concentrations, again showed the RUF what they would be up against if they took on the British forces or the UN troops they were there to support. It is fair to say that if the British forces had arrived even twelve hours later, the advancing rebels would have entered Freetown almost unopposed and captured the airport. If the airport had fallen it would have been impossible for the UN to evacuate unarmed personnel or for armed reinforcements to arrive. With no armed militias ready to stand up against the RUF, there would have been a horrendous bloodbath.

We were constantly aware of the RUF's repeated intention to 'do a Somalia'. It was common knowledge that the RUF were trying to snatch or kill a British soldier, both for propaganda reasons and to test the resolve of UK public opinion to tolerate casualties. The commander of the British task force, Brigadier David Richards, repeatedly urged all his personnel to stay alert to prevent this happening. On 19 May 2000, this vigilance paid dividends.

The Parachute Regiment's Pathfinder Platoon (16 Air Assault Brigade's specialist reconnaissance unit) were deployed in a village called Lungi Loi, north-east of the Lungi International Airport. At 0300 hours, an alert sentry spotted a large group of rebels trying to infiltrate the Pathfinders' position, and the platoon stood to. The RUF raiding force outnumbered the Paras by five to one, but they had picked a fight with the wrong people. The Pathfinder Platoon – highly trained, well led, heavily armed and, crucially, using night sights on their weapons – stood their ground. The ensuing fire-fight was fierce. No Paras were killed or injured but over twenty RUF combatants were killed. The Pathfinders' Platoon Sergeant, Stephen Heaney, was awarded the Military Cross.

This incident sent a strong message to the RUF: 'Don't mess with the Brits.' Since then, the RUF has done its best to avoid physical confrontation with British troops in Sierra Leone.

The RUF militiamen from the failed attack at Lungi Loi were not the only rebels having a hard time of it. Two weeks after he fled into the bush, Foday Sankoh turned up in Freetown. With a group of bodyguards, he had tried to link up with his RUF fighters as they advanced towards Freetown. This was one of the reasons why the RUF had been so keen to reach the capital. Sankoh, however, never made it off the Freetown peninsula, as the arrival of the UK forces had effectively stopped the RUF in their tracks. On 17 May, Sankoh was captured. He had re-entered Freetown, disguised as a woman, intending to bribe some Nigerians to smuggle him out of the country. Not surprisingly, some locals saw through his disguise. He was handed over to an angry mob who beat him severely and shot him in the leg. They were about to rip him to pieces when a British patrol drove past and (grudgingly) saved him from the lynch mob. Ironic, given the RUF's hatred of all things British. At the time of writing, Sankoh is still in prison, a fallen man awaiting trial for treason.

While the international community lobbied for the release of the UN hostages, UN reinforcements were hurriedly brought into play. Of the UNAMSIL reinforcements that had started arriving, some were more impressive than others. A minor hiccup occurred when a newly arrived battalion of Bangladeshi conscripts refused to get off their aircraft when they landed at Lungi airport. They were terrified by stories that had reached their country of the RUF's barbarism and were found literally clinging to the seats of their aeroplane. The arrival of all UNAMSIL reinforcements was being organized by a team of British movement controllers from the Royal Logistics Corps. To avoid a delay to their slick schedule, one of their team, a no-nonsense staff sergeant called Andy, was tasked to persuade the Bangladeshis to disembark. Ever the diplomat, he described in gruff Scottish tones how he encouraged them to disembark 'using the technique of shouting and dragging'. It seemed to work.

The Parachute Regiment's ethos is to get in and out of an operation as quickly as possible, and they had reacted to this crisis with impressive speed. Having arrived, though, with only the kit they could carry on their backs, they lacked the logistical support for a prolonged stay. So 500 Marines from 42 Commando were now arriving to take over from the Paras. They travelled on board the helicopter carrier HMS *Ocean*, the Royal Navy's largest ship, which carries up to twelve helicopters and 800 Royal Marines. Thanks to HMS *Ocean*, the Marines had the self-sufficiency to stay as long as it took for the situation to stabilize.

I spent a couple of days showing an advance party of Marines around Freetown. Having spent so long as the unarmed underdog, I enjoyed being a part of what now felt like the strongest gang in town. I made a point of sewing my Commando flashes back on to my uniform. I also took up an invitation to spend a couple of days on board HMS *Ocean* having a small but welcome fix of Britain – a roast dinner, warm beer and the football highlights as Chelsea beat Aston Villa 1–0 to win the FA Cup. Plus I was able to draw some clothes from the quartermaster to replace the kit stolen from me by the rebels in Makeni.

After a few days sleeping on someone's office floor in the UN HQ, Andy, Paul and I moved back into the rented house we had shared with the other Brits working for the UN in Freetown. This was a little risky, as our nightwatchman was very good at sleeping but not very good at watching. What's more, the rebels knew exactly where we lived. But we wanted to move back into our house. Just to be safe, we invited several heavily armed Royal Marines from 42 Commando to come and live with us. With British soldiers now occupying their country, the RUF saw any British serviceman as a legitimate target. I'd learnt my lesson the hard way and, given Sierra Leone's gun culture, reasoned: 'If you can't beat them, join them.' So I bought myself a Chinese-made AK47 for $10 and felt a little safer.

I was worried to see RUF sympathizers hanging around outside the UN headquarters. Being in the RUF was not a crime in itself as the Peace Process was technically still ongoing. Some Sierra Leonean friends of mine offered to make these rebels 'go away' for a small fee ($5). I thanked them for the offer but decided that sponsoring extra-judicial assassinations might be deemed inappropriate and not the best career move. Instead, I paid them $5 to help me find a guard dog. This was not easy as most Sierra Leonean dogs seem to have had all the aggression beaten out of them and we couldn't find many suitable candidates. We cruised the backstreets of Freetown and eventually tracked down a dog that at least had the guts to bark loudly at strangers. I suggested we gave it a macho-sounding name, like Ripper or Fangs. Unfortunately she would only answer to her existing name: Topsy. When we brought her into our compound for the first time, the change of environment completely freaked her out to the extent that she wet herself whenever she saw a stranger. With a little loving care and training, though, she soon regained her nerve and became a passable burglar alarm.

Andy, Paul and I were asked if we wanted to return to the UK to recuperate. We all declined the offer. We had an important role to play here, liaising between the UN and the newly arrived British forces. The military situation was still finely balanced: hundreds of UN soldiers were still being held hostage, including my friend and neighbour Andy, and we were all keen to do what we could to help.

There was another, less positive reason for not returning home straight away: we needed to cool down emotionally and psychologically. I don't think I'd have been good company if I'd come home immediately. Going straight from the madness of Makeni to the creature comforts of home was tempting but I think it would have screwed me up mentally. I spoke to Anna at length and she agreed with me. I was longing to see her again, but not until I had calmed down a bit. Every kid I saw still looked like a rebel and I didn't want this to happen at home. The best form of therapy after our experiences was to keep busy and stay involved with what was going on.

A week after the British forces arrived, the UN started to find its feet again and, as UN Military Observers, we still had a job to do. We received reports about the West Side Boys militia who, at this stage, were co-operating with the UN and UK forces. The West Side Boys had managed to recapture the town of Rogberi Junction from the RUF. Rogberi Junction was no more than a collection of mud huts but it was strategically important as Sierra Leone's two main highways met there. This was the place where the RUF had previously used 'Trojan Horse' tactics to overcome the Nigerian peacekeepers stationed there. The RUF had donned the uniforms of captured Zambian soldiers and forced their drivers to take them in Zambian armoured cars through UN checkpoints. The Nigerian soldiers had not realized what was happening and several of them had paid for this deception with their lives. The West Side Boys now claimed to have discovered the bodies of executed UN soldiers in Rogberi Junction and Andy and I were given the task of going to investigate. We were accompanied by a heavily armed patrol of Nigerians, who had temporarily abandoned all their UN insignia and re-adopted their Nigerian Army colours. They were never ones to mess around and trigger-happy at the best of times, so I was glad they were on my side.

We headed for Rogberi Junction in the Nigerian armoured cars, driving at breakneck speed through bandit country. When we reached our destination, the town had been burnt to the ground as a final spiteful gesture by the RUF before they retreated. Among the smouldering remains of a previously peaceful village, the only things left were a few burnt-out vehicles, mangled bicycle frames and some abandoned cooking pots.

The West Side Boys took us to the edge of the village, a couple of hundred metres behind the front line. The stench of rotting flesh made us gag, made worse by the knowledge that this was human flesh. The bodies had been lying in the hot tropical sun for nearly two weeks and there was not much left of them. You didn't have to be a forensic scientist to work out what had happened here. Some of the bodies were dressed in Nigerian uniforms and were still propped up in their trenches where they had been shot. At least these guys had died fighting. Other bodies found nearby in Zambian battle dress had been tied to trees and dismembered. This is what the RUF had done to the Zambian drivers after they no longer needed them.

I picked up a torso. Its insides had turned to liquid, which now drained out on to my feet. Fighting the urge to vomit, I searched the dead man's pockets and found his passport and ID card. We moved quickly from body to body and extracted whatever documentation we could. It was not a healthy place to hang around for long and we had no idea how long the lull in the battle would last. I asked a few local militiamen to help Andy and me collect the human remains and bury them in one of the abandoned trenches. We made a sketch map of where the mass grave was, so that the bodies could be disinterred and repatriated when the security situation allowed. As I left, I caught sight of two bored-looking combatants playing football with a skull.

This made me angry and I shouted over to them: 'What the hell d'you think you're doing? Show some respect!'

The man with the 'ball' misunderstood me, maybe thinking I was asking to join in their kick-about, and he neatly flicked the skull in my direction. I resisted the urge to kick it back, instead picking it up and placing it in the temporary grave. The sad fact was it was easier to get hold of a human skull than a football. This was just another sorry example of how cheap life had become in Sierra Leone.

Less than a week later, on 24 May 2000, two Western journalists, Kurt Schork of Reuters and a cameraman called Miguel Morena, had made their way to Rogberi Junction, looking for a story – and they found one. They wandered into an RUF ambush and were hacked to death.

On another patrol we passed through a sector controlled by the Jordanian contingent. Their frontline positions were occupied by a Special Forces Company who possessed some impressive weaponry and all wore balaclavas despite the heat. The Jordanians had already abandoned their positions on a number of occasions and a British liaison officer had been assigned the task of trying to persuade them to stand and fight. Andy and I tracked down the liaison officer to try to offer him some moral support during his delicate diplomatic dealings. He explained that the Jordanians were terrified of rain, trees and the noise of frogs croaking at night, none of which they had come across before in the deserts of Jordan. Worse, every time they saw a black person they claimed they were being attacked and opened fire with an assortment of weapons, including multi-barrelled rocket launchers. This approach did not endear them to the local population. The Jordanian contingent withdrew from Sierra Leone shortly afterwards.

Catching up with old friends

I had fully expected never to see the armed Kenyans from Makeni again. On the day we reached Freetown, the Kenyans had sent a radio message to the UN HQ reporting that they would attempt to fight their way out of Makeni. We knew some of them had had nothing to eat or drink for over a week and they were on their last legs. We waited anxiously for news.

We later heard the full story. With no formal direction from UN HQ, the Kenyan commanding officer had ordered his exhausted men to attempt to fight their way out. Under cover of the first decent rainstorm of the wet season, 'A' Company were able to bulldoze their way out of the compound, driving straight through the mud-brick wall to fool the waiting rebels. They burst out, all guns firing, and drove in a convoy through the backstreets of Makeni to link up with 'D' Company and their Battalion HQ on the north side of town. As a column, they then fought their way north to Kabala, which was still being held by the Sierra Leonean Army. They were ambushed a total of eleven times and took heavy casualties. The survivors were then stuck in Kabala for another three weeks before being airlifted out by a combination of Russian-piloted UN helicopters and British Chinooks.

I had an emotional reunion with my Kenyan colleagues, all the more so as several of their number hadn't made it. Some of their accounts were heart-rending. Like the Kenyan who'd been badly injured during the RUF attack on the DDR camp. His colleagues thought he was dead but friendly civilians had rescued him and were nursing him in their house. The injured Kenyan had sent a messenger with a letter to his comrades, asking them to come and find him or at least give the messenger money or medicine to pass to him. The Kenyans gave the messenger some money and asked him to bring their injured colleague to the camp. The brave messenger later returned with the injured Kenyan lashed to the back of a motorbike. But word of this had leaked to the rebels and, as the motorbike 'ambulance' tried to enter the compound, both messenger and casualty were gunned down. For good measure, the rebels also slaughtered all the members of the messenger's immediate family.

After everything the Kenyan soldiers had been through, the UN system unbelievably did not allow the survivors a free phone call home. And even a short call on a satellite phone cost more than their monthly wages. So Jim and I let them use our British Army-issue phone instead. Some of their families back in Kenya had been wrongly informed that their loved ones were dead and it was moving to hear these battle-hardened Masai warriors telling their shocked and happy wives that they weren't widows after all.

As for Fergus, he and his colleagues from DfID had also escaped from Makeni by the skin of their teeth. At first light on the same day we made a break for it, Fergus walked boldly and calmly out of the compound into the hands of the waiting rebels. Showing astonishing nerve, Fergus somehow persuaded Colonel Kallon to let him and his fellow aid workers go. Everyone else who had tried appealing to the rebels had either been killed or was still being held captive. I don't know exactly what Fergus said but his charm – and several thousand dollars – obviously did the trick. Escorted by Kallon, Fergus and his team then drove out of rebel territory. Their luck held as they crashed through the front line in a Toyota pick-up truck and were eventually picked up by helicopter.

I received a message from a Nigerian sentry in Freetown that a man called Usman Kamara had turned up at the checkpoint outside the Mammy Yoko Hotel and was asking to see me. It was Usman, my teacher friend. The last time I had seen him was three weeks before, when he had offered to try to smuggle us out of Makeni dressed as holy men. We went for a drink together and he told me what had happened to him and his family, who had been forced to flee their home.

Like most Sierra Leoneans, Usman knew from bitter experience that it was always civilians who suffered the most during fighting. He had chosen, not for the first time in his life, to take his wife and family into a squalid refugee camp rather than live under the RUF. As soon as the civil war had started up again, the RUF had begun 'recruiting' in Makeni. Both Usman and his six-year-old son Mohammed were in the right age bracket for recruitment. Rather than join them, Usman had joined a 10,000-strong column of refugees from Makeni and walked with his family to safety, carrying what possessions they could. Usman's wife, Mariatu, had given birth to a baby boy half-way through their four-day trek. Gobsmacked by this, I asked if there was anything I could do to help. I certainly owed him a favour as he had risked his life to pass us information while we were surrounded in Makeni. He thanked me but said no. Before I left for the UK I gave him some money to set himself up with a small business – as a teacher, he had not earned a penny for three years.

What of Andy Harrison, the Parachute Regiment major captured by the rebels? I had been following developments closely and his full story now came out. He had been working in an UNMO team in Kailahun, a desolate town in the south-east corner of the country. Just as I had done in Makeni, he had enjoyed relatively cordial relations with the local RUF commanders until the day I disarmed the rebels in Makeni. That day, Andy was invited to the house of the commanding officer of the RUF Kailahun Battalion with his UN team leader and some Indian peacekeepers. The meeting started amicably enough but, half-way through, the RUF commander announced there would be a 'peaceful protest' and that all the UN personnel present would be detained. At this point, around fifty armed rebels stormed the room and overpowered the Indian peacekeepers, Andy and his team leader. The RUF stated that the UN personnel would be held in retaliation for the alleged UN detention of the ten RUF 'deserters' in Makeni. These were the ten rebels we had disarmed in good faith.

Andy and his colleagues were dragged from the room and driven to a rebel stronghold in the village of Geima, on the Sierra Leone/Liberia border. The volatile atmosphere came to a head when guards severely beat one of their colleagues for stealing a watch from one of Andy's group. The rebel soldier was taken away and executed. Andy found it worrying that the rebels were prepared to kill one of their own over such a trivial issue. This did not bode well for his own safety.

That afternoon, Andy was told he was going to be released but, as he drove back towards Kailahun, escorted by the rebels, he was suddenly ordered back to Geima at gunpoint. He was thrown into a shed on the outskirts of the village. That evening, Andy was joined by other UN hostages, including a Russian naval officer called Andre who was to become Andy's closest friend for the next two months.

As the security situation across the country deteriorated and we had started fighting for our lives in Makeni, so the atmosphere in Geima worsened. Andy and Andre, the two white officers, received the brunt of the harsh treatment. Andy was told on several occasions that he was about to be executed in retaliation for the deaths of the RUF soldiers killed by my Kenyan colleagues, and he was beaten repeatedly. On one occasion a rifle was held to his head and he was told to 'kneel down and prepare to die'. Andy refused, saying if they were going to shoot him, they would have to shoot him standing up. This act of defiance earned him a savage beating but ultimately his bravery impressed even his captors and he was given a stay of execution.

Nationwide, frantic efforts were being made behind the scenes to split the RUF leadership. Britain and the UN were conducting

PsyOps – psychological operations or military spin doctoring – to convince Andy's RUF captors that the rebels in Makeni were acting against the wishes of the overall RUF leadership. A wedge was being driven between the RUF in the Northern Province (Makeni) and the RUF in the Eastern Province (Kailahun and Geima). The Revolutionary United Front turned out not to be particularly 'united'. This PsyOps campaign, together with Andy's cool-headedness, was to save his life.

The rebels made it clear that if any of the UN personnel escaped, the remainder would be executed. Andy's team agreed that if they were to attempt an escape, then it would only be if they could all get out together. If any one of the team was shot, then escaping would become an individual decision.

The news that 1 Para had landed in Freetown was not good news for Andy. If the Paras came to blows with the RUF in Freetown, their Kailahun counterparts would surely not miss the chance to exact personal revenge on the British paratrooper in their clutches. Andy passed a message to the rest of his captured team, telling them that if 1 Para inflicted any casualties on the RUF, he would have to attempt to escape. He spent the next few days straining to hear each BBC World Service news report on the guards' radio.

In Kailahun, the rest of Andy's team had also been overpowered, beaten and held in their own house until 9 May when they too were moved to Geima. As had happened to the Kenyans and us in Makeni, the two companies of armed Indian peacekeepers in Kailahun were surrounded in their camps. Andy's team tried repeatedly to persuade their captors to let them return to their house in Kailahun. After eleven days in captivity, a groundswell of local opinion demanded that the RUF move Andy and his fellow captives back to their empty house in Kailahun. Here, their conditions improved slightly but they were still hostages.

With the British troops in Freetown becoming more active, Andy knew that to stay isolated in town was becoming increasingly dangerous. With two colleagues, he decided he had to try to reach the Indian peacekeepers' defended location. In the end, the three of them simply told their guards that they had been summoned to see the RUF commanding officer then walked boldly out of the house and into town. As they strode off, resisting the overriding urge to look back, they realized that their bluff had worked.

The other two made their way to the Indian peacekeepers, but Andy actually did go and speak to the RUF commanding officer in an attempt to secure the release of those left in the house. Amazingly, he persuaded the rebel warlord to allow the whole team to visit the Indians' position 'to wash'. Andy shepherded his somewhat confused colleagues into the Indian compound. Once in, they were not going to leave. Not surprisingly, the RUF were furious and repeatedly attempted to force them out. But the Indian troops, all Gurkhas, were well armed and had a strong defensive position which the rebels failed to overrun. Two days later, the Pathfinder Platoon (the Paras' specialist reconnaissance unit) killed a number of rebels near Freetown. Andy had removed himself from the rebels' clutches just in time.

Andy and the Indians were besieged in their new location for another two months. The RUF did occasionally let resupply convoys into the town and we had managed to smuggle a satphone in to him, hidden in a container of cooking oil. From then on, Andy could at least speak to the outside world. He was adamant that there should be no attempt to rescue him that might in any way jeopardize any other UN personnel.

Eventually – when the RUF refused to allow in any more convoys – the UN, with British support, mounted an operation to extract all the UN soldiers in Kailahun, including Andy. The operation was codenamed Op Kukri (the name of the Gurkhas' fighting knife). At dawn on Friday 14 July 2000, in a driving rainstorm, two British Chinooks extracted Andy's team and nineteen injured Indians. With helicopter gunship and artillery support, the remaining Indians broke out and linked up with the rest of their battalion in the nearby town of Daru. The Indians suffered one fatal casualty and several wounded, but inflicted heavy casualties on the RUF, and Op Kukri went some way to restoring damaged UNAMSIL credibility.

Andy was subsequently awarded an MBE for his exemplary conduct throughout these episodes.

Over a year later, the RUF has been brought back into the Peace Process. While Sankoh remains in prison, awaiting trial for treason, other RUF commanders have fared a little better. The self-styled General Issa Sesay took over as leader of the RUF, though he now calls himself Mr Issa and presents himself as a politician. Colonel Bao is still the RUF's Head of Security. Colonel Kallon, the RUF commander who led the attack on the UN and killed my Kenyan colleagues, was recently promoted to brigadier.

Major-General Jetley, the Indian officer in charge of UNAMSIL, was short-toured as the overall military commander. He was replaced by Lieutenant General Daniel Opande who – perhaps coincidentally – is a Kenyan officer.

As of September 2001, UNAMSIL and the Disarmament Process appear to be back on track. UNAMSIL's strength has increased from 12,000 to nearly 17,000. As I write, it is still the biggest UN mission in the world. The RUF still controls two-thirds of Sierra Leone but they have now allowed UNAMSIL back into their territory and some have even disarmed. Why the apparent change in attitude? When the main body of British troops withdrew in June 2000 a British Military and Advisory Training Team (BMATT) stayed behind in Sierra Leone. Several hundred strong, it has provided the backbone needed to shore up the previously ramshackle Sierra Leone Army. The BMATT has trained several thousand soldiers since then and has helped reorganize the command infrastructure of the Sierra Leonean Ministry of Defence. For the first time in over a decade, the Sierra Leone Army is once again a credible force and the RUF realize that ultimately they're not going to win the war. Faced with a choice of either military defeat at the hands of the Sierra Leonean Army or co-operation with UNAMSIL, it's not surprising that the rebels are at least going through the motions of re-entering the Peace Process.

One thing is sure though: the RUF still hold the diamond mines and they are unlikely to give them up without a fight.

My six-month tour in Sierra Leone was over at the end of June. On the morning I was to leave Freetown, I awoke in a feverish sweat with a headache from hell. For a moment, I feared another malarial attack – until I noticed I was still fully dressed, and remembered I had been trying to have a drink the night before with every different nationality involved with UNAMSIL. Given that there were twenty-five different nationalities, that meant a lot of beer. Then I noticed I was wearing a Chinese Red Army uniform. Andy brought me a coffee and explained that I'd swapped clothes with a Red Army major called 'Harry the Spy' half-way through the evening... I stuck to mineral water and orange juice on the flight home.

After everything I'd been through, I was happy to finish my tour with nothing worse than a bad hangover. I had survived essentially unscathed the threat of armed and hostile rebels, and the punishing rigours of heat and thirst. I was now looking forward to going home. But a tiny part of Sierra Leone had got through my defences. It was invisible and, for now, lying low.

A FINAL TEST
OF NERVE

'Be happy while ye're livin'. For ye're a lang time deid.'
SCOTS PROVERB

Our tours in Sierra Leone over, we all took up other posts. Dave is back with his regiment in New Zealand. Paul is an instructor at Britannia Royal Naval Academy, teaching new entry naval officers. Andy has completed a six-month tour in Kosovo and is currently back out in Sierra Leone with his regiment, training new recruits in the Sierra Leone Army. Looking back, I realize the four of us were an assortment of servicemen with totally different areas of experience and expertise thrown together in an extraordinary situation. And I couldn't have asked for a braver group of men to break out with. Had one of us dithered as we climbed over that mud wall, I don't believe that any of us would have made it.

I meet up with Andy and Paul from time to time, to catch up over a beer. We've always got plenty to talk about – it's easier to get stuff off your chest with someone who has been through the same things as you. Even if this means joking about events that would seem taboo or shocking in normal conversation – you get some odd looks in the pub when you are casually discussing cannibalism.

The first thing I did when I got back from Sierra Leone was to have a belated thirtieth birthday party (three different people gave me Frisbees). Then I returned to Africa for my summer holidays, on a climbing trip to Kenya with Anna. We trekked up Kilimanjaro to acclimatize, then attempted a technical, multi-day rock climb on the North Face of Mount Kenya. We were forced to retreat after it snowed heavily while we were bivvying on a small ledge, but summited by another, easier route. From the friends I had made in Sierra Leone, I was able to do some handy name-dropping among Kenyan soldiers at the numerous army checkpoints near Nairobi. The Kenyan Battalion I had been with had, deservedly, been hailed as heroes in their home country and I enjoyed being associated with them.

After Kenya, I was well acclimatized and climbing strongly. Now in my thirties, I was feeling stronger, fitter and tougher than ever before. Unfortunately for me, however, this was not to last.

At the beginning of September 2000, I began my next posting – as a staff officer in the Directorate of Naval Manning in Portsmouth. Three weeks in, the intricacies of 'strategic manpower planning' were just starting to make some sense. After a particularly mind-bending Thursday morning I had gone for a run at lunchtime to clear my mind. It was a wet and windy day and I remember deliberately jumping in all the puddles as I ran around the Dockyard. I felt a slight pain between my shoulder blades, but thought nothing of it. I had a shower and went back to the office. An hour later, I was sitting behind my desk, staring at a computer screen full of numbers, when I felt my left leg go numb. I assumed it was just the way I was sitting so got up off my seat, strolled around the office and sat back down. Then my right leg went to sleep. Then the numbness began spreading up my body and my vision started going funny.

By the time I was rushed to hospital later that night, I was effectively paralysed from the waist down, with shooting pains in my back and head. In Accident and Emergency, I was initially told I had broken my back. I thought this unlikely as I'd been sitting at my desk when it happened, and an X-ray soon confirmed my scepticism. Next my legs went into spasm. There was something pressing on my spinal cord that was affecting my nervous system. If it were a tumour, they would have to operate that night. This sounded serious. For the second time in a couple of months, I phoned my father and asked him to tell my mother a little white lie so as not to worry her unduly. Anna, no stranger to spinal injuries herself, did her best to reassure me.

I lay awake on my hospital bed all night, worried but grimly amused that my luck appeared to have run out in this way. I entertained myself with thoughts of Sierra Leonean witch doctors pushing pins into my effigy.

The next morning, British doctors were pushing pins into my body for real. They were checking for loss of sensation and I couldn't feel a thing below my waist. I had one of the country's top neurologists looking after me, but it seemed the most sophisticated method of checking for nerve damage was to stick a needle in my arse and watch to see if I flinched. I didn't.

The doctors carried out dozens of tests over the next few weeks: more X-rays, brain scans, blood tests, lumbar punctures and general proddings. Samples of my blood and spinal fluid were sent to laboratories around the country including the School of Tropical Medicine and even Porton Down, Britain's research establishment for biological warfare. One by one, the doctors eliminated possible causes of the symptoms: spinal fracture, meningitis, tuberculosis, cancerous tumours on my brain and spine, Guillain-Barré syndrome, multiple sclerosis and Aids.

They eventually concluded that I had carried back an unwanted memento of Sierra Leone in the form of a tropical virus, which was now living in my spine. The resulting swelling in my spinal cord was causing nerve damage – a condition called virally induced acute transverse myelitis. Whether this was from something I had eaten, drunk, been bitten by, or caught from my rodent roommates back in Makeni, I shall probably never know.

After a few days, the spasms had worn off sufficiently for Anna to be able to push me around in a wheelchair, but more than anything I wanted to get out of hospital and go home. The doctors told me they would let me go when I could make my own way to the toilet, twenty feet away. After a week of practicing with sticks I could manage it, but that twenty foot felt as difficult as fifty miles through the jungle in Sierra Leone. In the end, my body fought off the virus on its own, but I have been left with significant neurological damage.

A year later, it's like recovering from a stroke. My left leg is especially weak and I have almost no feeling in either leg from the knee down. Every morning when I wake up it feels like my feet have been in a bucket of ice-cold water. Sometimes they tingle, sometimes they ache and sometimes they feel nothing at all. On occasions my legs shake uncontrollably. I am told that these symptoms may continue to wear off slowly but some of the damage will be permanent. The physical part I can cope with, but tests have shown that the virus also attacked my brain. When I was told I had minor brain damage, it at least helped explain the short-term memory loss, poor concentration span and insomnia I have been suffering. None of these made an ideal starting point for the master's degree I've just embarked upon! I feel like I have a permanent hangover. It is all very frustrating.

Despite my condition, I can think of nothing more demoralizing than complete inactivity, so I've been 'back on the rock' – an interesting experience with numb feet and wobbly legs. Scary for me, but worse for Anna on the other end of the rope faced with the prospect of fifteen stone of damaged Royal Marine landing on her head! Still, I have been determined to continue life as normal as much as possible.

The novelty of sick leave soon wore off and I found that work was the best therapy, and kept me sane, despite not firing on all cylinders. The Marines have been immensely supportive, especially my last boss, Joss, who not only did my job for me when I was off work, but had the patience to bear with me when I went back to work and spent the best part of six months asking him stupid questions.

In some ways, I would rather have had a concrete, visible injury that I could point to and come to terms with – even a missing limb. Not knowing exactly what is wrong with you, or how bad or good it is going to get, is mentally as well as physically debilitating. It sounds big-headed, but I was used to being one of the best at whatever I set out to do and the thought of not being able to work hard and play hard is a pretty desperate prospect.

I still consider myself lucky, though; West Africans with 'wobbly leg syndrome' don't even have access to a doctor, let alone the safety net that I have had to catch me and look after me, and I try to look on the bright side. I know that when you go climbing, you can get a buzz from performing near your limits, regardless of what those limits are. I hope this applies to other walks of life.

I like to think that in a couple of years I'll be able to look back on the whole setback and see it as just another life-enriching experience. Anna has been a great role model in this respect; she has shown nothing but determination and optimism in overcoming her own physical trauma. I'm inspired by her zest for life following the accident, which threw things into perspective for both of us. And whatever else happens, we know we'll always have each other.

I may not be climbing many physical mountains right now, but I will do my best to scale the other peaks ahead of me. As far as I'm concerned there are plenty more adventures to come.

INDEX